Songs of the Saints of India

Songs of the Saints of India

TEXT AND NOTES BY
John Stratton Hawley

TRANSLATIONS BY
J. S. Hawley AND
Mark Juergensmeyer

New York Oxford
OXFORD UNIVERSITY PRESS
1988

Oxford University Press

Oxford New York Toronto
Delhi Bombay Calcutta Madras Karachi
Petaling Jaya Singapore Hong Kong Tokyo
Nairobi Dar es Salaam Cape Town
Melbourne Auckland

and associated companies in
Berlin Ibadan

Published by Oxford University Press, Inc.,
198 Madison Avenue, New York, New York 10016-4314

Library of Congress Cataloging-in-Publication Data
Songs of the saints of India / text and notes by John Stratton Hawley;
translations by J. S. Hawley and Mark Juergensmeyer.
p. cm.
Bibliography: p.
Includes index.
ISBN 0-19-505220-X; ISBN 0-19-505221-8 (pbk.)
1. Religious poetry, Hindi—1500–1800—Translations into English.
2. Religious poetry, English—Translations from Hindi.
3. Poets, Hindi—1500–1800—Biography. 4. Hindu saints—Biography.
I. Hawley, John Stratton, 1941– . II. Juergensmeyer, Mark.
PK2141.E3S66 1988
891'.4312'080382—dc19 87-24155
CIP

11 13 15 17 19 18 16 14 12 10

Printed in the United States of America
on acid-free paper

For Ainslie Embree

Acknowledgments

The help of a number of friends and institutions has been essential in the preparation of this book. For their critical but sympathetic reading of the manuscript, in part or in whole, we sincerely thank Ainslie Embree, Linda Hess, Lindsey Harlan, David Lorenzen, Philip Lutgendorf, Gurinder Singh Mann, W. H. McLeod, Frances Pritchett, and Michael Shapiro. The illustrations, a last-minute surprise, are from the hand of Braj Vallabh Mishra, to whom we are most grateful. For assistance in translation we are indebted to Sandhya and Shrivatsa Goswami, Om Prakash Jaiswal, and especially Krishna Caitanya Bhatt. A great debt is also owed to the John Simon Guggenheim Memorial Foundation and the Woodrow Wilson International Center for Scholars for helping to provide us with the time away from teaching that enabled us to bring the book to completion. The National Endowment for the Humanities has given generous support for the critical edition and verse translation of the poems of Surdas, upon which one chapter of this book is based, and the American Institute of Indian Studies has made possible the research in India upon which the entire edifice rests. Cynthia Read of Oxford University Press has been the soul of patience and encouragement. Laura Shapiro is owed a special debt for giving the whole manuscript the benefit of her consummate editorial eye on two separate occasions, and both she and Sucheng Chan have endured a fair amount of talk about it in between.

Several of the translations have appeared—often in an altered form—in earlier publications, and we are grateful for permission to draw upon them here. The books are as follows: Ainslie T. Embree, ed., *Sources of Indian Tradition,* vol. 1 (New York: Columbia University Press, 1988); John Stratton Hawley, *Krishna, the Butter Thief* (Princeton: Princeton University Press, 1983) and *Sūr Dās: Poet, Singer, Saint* (Seattle: University of Washington Press and Delhi: Oxford University Press, 1984); and Caroline Walker Bynum, Stevan Harrell, and Paula Richman, eds., *Gender and Religion* (Boston: Beacon Press, 1986).

Finally, a word is in order to explain which of us did what. For years we have worked together as mutual editors—Hawley for prose and Juergensmeyer for poetry—and this volume grew out of that collaboration. We decided to expand our efforts from Surdas to his medieval poet-peers, and we did some of the field research as a team, discussing the shape and content of the book at various stages. Ultimately it was Hawley who wrote the prose portions of the book; we did the poems together. Typically, Juergensmeyer worked "from the ground up" on the basis of a literal translation provided by Hawley, though Hawley's verse translation is in the background on several occasions. Then, of course, we argued about the whole thing, not just the poetry but the prose as well. Each of us happily acknowledges the other's sometimes irksome help in a friendship that is now many years old.

This book is dedicated to Ainslie Embree, a friend to both of us and to India in ways too numerous to record.

New York and Berkeley J.S.H.
October 1987 M.J.

Contents

GUIDE TO TRANSLITERATION AND PRONUNCIATION

In rendering Hindi into the Latin alphabet we have departed from the standard method of transliterating devanagari script, which was designed to render Sanskrit usage, where it seemed to misrepresent the sounds produced in spoken Hindi. The neutral vowel is omitted at the ends of words (*nām,* Rām) except where it is audible in Hindi speech (*viraha, vinaya*). For consistency's sake we have done the same in translitering poetry, even though such a vowel can sometimes be metrically significant. The vocalic *r* is retained, as in Sanskrit (*amṛt*). Words that appear in various spellings in manuscripts and dialects are reduced to their common Hindi form (*śabad* > *śabd*) when discussed in the text; in the notes and glossary, however, an effort has been made to cite the form actually used as well. The nasalization of open vowels is indicated with a tilde (*gosā̃ī̃*); otherwise an "m" or "n" is employed (*saṃvād, sārang, pañcvāṇī*). Words that have come into standard English usage are given in their most easily recognized form (Krishna, Vishnu, Śiva, Kāma), and several words familiar to Indic readers are retained in their *tatsam* Sanskrit form (*saguṇa, nirguṇa*). Place names are given in their anglicized form if a familiar designation exists (Benares, Cittor, Brindavan), as are the names of authors and speakers when the context is English; otherwise they appear in full transliteration.

For ease of reading, the text and translations have been kept free of diacritical marks. In the notes and glossary, however, diacritics are used. Readers concerned about accurate pronunciation are therefore referred to those sections of the book. In the transliteration system we employ, the long vowels *ā, ī, ū, e,* and *o* are pronounced approximately like the corresponding vowels in the English words f*a*ther, mar*i*ne, r*u*le, pr*e*y, and m*o*w. The diphthongs *ai* and *au,* though sometimes given the length of the vowels in the English words str*i*de and tr*ou*t, are more usually shortened, yielding the vowel sounds contained in m*a*d and cr*aw*l. The vowels *a, i,* and *u* are short and are pronounced like the vowels in the words b*u*t, f*i*ll, and b*u*ll. Vocalic *r* is also short; in modern speech it is rendered as if it were *ri,* as in *ri*b.

The consonant *c* sounds like *ch* in the English word *ch*arm, except that it has less aspiration; the consonant transliterated as *ch* has correspondingly greater aspiration. The aspirated consonants *th* and *ph* should be pronounced like the clusters in goa*th*erd and mor*ph*ium. The distinction between the sibilants *ś* and *ṣ* is not usually made in modern Hindi usage; both sound like *sh* in English *sh*ort. For the retroflex consonants, produced by curling the tip of the tongue toward the roof of the mouth (*ṭ, ṭh, ḍ, ḍh, ṇ*), there are no genuine English equivalents. To some they sound as if the corresponding English consonants had been preceded by an American *r* (ha*rd,* hea*rt*), though the placement is slightly farther back in the mouth.

Songs of the Saints of India

INTRODUCTION

A Family of Poets and Saints

THE VERSES of the great poets of medieval north India stand at the fount of the Hindi language, and many would say that they also represent its greatest flowering. Unlike the poems of Chaucer or Donne, which occupy a somewhat similar place in the history of the English language, these Hindi verses are as lively and familiar to Indians today as they were four hundred years ago. Any schoolchild, any rickshaw driver, any businessman can recite something from the poetry of Mirabai or Nanak or Kabir, and the compositions of Surdas and Tulsidas provide the basis for dramatic performances that attract millions of people every year. These poems, though religious in context, are universal in theme. They speak of the trials of life in society, the hollow shell of the body, friendship, betrayal, beauty, birth, death, and the pains and exaltations of love.

This book is an introduction to six of these poets: Ravidas, Kabir, Nanak, Surdas, Mirabai, and Tulsidas. Each poet is represented by translations based on compositions that have a cogent claim to authenticity, as well as by a biographical sketch, for in the Indian view it is often the life that makes the word believable. These beloved figures are regarded not just as poets but as saints. At about the same time that their poems began to be written down and collected, therefore, a considerable hagiographical literature about them began to flower. It continues to proliferate today, in forms ranging from scholarly tomes that depict the "Lives of the Saints" to the recitations of bards, who walk from village to village recounting the stories and singing the songs. Religious communities, too, have played a part in immortalizing these poet-saints by adopting one or another as their patrons, and of late the major organs of popular culture have joined the hagiographical chorus. Comic books show the saints singing their way from miracle to miracle, and the film industry has warmed to the challenge of bringing their supernatural virtuosity to the screen.

For all the diversity of expression, however, we are talking about a single family of saints. It is usually referred to as the family of *bhakti*, a word that means passionate love for God and implies a sense of close engagement with other people. The word *bhakti* is derived from a Sanskrit root meaning "to share," and it points to the importance of relationship—both to God and to human beings—in the kind of enthusiastic, often congregational, religion it describes. Another term that is sometimes used to describe this family is *sant*, deriving from the Sanskrit verb "to be." This verb and its derivatives connote not only what is real but what is true; hence a *sant* is someone true or good as well as someone who incarnates what is essential about life. Though the etymology is unrelated, the English word "saint" is often the best translation of *sant;* and the word *bhakta,* though it means "devotee" or "lover of God," can also be used in an honorific sense that makes it a rough Hindi analogue for "saint."

In medieval times both these terms were used to designate all six saints in our group, with no distinction as to theological leaning. In more recent days, however, a distinction has been made between *sants* and *bhaktas* to clarify the outlines of the two branches in the *bhakti* family they form. The *sants* are the clan that prefers to worship God "without attributes" or "without form"; they have a tendency to be critical of anyone who approaches God through icon and legend, as most Hindus do. Those who take the opposite, or "with attributes," position affirm that God has indeed entered history and taken form—even the form of an image in a temple—to guide and aid earthly beings. Members of this clan are called either *bhaktas* or Vaishnavas, the latter term being appropriate because as a group they tend to be worshipers of one of the two major expressions of the high god Vishnu: his avatars Krishna and Ram.

Of the six saints we will meet, three belong to the "without attributes" (*nirguna*) school—Ravidas, Kabir, and Nanak—and three—

School	"Without attributes" (*nirguna*)	"With attributes" (*saguna*)
Deity	(nameless)	Krishna Ram
Saints	*sants* Ravidas Kabir Nanak	*bhaktas* Surdas Tulsidas Mirabai

Surdas, Mirabai, and Tulsidas—are of the "with attributes" (*saguna*) persuasion. Definite loyalties solidify each group. For instance, all three saints in the first branch are well represented in the *Adi Granth,* the poetic anthology that was created to serve as the scripture of the Sikhs; only sparse references are made to the *saguna* school. Moreover, both Nanak and Ravidas appear to have seen themselves explicitly in the lineage of Kabir, and all three were to some degree influenced by concepts developed among the Nath Yogis, the most important order of ascetics in medieval north India. Above all, these three are undying advocates of interior religion, and are as outspokenly suspicious of superficiality and hypocrisy as they are of the more formal expression of "with attributes" religion: worship through image and myth.

The imagists—the "with attributes" group—also share significant affinities. Two of them, Surdas and Mirabai, are primarily devotees of Krishna, and their descriptions of his world often draw them within close range of each other. The third, Tulsidas, is more closely identified with Ram, but tradition has made sure that we see an analogy between him and his Krishnaite colleague, Sur. Despite the fact that they came from different regions and different generations, there is a legend that these two did once meet. It is a logical enough connection to have posited, for Sur, the Krishna devotee, also composed poetry to Ram; and Tulsi, the poet of Ram, dedicated an entire collection of poetry to Krishna.

Despite the division between these two sets of saints—with the

Protestants, so to speak, on one side and the Catholics on the other—they all inherited a single, massive *bhakti* movement that had been gathering force in other parts of India for a millennium. A favorite Sanskrit passage personifies it as a lovely woman who was born in the south (about the sixth century A.D.), gained strength and maturity in the middle regions of the west (from the twelfth century onward), grew decrepit, and was revived to experience her full flowering when she reached the north. The tenor of the movement remained recognizably the same over the centuries. Its members, though part of no overarching formal organization, were united in their commitment to the value of personal experience in religion. Therefore they questioned the *ex opere operata* ritualism characteristic of the sort of Hindu worship superintended by Brahmins, and they often criticized the caste conceits that went with it. Another consequence of their belief in the value of personal experience was their use of vernacular, regional languages as the appropriate expression of faith. Sanskrit, with its elaborate archaisms, seemed of little use as a medium to reach the heart.

This was the common past our six poets inherited, and they participated in a common poetic environment in their own time, too. Although their individual emphases differed greatly, they all composed poetry in a petitionary genre called *vinaya,* "humble submission," and this made their poems apt to be included in the same anthologies no matter which side of the "with attributes" or "without attributes" divide they stood on. The sense that they belonged together was also acknowledged in the hagiographical traditions that grew up around them. We have already mentioned the anachronistic meeting that was invented to tie Tulsi and Sur together, and similar encounters were formulated to link Kabir, Ravidas, and Nanak. These imagined interviews give definition to the two great branches on the *bhakti* family tree, but others reinforce its unity as well. Mirabai is commonly construed as having been a pupil of Ravidas, who stands on the opposite side of the tree from her, and Tulsidas is made part of the same guru-disciple lineage (the one going back to Ramanand) that Ravidas and Kabir are believed to share.

In introducing these poets, we will stress the traits that made each stand out as an individual, but we will also touch on issues that affect the entire group. For example, we will speak of Ravidas's extremely low caste—it is a prominent feature of his hagiography—yet in doing so we will be focusing on the suspicion of caste society that runs through all these *bhakti* poets. One can even find it in the writings of Tulsidas, the Brahmin. Similarly, when we speak of Mirabai's womanhood and observe the particular slant it gives her poetry, we will be exploring the sense of femininity that poets as distant as Sur and Kabir shared when confronted with the presence—or, more often, absence—of God. Finally, although we will draw attention to the surprising variety of ways in which a poet-saint can be revered, we will also see that a community that celebrates the memory of one saint often bears close resemblances to a group that aligns itself with someone quite different.

The six poet-saints presented here have contributed more to the religious vocabulary of Hinduism in north India today than any voices before or since. In its style of worship, in its institutions, even in its political ramifications, modern Hinduism sings their tune. For half a millennium these saints' poems have circulated from the banks of the Jumna to the rice fields of Bihar and back to the deserts of Rajasthan, and have played a crucial role in making all of north India a place where *bhakti* is spoken. Their influence is religious, to be sure, but it is much more. These poems have provided a language in which many of life's most vivid concerns can be expressed: cruelty and loneliness, status and intimacy, hope and infatuation, and the maddening transitoriness of it all. Such realities go quickly beyond the boundaries we associate with religion, and go beyond the boundaries of India as well.

ONE

Ravidas

Oh well-born of Benares, I too am born well known:
my labor is with leather. But my heart can boast the Lord.

BENARES, Hinduism's oldest city and a citadel of the Brahmin caste, fits along the left bank of the Ganges as if it were an elaborately embroidered sleeve. A long and complicated city, like the religious tradition it symbolizes, it opens at its southern extremity onto the spacious grounds of Banaras Hindu University, and for most people it stops there. But just beyond the high wall that surrounds the university, at its back gate, there is one more settlement, a dusty little enclave called Sri Govardhanpur. It is the last collection of houses before the country begins, and there is a reason that it has grown up where it has. This is a village inhabited almost entirely by Untouchables, outcastes. Even in a secular India committed by its constitution to the abolition of untouchability, their pariah identity still has its geographical symbol.

The people of Sri Govardhanpur have no intention of accepting their lot as if it were decreed by fate or religion. Since 1967 they have devoted many of their efforts toward the completion of a large temple that is designed to put Sri Govardhanpur on the religious map of Benares. They hope that their four-story edifice will rival temples in other sectors of the city and become a familiar part of the pilgrims' circuit—or if not that, at least serve as a magnet for low-caste people who are not always welcome in the city's other temples. The project by no means belongs to the people of Sri Govardhanpur alone. Much of the organization has come from a "mission" headquartered in New Delhi that is dedicated to advancing the Untouchables' cause, and financial support has been largely provided by urbanites of Untouchable background who live in the distant but prosperous province of Punjab or lead even more comfortable lives in far-off England. Clearly, even people who have managed to escape the worst strictures of caste care about erasing the shame of untouchability.[1]

The new edifice in Sri Govardhanpur is not just another Hindu temple. In fact, there is some debate about whether it should be called Hindu at all, for it is dedicated to the remembrance of a saint whose person, perspective, and teachings place him in a sense outside the Hindu pale. His name is Ravidas; he was a man of Benares; and though he lived in the fifteenth or sixteenth century, he still qualifies today as the great Untouchable saint of north India. If one means by Hinduism the religious system whose central rituals are entrusted to Brahmins, whose central institutions require a set of reciprocal but unequal social relationships, and whose guiding ideas set forth what life should be within this hierarchically variegated world and how it may rightly be transcended, then Ravidas was not really a Hindu. As he saw it, there was nothing fundamental about the institutions of caste. His position in society helped him see the point, for he was a leatherworker, a *camar,* a shoemaker, someone whose work brought him into daily contact with the hides of dead animals. Strict Hindus either shun the touch of such skins altogether, believing them to be polluting, or contact them only with the lowest portion of their bodies, the bottom of their feet. And that, by extension, is what the *camar* is in relation to almost all of Hindu society.

But Ravidas was special: he was a poet and singer, and the hymns he sang evidently had such a ring of truth that even Brahmins came to hear them. His poet's charisma must have been equally powerful, for he says that the Brahmins actually bowed before him, in a total inversion of religious and social protocol.[2] Yet he never forgot his own condition. In praising God he habitually contrasted the divine presence to his own: God, he said, was finer than he, as silk was to a worm, and more fragrant than he, as sandalwood was to the stinking castor oil plant.[3]

His clear perception of his lowly condition made him poignantly aware that it did not belong just to him, but to every shoemaker and scavenger of this world. These, he felt, included not only his castefellows but everyone who exists inside a body. No living being is spared the degradations of the flesh, and whoever prefers to think otherwise is dwelling in a world of make-believe.[4] Ravidas thought it ridiculous that caste Hindus could set such store by rituals demanding the use of pure substances, when in truth there is nothing on earth that is not polluted. "Can I offer milk?" he asked in one poem, referring to the substance Hindus regard as purest of them all, since it emerges straight from the holy cow. His answer was that even it had been polluted by prior use: "The calf has dirtied it in sucking its mother's teat."[5] Nothing is spared the taint of the flesh, so he railed against anyone who treated another person as trash.[6] Even kings, he said, dream that they are beggars; only the absence of love in one's life makes one truly an Untouchable.[7]

For the wonder is that God is precisely the sort of being who cares for those who are troubled and lowly. As Ravidas puts it, he "rescues even tanners of hides."[8] In relation to God, every person is untouchable; yet because God is who he is, every person is touched.

An Outcaste in the Family of Saints

Such a message appeals on every front to the hard working, socially oppressed people of Sri Govardhanpur; that Ravidas was a Benarsi makes him even more naturally their patron. But he does not belong to Untouchables alone. Ravidas is one of the *bhakti* family, and as such he is venerated by Hindus of all backgrounds and stations. The sharing in God that *bhakti* implies creates networks of human beings that cut across the divisions society erects—even those that it dignifies with religious significance. In many of its expressions *bhakti* has called into question that version of Hinduism that ties itself intimately to the caste system. Hence even upper-caste Hindus who regard themselves as its beneficiaries take care to include in the hagiographical pantheon at least one representative of caste groups normally considered too low to qualify as "twice-born"—ritually pure—members of society. When the *camars* of Sri Govardhanpur began building their temple to Ravidas, then, there was an aspect of Hindu religion to which they could appeal. On a *bhakti* construction of what Hindu religion is about, a temple to Ravidas had a genuine claim to being included in the religious universe of Benares.

Ravidas himself indicates the *bhakti* family in which he felt he belonged by naming in his poetry several of his predecessors in the faith. One of the names he gives is that of Namdev, a fourteenth-century saint of western India who was a tailor and a member of the relatively low caste associated with that profession.[9] Another was Trilocan, also from the west.[10] A third—and the name he mentions more frequently than any other—was Kabir, the crusty fifteenth-century iconoclast who, like Ravidas, lived in Benares.[11] Kabir too came from the lower echelons of society. He was a weaver and belonged to a caste, the *julahas,* many of whose members had found their place in Hindu society sufficiently distasteful that they had turned to Islam. In mentioning these three as recipients of divine grace along with himself, Ravidas underscored his sense of solidarity with a tradition of *bhakti* that flowed with particular animation in the lower ranks of society.

This, however, is only Ravidas's immediate *bhakti* family, the one that he constructs for himself in several of the poems that have a good claim to being regarded as authentically his. These compositions are included in the *Adi Granth,* the *bhakti* anthology that serves as scripture to the Sikh community. The *Adi Granth* was compiled in A.D. 1604 by the fifth in the lineage of Sikh gurus, Guru Arjun, and contains the oldest substantial collection of poetry attributed to Ravidas: forty full-length poems (*pads*) and an epigrammatic couplet.

But many more poems than these are generally thought to have been sung by Ravidas,[12] and many more connections between him and other *bhakti* figures are accepted by tradition. One of these traditional links is with Nanak—a connection that Sikhs see as almost a tenet of faith, since they understand Nanak, whom they regard as their founding guru, to have been inspired by the other poets anthologized in the *Adi Granth.* It is commonly accepted that Nanak and Ravidas were contemporaries who met at a place in Benares that is now called, fittingly, Guru Bagh—"The Gurus' Garden"—but the estimation of who learned more from whom depends upon whether one is primarily a follower of Nanak or of Ravidas.[13]

Another saint mentioned in Ravidas's company is Mirabai, the woman poet of Rajasthan, who is said in a modern text called the *Ravidas Ramayana* to have traveled all the way to Benares to obtain initiation from Ravidas.[14] Another is Gorakhnath, a renowned yogi who is usually thought to have lived several centuries earlier.[15] Still another is Ramanand, the Brahmin who is said to have played a critical role in the expansion of *bhakti* Hinduism by transferring it from its original home in south India to Benares, where he came to live. To judge by the account of Priyadas, the influential commentator who in A.D. 1712 fleshed out the skeleton provided by Nabhadas's somewhat earlier anthology of *bhakti* saints (the *Bhaktamal,* ca. A.D. 1600), Ramanand managed to gather around himself a more dynamic circle of devotees than north India has seen before or since. As indicated in a list given by Nabhadas himself, both Kabir and Ravidas were included in their number.[16]

These and many other traditions about Ravidas's place in the community of *bhakti* saints abound. Unfortunately, they cannot all be taken at face value. There is some indication, for example, that Ramanand lived a full century before Ravidas, which makes it hard for any but the most committed (who are willing to grant Ravidas a lifespan of 150 years or so) to think that the two could have met.[17] Nor is there anything in the oldest collection of Ravidas's poetry to point to Ramanand. With the Mirabai story too there are problems. It appears that the tale concerning her was grafted onto Priyadas's similar but earlier account of a Rajput queen called Jhali who, like Mira, came to Ravidas from the city of Cittor to be initiated by him as his spiritual child. In the course of time Jhali was forgotten as the fame of Mira, the queen's musical counterpart, grew.[18] But the debatable accuracy of these stories matters less than the spirit that gave them rise. What is important is that for many centuries after Ravidas, and right down to the present day, there has been a persistent desire to connect the cobbler poet with a larger network of *bhakti* heroes. Ravidas's low-caste followers are not the only ones to have felt this urge; other writers, including Brahmins, have done the same.[19]

The reason is that the *bhakti* tradition by nature runs in families—this is a piety of shared experience, of singing and enthusiastic communication—and each clan, to be inclusive, needs to have at least one representative from the Untouchable castes. In south India, where the *bhakti* movement can be traced back much farther than in the north, this meant that Tiruppan, an Untouchable, and Tirumankai, a member of the thief caste, were set alongside Brahmins and high-status *velalas* in building the family of Alvars—

devotees to Vishnu who lived from the sixth to ninth centuries A.D. In the west of India one found Cokhamela, the Untouchable who on occasion transported carrion, and Namdev, the lowly tailor, in the company of such higher-caste divines as Jnandev and Eknath. And in north India, Kabir and especially Ravidas filled out the family of saints by providing it with poor cousins from the lower end of the social spectrum. The message proclaimed by this tradition of family associations in that the love of God transcends the givens of the social order, bringing together people who otherwise could not have met and creating an alternate, more truly religious society capable of complementing and challenging the one established by caste. It was often the saints situated on the lower rungs of the social ladder who envisioned this other society most clearly.

Some of the most vivid episodes in the traditional life stories of Ravidas take up this point. They reconstitute society according to a *bhakti* definition by showing that Ravidas belongs at its religious apex, that is, in the company of Brahmins. In all of these tales, those who are Brahmins by blood are the last to see the point.

The story of Queen Jhali is a good example. According to Priyadas, this pious woman traveled to Benares in the company of a number of her court Brahmins, who were then scandalized at her choice of gurus. They went to the king of Benares for justice, expecting a sympathetic ear, but the wise ruler, who had already had some experience with Brahmins jealous of Ravidas, submitted the matter to even higher arbitration. He brought both the Brahmins and Ravidas into the presence of the royal icon and announced that he would value the claim of whoever could show that the Lord inclined in his direction. The Brahmins chanted the correct Vedic verses, but these seemed to have no effect. When Ravidas began to sing, however, intoning a verse in which he asked God to reveal himself as the one whose nature is to rescue the fallen (*patit pavan*), the image responded by jumping directly into the poet's lap.[20]

Queen Jhali insisted on taking Ravidas to her home in Rajasthan for a time, and the disgruntled Brahmins could do no more by way of protest. Yet nothing could persuade them to share a meal with the Untouchable saint. When the queen prepared a great feast to honor her newfound teacher, these religious aristocrats declined to eat from the same vessels that he did. Jhali bowed to their compunctions by giving them the ingredients separately, so that they could cook their own meal, and Ravidas issued no protest. When they all sat down, however—Ravidas on his side of the hall and the Brahmins on theirs—and the Brahmins raised the food to their mouths, they discovered to their horror that between each of them a Ravidas had miraculously materialized. Evidently he belonged in their row after all. They fled in consternation and challenged him on his right to be there, but when they did so he peeled back the skin from his chest and revealed a golden sacred thread that lay within, clear evidence of his inner brahminhood.[21]

The *camars* of Sri Govardhanpur love to tell this story, along with others testifying to Ravidas's spiritual superiority. Another favorite is the tale of how the Ganges herself, a Hindu goddess with intimate ties to a wide range of brahminical rituals, acknowledged Ravidas's claim. When the Brahmins of Benares challenged Ravidas's right to preach as he did, the two sides agreed to let the river goddess decide the case: if each threw something into the water, which would she support on her surface? The Brahmins tossed in a piece of wood, but it sank like a stone. Yet when Ravidas threw a stone into the river, it floated.[22]

The people of Sri Govardhanpur find such stories about spiritual brahminhood congenial enough, but they are understandably reluctant to accept any hint that Ravidas was physically a Brahmin or even that he desired to be adopted into the spiritual care of Brahmins. The story that Ravidas sought initiation at the hands of Ramanand, a Brahmin, is an old one—it is told by Priyadas—but the Untouchables of Sri Govardhanpur deny it. Pursuing the new historical connections first suggested by B. R. Ghera, a retired civil servant living in Delhi who is the intellectual spearhead of the Ravidas mission in Sri Govardhanpur, they insist that Ravidas's teacher was instead a certain Saradanand, about whom little has hitherto been heard.[23]

They are even more vehement in contesting the validity of another story told by Priyadas. They refuse to accept that Ravidas was a Brahmin in the life that preceded his incarnation as a *camar*. That they should find such a story offensive is no surprise, since it suggests that no leatherworker can become a saint unaided, but several details reported by Priyadas are particularly heinous. His explanation of why Ravidas was born a *camar* is that in the saint's former life as a pupil of Ramanand he compromised his teacher's Brahmin purity by offering him food donated by a merchant who had been tainted by business dealings with *camars*. According to the story, Ramanand could tell instantly that the food was contaminated by its distant association with Untouchables. Equally offensive is Priyadas's depiction of what happened when this Brahmin pupil died and was reborn into a family of leatherworkers. He says that as a baby Ravidas refused to receive milk from his own *camar* mother. Only when Ramanand heard of the newborn's distress and came to adopt him would the child take sustenance.[24]

No one can deny that such stories are *ex post facto* attempts to brahminize Ravidas, and it is hard not to feel exactly the way the people of Sri Govardhanpur do about the light that they cast on *camars*. Still, the desire of Brahmins to claim Ravidas's charisma as their own is worthy of note. What galls the inhabitants of Sri Govardhanpur and other low-caste communities, however, is that this ecumenical spirit is almost never extended from the realm of *bhakti* hagiography into the real world. They had to appeal to the city government for more than a decade before the road that passes by the new temple was grudgingly paved. They know, too, that many of the Brahmins of Benares scoff at the procession that passes through the city each year on the day they celebrate Ravidas's birth. And they have often had to endure humiliations such as those suffered by a group of Ravidasis who not long ago traveled to far-off Rajasthan to visit the temple of Mirabai in her natal village of Merta, only to be denied entrance once they arrived.

Bhakti and Social Protest

The question that lingers here is whether the message of *bhakti* is a message of social protest. Is the equality it celebrates fundamentally a social reality—and therefore something revolutionary in its Indian context—or is it only spiritual, in which case it can coexist with brahminical Hinduism even if it does not endorse it?

On the one hand it seems clear that a poet like Ravidas raises crucial questions about the social order. His perception of Brahmins and others who set store by standard Hindu texts and rituals is scarcely complimentary, and he has contempt for all who denigrate people belonging to other sectors of society than their own.[25] He insists that

> A family that has a true follower of the Lord
> Is neither high caste nor low caste, lordly or poor.[26]

The number of times he refers to his own caste position suggests that he was always mindful of it.[27] On the other hand, he does not propose any religious legislation that would change the current social order. To the contrary, it often seems that he values his own lowly position as a vantage point from which the truth about everyone comes more clearly into view. His *bhakti* vision seems to be not so much that God desires to reform society as that he transcends it utterly, and that in the light of the experience of sharing in God, all social distinctions lose their importance. At the end of the poem most recently quoted he speaks of how the person of faith may "flower above the world of his birth" as lotuses float upon the water.[28] And he often dwells on the miracle that God has come to him as an implicit sign of how remarkable it is that the holy should touch any human life.[29]

Ravidas's *bhakti,* then, is an answer to caste Hinduism, but not explicitly a call for its reform. Even though he speaks of a kingdom "where none are third or second—all are one" and where the residents "do this or that, they walk where they wish," still he admits that it is his "distant home," and he issues no direct call for realizing it here on earth.[30]

Indeed, when he speaks of earth his emphasis is quite different. He characterizes life in this world as an inevitably difficult journey and asks God for help along the way.[31] Death stands waiting at the end of the road, he knows,[32] and when it strikes, even one's closest relatives scurry to keep their distance.[33] As for the body, it is a fiction of air and water, nothing more than a hollow clay puppet.[34] About all there is to do in such circumstances—as bewildering to human beings as the wider world is to a frog in a well—is cry for help.[35] Fortunately, remarkably, there is a friend who answers that lonely call, someone who is at times confusingly, disconcertingly near, someone to whom people are tied by what Ravidas calls on several occasions "the bonds of love."[36] That friend, of course, is God.

The Ravidas Legacy

The *bhakti* of Ravidas, then, is a gritty, personal faith, so it is fitting that the response of Untouchables to it and to him has a number of facets—social, liturgical, conceptual, and, of course, personal. The first of these responses is indeed the demand for social reform, and at various points over the past several decades it has been couched in frankly political terms. The organization responsible for building a temple to Ravidas in Sri Govardhanpur is called the All India Adi Dharm Mission, a body established in 1957. Building on a heritage that extends back into the early years of the twentieth century, it has at its core the idea that the lowest echelons of modern Indian society are the survivors of a noble race who inhabited the subcontinent long before the Aryan Hindus arrived from central Asia. They were a people who "worshiped truthfulness, justice, simplicity and who were benevolent and helped one another at the time of difficulty. . . ."[37] This was India's *adi dharm,* its "original religion" or "original moral order," something that was substantially destroyed by the Aryan incursion, but that God saw fit to revive by raising up sages and gurus such as Nanak, Kabir, and preeminently Ravidas.[38]

Over the course of its episodic but now relatively long history, the Adi Dharm (or as it is sometimes called, Ad Dharm) movement has attempted to mobilize the lower castes of north India, particularly in the Punjab, to achieve greater social justice.[39] Even the establishment of the Ravidas temple in Sri Govardhanpur serves a potentially political purpose. The current plan to extend the educational activities of the temple by founding a Ravidas college in Sri Govardhanpur is aimed at preparing lower-caste people for jobs in a literate society and enlarging the pool of candidates available to fill positions in government service that are reserved for members of the lower castes.[40]

When Ravidas's name is sounded in religious circles, then, the social message associated with him is never inaudible—even if, to judge from the compositions anthologized in the *Adi Granth,* the saint himself was not entirely preoccupied with the matter. But this is only one facet of the modern response to Ravidas. Another is more specifically cultic and ceremonial: at Sri Govardhanpur and a number of Ravidas *deras* (sacred compounds) in the Punjab, he serves as the actual focus of the community's worship.

Considering the liturgical importance of Ravidas, it is surprising that none of the verses that can best claim to have come from the mouth of the master himself play a role in the worship services that take place at Sri Govardhanpur. When the old liturgist sits down in front of the large, handwritten book from which he chants, the turgid verse he intones has almost no relation to the vivid compositions collected in the *Adi Granth*. Though each of the poems he recites bears Ravidas's oral signature, as is customary in the *pad* genre he employed,[41] these dutiful compositions seem to be about Ravidas, rather than by him. Each of them praises the greatness of one's guru and underscores the importance of preserving one's fealty to the master. The following, the second in the book, is typical:

> Project the guru's image in your mind,
>   hold it ever steady in your thought.
> Purity, charity, making yourself a name—
>   these only bolster your pride,
> But to utter the name of the guru in your heart
>   will make you unshakeably wise. . . .

And so forth, ending with the phrase, "so says Ravidas."[42] The language of this poem is flatter and more plodding than what one meets in the *Adi Granth*. Its simplicity has the advantage of making the verse easily intelligible to its hearers, but because its style is so different from those likely to be authentic, the chances are that the poem is not very old. Though it purports to be the verbiage of Ravidas himself, it has a flaccid, contemporary ring and could scarcely have been produced before the nineteenth century. Even that seems improbably early.

To understand this poetry, one must know who created the book in which it is inscribed. It was B. R. Ghera, the retired civil servant who has had so much to do with launching Ravidas on his most recent career. His intention, like several Adi Dharmis before him, was to draw together the poems of Ravidas into a collection that would rival the anthology of poems that Sikhs take as their scripture, the *Adi Granth*. To do so, he made frequent trips between 1963 and 1967 to a teacher named Harnam who lived in a *dera* in Moradabad district, not far east of Delhi. Ghera reports that Harnam, who himself came from a lower-caste background, was exclusively a follower of Ravidas, so his collection of Ravidas poems was to be trusted as authentic. Ghera reproduced it in a series of volumes that he entitled the *Guru Ravidas Granth*. Only the first volume has so far been issued, but the hope is that when the whole set emerges before the public eye it will indeed be received as comparable in size and depth to its Sikh namesake.[43]

There is no need to prejudge the literary merits of Ghera's effort. What is important is that Ghera tried to create for his castefellows a focus of communal and religious loyalty that would give them the sort of group cohesion for which the Sikhs are well known both in India and abroad. Equally important, he hoped the book would convince them that theirs was a scriptural tradition to rival the best in the *bhakti* heritage, just as the guru that stood at the heart of it was the quintessential expression of the pristine, original faith of India.

These efforts have not yet been entirely successful. While it is the aim of the man in charge of liturgy at the Sri Govardhanpur temple that all forty hymns now included in the *Guru Ravidas Granth* should be recited morning and night, in practice the audience that assembles usually hears only a small selection of didactic verses.[44] The reading of the entire book is reserved for festival occasions. Still, the consolidation of this community's identity behind the figure of Ravidas is well under way. He has become their guru—the founder of their faith and the source of their inspiration—as Nanak is for Sikhs. But he has also become the sort of guru that would be familiar in many Hindu communities. For whereas Sikhs proscribe the use of any image in their places of worship (*gurudvaras*), preferring to meet Nanak and his successors entirely through their words, the Ravidasis of Sri Govardhanpur can establish visual contact with the master, as Hindus typically do. A multicolored, life-size image of the great saint is installed at the center of the altar area, just behind the little stand upon which the book rests. As songs praising the guru's greatness are sung, he receives the community's adoration in person.

A third way in which the fifteenth-century *camar* saint matters in the lives of his latter-day castefellows goes beyond social reform and religious cult. Through Ravidas, Untouchables are able to map out their relation to other aspects of Indian society in a manner that is clearer and more satisfying to them than the conceptual grids through which others are apt to see them.

One expression of this process of conceptual clarification is an enormous construction effort now under way on the opposite side of Benares from Sri Govardhanpur. There, on a bluff overlooking the Ganges, the most important Untouchable political figure of recent times, the late Deputy Prime Minister Jagjivan Ram, began building a temple to Ravidas as the last great project of his career. Work proceeds apace, and when finished, the edifice will be a splendid one indeed. It will be covered entirely with marble; it will contain a vast sanctuary, a huge kitchen, and quarters for ascetics and visiting scholars; and it will house a museum in which will be deposited not only memorabilia relating to Ravidas but those documenting the life of Jagjivan Ram as well. In the circular appealing for funds, in fact, these two share the spotlight: a picture of Jagjivan Ram is on one side of the page and a picture of Ravidas is on the other.[45]

Jagjivan Ram's temple says many things. First and foremost, of course, it says that Ravidas belongs on the highlands along the Ganges as much as any other Hindu god or saint. Fortunately Jagjivan Ram's political connections enabled him to acquire from the government the land necessary to make such a statement. Second, the temple says something about Ravidas's place among the other *bhakti* saints of north India: it puts him right in the center. In the tea stall at the temple's entrance, Ravidas's picture is flanked by others depicting Kabir and Surdas, and in the sanctuary one finds not only a central altar dedicated to Ravidas but an ancillary shrine to Mirabai. Third, the structure states the relation between the veneration of Ravidas and India's major religious communities. Spires on each of the corners will commemorate Hinduism, Buddhism, Christianity, and Islam, and in their midst will rise the great spire to Ravidas. The message is that Ravidas is open to all the great religions, and illumines them equally.

Finally there is a political message. The man in charge of day-to-day operations at the temple, Ram Lakhan, a former member of parliament and minister in Indira Gandhi's government, declares it to be "the people's temple," with the implication that the people provide the basis upon which all other structures rest. To speak this way is to cast Ravidas in the role of vox populi and to suggest not too subliminally that the Congress Party, in which both Jagjivan Ram and Ram Lakhan served, is the organization capable of bringing together adherents of all communities in a way that transcends caste and religious affiliation.[46]

The people of Sri Govardhanpur say that they will surely visit this new monument when it is finished, but they are well aware that it was Jagjivan Ram's establishment connections that made its construction possible. Some quip that it is less a temple to their saint than to the political figure who posed as his devotee. And they have their own way of charting the territory that ties them, through Ravidas, to the wider world. The contents of their own Ravidas edifice may be less imposing than what is being assembled across town, but they serve essentially the same function.

First of all, there is a life-size statue of the bespectacled Sant Sarvan Das, the Punjabi religious leader whose Ravidas following contributed the financial means that made the temple possible and whose far-off *dera* welcomes pilgrims from Sri Govardhanpur into what seems a pan-Indian community.[47] Other aspects of the sanctuary serve a similar purpose by placing Ravidas himself in a broader context. There is, for example, a map of India that records in careful detail the journeys that Ravidas took around the subcontinent. It shows how he traveled from Kashmir in the north to the Deccan in the south and spanned the distance between Puri and Dvaraka, two great hubs of pilgrimage on the east and west coasts—a total journey of 5,946 kilometers, as the legend announces. This map has the effect of placing Ravidas in the great tradition of philosophers and theologians who circled the land to establish the paramount legitimacy of their views.

Other illustrations do the same thing in other ways. One painting, for instance, depicts the moment in which Ravidas initiated Mirabai. It relates him to the figure who is probably the most popular member of the north Indian *bhakti* family, but who stands at the head of no formalized cult or community of her own. This makes it less dangerous than it otherwise would be for these lower-caste people to assert their guru's primacy over her, and thereby suggest that he is the ultimate cause of her celebrity. Another illustration shows the master's own lineage, situating him as the central figure in a genealogy of revelation that extends from the present era of world history all the way back to the beginning of time.[48]

Of course, the people of Sri Govardhanpur are aware that other people see things other ways and would not necessarily agree with all that these pictures imply. But that is no great problem. They see that history has a tendency to be forged after the fact by communities who wish to shape it: after all, how many stories of Ravidas himself have been suppressed or twisted by upper-caste groups eager to rewrite history so that it serves their own interest? Furthermore, they take it as given that things seem different from different perspectives, and that people emphasize what matters most to them. In this perception they are not alone. This feature of Hindu thinking seemed so pervasive to the pioneering Indologist Max Müller that he felt he had to coin new words to describe it. He spoke of "kathenotheism" and "henotheism," both referring to the Hindu tendency to worship gods one at a time, yet regard each as ultimate for the period during which that god is at the forefront of the believer's attention.[49] Similarly, when it comes to saints and society, Hindus find it natural that people should draw toward their own point of focus all that concerns them, as the Untouchables of north India have consolidated much of the general *bhakti* heritage around Ravidas.

The henotheistic habit of mind makes it possible for people like those who live in Sri Govardhanpur to assign themselves a convincingly important position in the broad sweep of Indian society and religion. If others do not orient themselves by the same map, it does not greatly matter. For these Benarsis the figure of Ravidas, a gift from the past, serves as a major point of reference, and for that reason he is very much alive in the present, shaping the world half a millennium after his death.

POEMS OF RAVIDAS

I've never known how to tan or sew,
  though people come to me for shoes.
I haven't the needle to make the holes
  or even the tool to cut the thread.
Others stitch and knot, and tie themselves in knots
  while I, who do not knot, break free.
I keep saying Ram and Ram, says Ravidas,
  and Death keeps his business to himself.

[AG 20]

Who could long for anything but you?
My master, you are merciful to the poor;
  you have shielded my head with a regal parasol.
Someone whose touch offends the world
  you have enveloped with yourself.
It is the lowly my Govind makes high—
  he does not fear anyone at all—
And he has exalted Namdev and Kabir,
  Trilocan, Sadhna, and Sen.
Listen saints, says Ravidas,
  Hari accomplishes everything.

[AG 33]

Oh well born of Benares, I too am born well known:
  my labor is with leather. But my heart can boast the Lord.
See how you honor the purest of the pure,
  water from the Ganges, which no saint will touch
If it has been made into intoxicating drink—
  liquor is liquor whatever its source;
And this toddy tree you consider impure
  since the sacred writings have branded it that way,
But see what writings are written on its leaves:
  the Bhagavata Purana you so greatly revere.
And I, born among those who carry carrion
  in daily rounds around Benares, am now
    the lowly one to whom the mighty Brahmins come
And lowly bow. Your name, says Ravidas,
  is the shelter of your slave.

[AG 38]

A family that has a true follower of the Lord
Is neither high caste nor low caste, lordly or poor.
  The world will know it by its fragrance.
Priests or merchants, laborers or warriors,
  halfbreeds, outcastes, and those who tend cremation fires—
    their hearts are all the same.
He who becomes pure through love of the Lord
  exalts himself and his family as well.
Thanks be to his village, thanks to his home,
  thanks to that pure family, each and every one,
For he's drunk with the essence of the liquid of life
  and he pours away all the poisons.
No one equals someone so pure and devoted—
  not priests, not heroes, not parasolled kings.
As the lotus leaf floats above the water, Ravidas says,
  so he flowers above the world of his birth.

[AG 29]

Mother, she asks, with what can I worship?
  All the pure is impure. Can I offer milk?
The calf has dirtied it in sucking its mother's teat.
  Water, the fish have muddied; flowers, the bees—
No other flowers could be offered than these.
  The sandalwood tree, where the snake has coiled, is spoiled.
The same act formed both nectar and poison.
  Everything's tainted—candles, incense, rice—
But still I can worship with my body and my mind
  and I have the guru's grace to find the formless Lord.
Rituals and offerings—I can't do any of these.
  What, says Ravidas, will you do with me?

[AG 13]

Your name: the act of worship
with the lifted lamp, Murari;
without the name of Hari all the universe is a lie.

Your name: the throne on which
the deity sits, your name the grinding stone,
the saffron that is ground and daubed upon the gods.

Your name: the holy water,
your name the sandal for sandalwood paste.
Grinding, chanting, I take that name and offer it to you.

Your name: the little lamp, the cruse,
your name the wick.
Your name is the oil that I pour into the ritual lamp.

Lighting your name:
the flame in the lamp
brings the glow that lightens all the corners of the house.

Your name: the garland;
your name the string, the flowers.
Beside them wither all the blossoms of the wilds.

Your handiwork: the world;
what could I offer more?
I can only wave your name like the whisk before the gods.

The world contains the vessels
for your sacred rites—
the scriptures, the direction points, and all the sacred sites—

But your name, says Ravidas,
is the lifting of the lamp;
your true name, O Hari, your food.

[AG 23]

The walls are made of water, pillared by air,
  sealed together with the mortar of blood,
A cell of veins and meat and bones,
  a cage to hold this poor bird.
Who cares what is yours or mine?—
  for we nest in this tree only briefly.
As high as you can build, as low as you can dig,
  your size will never swell the dimensions of a grave;
Those lovely curls, that turban tied so rakishly—
  they'll soon be turned to ash.
If you've counted on the beauty of your wife and home
  without the name of Ram, you've already lost the game.
And me: even though my birth is mean,
  my ancestry by everyone despised,
I have always trusted in you, King Ram,
  says Ravidas, a tanner of hides.

[AG 19]

It's just a clay puppet, but how it can dance!
It looks here, looks there, listens and talks,
  races off this way and that;
It comes on something and it swells with pride,
  but if fortune fades it starts to cry.
It gets tangled in its lusts, in tastes
    of mind, word, and deed,
  and then it meets its end and takes some other form.
Brother, says Ravidas, the world's a game, a magic show,
  and I'm in love with the gamester,
    the magician who makes it go.

[AG 12]

The house is large, its kitchen vast,
  but after only a moment's passed, it's vacant.
This body is like a scaffold made of grass:
  the flames will consume it and render it dust.
Even your family—your brothers and friends—
  clamor to have you removed at dawn.
The lady of the house, who once clung to your chest,
  shouts "Ghost! Ghost!" now and runs away.
The world, says Ravidas, loots and plunders all—
  except me, for I have slipped away
    by saying the name of God.

[AG 27]

This bodily world is a difficult road—hilly, overgrown—
  and I've only this worthless bullock to rely on.
This request I make of Ram:
  protect my wealth as I go along.
Who is a peddler for Ram?
  My daily pack is loaded—
I am a peddler for Ram;
  I traffic in his easy ecstasy:
I've loaded myself with the wealth of Ram's name
  while the world is loaded down with poison.
You who know both shores of the sea,
  chart my course through heaven and hell
So Death will not ambush me with his stick
  nor trap me in his snare.
The world's a fading yellow dye, says the tanner Ravidas,
  but Ram is an indelible red.

[AG 4]

Peddler,
  the first watch of night.
  What's this body's business?
Hari, the child-god:
  you paid him no heed—
  simpleton, such a foolish, childish way to think!
Simpleton, such a foolish, childish way to think—
  you ignored the net of illusion,
  simply paid it no mind.
What's that? Why repent?
  All that water everywhere,
  and once the sails are loose, you're gone.
Peddler,
  so says Ravidas the slave:
  simpleton, such a foolish, childish way to think.

[Fatehpur, p. 190]

Peddler,
  the second watch of night.
  You went chasing shadows of yourself.
You paid him no heed—Hari,
  the child-god—
  didn't board his boat.
Didn't board Hari's name—
  you couldn't, all bloated up
  with youth.
Desire so dulled you,
  you couldn't see the line
  between the woman that was yours
  and someone else's.
Well, Hari will straighten the accounts;
  you'll pay in full.
  You'll burn if that's what's right.
Peddler,
  so says Ravidas the slave:
  you went chasing shadows of yourself.

[Fatehpur, p. 191]

Peddler,
  the third watch of night.
  The breath has gone slack.
Peddler, the body is bent
  and what to do?
  Bad thoughts have settled inside.
Bad thoughts have settled inside,
  evil fool—a life completely lost.
Now was the moment,
  but you shunned what was right
  and the time will never come again.
Your frame is weary,
  your body frail,
  and still you won't rethink your ways.
Peddler,
  so says Ravidas the slave:
  the breath has gone slack.

[Fatehpur, p. 191]

Peddler,
  the fourth watch of night.
  The body shivers, it quakes.
Peddler,
  the Master is going to settle accounts.
  Abandon your perverse old ways.
Get wise,
  abandon the old fort.
  He may adorn you, he may feed you to the fire.
Death himself is at large:
  he's sent to have you bound,
  you smuggler. It's death's door.
The road ahead is hard,
  and you'll travel it alone.
  Where are the ones you once loved?
Peddler,
  so says Ravidas the slave:
  the body shivers, it quakes.

[Fatehpur, p. 192]

The day it comes, it goes;
  whatever you do, nothing stays firm.
The group goes, and I go;
  the going is long, and death is overhead.
What! Are you sleeping? Wake up, fool,
  wake to the world you took to be true.
The one who gave you life daily feeds you, clothes you;
  inside every body, he runs the store.
So keep to your prayers, abandon "me" and "mine,"
  now's the time to nurture the name that's in the heart.
Life has slipped away. No one's left on the road,
  and in each direction the evening dark has come.
Madman, says Ravidas, here's the cause of it all—
  it's only a house of tricks. Ignore the world.

[AG 26]

The regal realm with the sorrowless name:
  they call it Queen City, a place with no pain,
No taxes or cares, none owns property there,
  no wrongdoing, worry, terror, or torture.
Oh my brother, I've come to take it as my own,
  my distant home, where everything is right.
That imperial kingdom is rich and secure,
  where none are third or second—all are one;
Its food and drink are famous, and those who live there
  dwell in satisfaction and in wealth.
They do this or that, they walk where they wish,
  they stroll through fabled palaces unchallenged.
Oh, says Ravidas, a tanner now set free,
  those who walk beside me are my friends.

[AG 3]

TWO

Kabir

Brother, if holding back your seed
Earned you a place in paradise,
eunuchs would be the first to arrive.

IN the whole sweep of north Indian religion there is no voice more stringent, more passionate, more confident than that of Kabir. If Hinduism has a prophet, an Amos or a Jeremiah, here he is—not in the sense that he forecast anything, but that he was ever at odds with the world around him, always ready to fling the dart of criticism in the direction of established religion. This cannot have endeared him to the slickly robed, nicely perfumed Muslim *qazis* who expounded matters of Muslim law in the mosques and courts of a Benares ruled by sultans of Turkish ancestry. Nor can it have earned him the affection of the argumentative, supercilious Brahmin pundits with whom they coexisted. And it had no chance of making him a great favorite among the sometimes dignified, sometimes unkempt yogis who filled the city with their message of renunciation, then as now. But his testy aphorisms did ensure that the common people would take in what he said—storekeepers, fishermen, housewives, and rickshaw drivers—and his words are on their tongues to this day.

Here is Kabir on things dear to Hindus:

Vedas, Puranas—why read them?
It's like loading an ass with sandalwood!

As for Muslim priorities, such as the necessity of circumcision:

If God had wanted to make me a Muslim,
  why didn't he make the incision?

Or the practices of naked mendicants:

If the union yogis seek
Came from roaming around in the buff,
  every deer in the forest would be saved.

Then there are his numerous reflections on life:

Your chance of human birth
Doesn't come time and again.
Once the ripe fruit falls
You can't stick it back
  on the branch.

And on death:

Bones: they burn like tinder
Hair: it burns like hay.
And still, says Kabir, people won't wake up—
Not until they feel death's club
  inside their skulls.

The Hagiography of Kabir

As in the case of Ravidas, we know very little with historical certainty about the life that produced attacks and meditations such as these. Kabir's name is a Muslim one, a Quranic title of Allah meaning "great," but in poems of his that have the best claim to authenticity one finds little to suggest that Kabir was a Muslim in the usual sense of the word. He criticized Islam rather than embracing it, and evidently had little appreciation for the niceties of Islamic theology. He seems more at home with Hindu ways, though they too receive his criticism, and there has been some speculation of late that he came from a social group that had recently and superficially converted to Islam.[1] Such a picture would fit well with his social station as it is described both in legend and in poems attributed to him. Apparently he belonged to the weaver (*julaha, kori*) caste, which had every reason to disown its lowly place in the caste hierarchy and turn to Islam. Beyond that there is little one can say, except that poetry and hagiography are united in asserting that Kabir's weavers were from Benares.

For centuries the weavers of Benares have beautified the streets and open places of the city with their work. People come from all over India to buy the richly woven, gold- and silver-bordered saris of Benares, and the production of these garments is one of its visual joys. Early in the morning these weavers, most of whom are Muslim, bring great skeins of brightly dyed thread and stretch them out to dry on racks, a hundred yards at a time. And if one passes through one of the weavers' neighborhoods, the aural pleasure is scarcely less intense. Behind courtyard walls and under open porches, the men sit at their looms skittering the shuttles back and forth across long, taut threads in a strangely addicting rhythm. Often they sing as they go. It is an occupation that gives one time to reflect on the noisy happenings that fill the city's twisted streets, and Kabir evidently did plenty of reflecting. His biographies and his own compositions suggest that his thoughts often got him so agitated that he couldn't sit still, so he jumped up and joined the fray.

It is easy to imagine that Kabir's tendency to get involved in debates about religion took him away from his loom more frequently than was good for the family's financial health, and this is affirmed in Priyadas's commentary on the *Bhaktamal,* which gives one of the oldest extant accounts of Kabir's life, as of Ravidas's.[2] But the reason for this state of affairs is quite different from what one might expect on the basis of the spicy, obdurate personality that emerges from the poems we have already quoted. In suggesting why Kabir's business habitually lost money, Priyadas seems eager to soften Kabir and make him conform to the kindly, abstracted type that lies at the core of Priyadas's own vision of sainthood. Part of the problem, says Priyadas, was that Kabir would often drift off into meditation as he worked; and even if he went to market to hawk a bolt of cloth, he would very likely be overcome with a wave of generosity and give the whole thing away to some needy beggar. Priyadas reports that once when this happened Kabir became so frightened of the reception he would get if he returned home that he simply did not go. He hid in the market for three days, while his family languished in hunger. In the end it all came out for the better. Enunciating a theme that is one of his favorites, Priyadas says that God responded to Kabir's unstinting generosity to others by sending an ox-cart full of provisions to his family.[3] But in recounting the event, he takes a moment to note that even when this great boon arrived at the door, Kabir's mother was not pleased. She suspected that someday they would be punished for accepting this unearned beneficence, and shouted at the merchant who delivered it to go away.

The story then develops into an account of how the saint's generosity and devotional charisma drew to him great crowds of followers, including even royalty. As usual in Priyadas's hagiographical portraits, this popularity provokes anger and jealousy among Brahmins, who feel that their influence is being eroded and their position displaced—the sort of feeling that inflamed them against Ravidas. In this case they are able to win the allegiance of Kabir's disgruntled mother, who joins them in complaining of the great pain he has caused to all.[4] In an effort to bring him to trial, the Brahmins take Kabir before the emperor Sikandar Lodi, who is said to have been visiting Benares from Delhi at the time. The *qazi* of Sikandar's court orders Kabir to bow before the potentate, but Kabir refuses, saying that he only knows how to bow to God. That is enough for the emperor to decree that Kabir be bound in chains and thrown in the middle of the Ganges, to be drowned. The order is carried out, but when the emperor's men return to the shore they find Kabir standing unharmed on the bank. (The cover of a modern comic book depicting Kabir's life shows him walking across the water to get there.)[5] Suspecting that witchcraft is involved, the soldiers place his body on a nearby funeral pyre. Then they ignite the pyre, but all that happens is that the body emits a luscious golden glow: the saint remains unhurt. These events are soon told at court, and it is not long before Kabir can number among his devotees the most powerful ruler in India.

Nothing, however, can placate the Brahmins. Having failed to win the ear of royalty, they resort to efforts to organize Kabir's own people against him. They invite Untouchables near and far to attend an elaborate feast at Kabir's house, expecting that there will be a great riot when the rabble arrive and find nothing to eat. As on former occasions Kabir, sensing the imminent press of a crowd, goes into hiding. But his patron, God himself, steps in to fill the breach, taking human form in the likeness of Kabir and tending to the guests' every need.[6] Thus the Brahmins' evil plans are foiled again; and again, as in the case of Queen Jhali of Cittor, it is in the gustatory arena that they meet defeat. Evidently Priyadas loves this theme: perhaps it is his commentary on the legendary appetites of Brahmins, whose traditional livelihood depends so much on food offerings paid for by members of other castes.

The end of Kabir's life is told in a surprisingly economical fashion, compared with the attention it has received almost everywhere else. Priyadas merely says that Kabir retired from Benares to live in the small town of Magahar, some miles to the north, near Gorakhpur. When he sensed that his death was at hand, he asked for some flowers, spread them out as a bed, and merged forever into the infinite love of God.[7]

This peaceful departure is not quite what the larger tradition reports. It is more usually said that Kabir's death was witnessed by great throngs of people, among whom could be found equal numbers of Hindus and Muslims. When the great saint finally passed away, these two camps set upon each other with brilliant fury, each trying to lay claim to the body. But their warfare was useless. After battling one another to get to the corpse, they found in its stead only a pile of flowers—or, according to another version, two piles of flowers. A voice from heaven—was it Kabir himself?—advised the Muslims present to bury one pile, as was their practice, and told the Hindus to cremate the other, as was their wont.[8] Either the purpose of this story is to show that religious practice, whether Hindu or Muslim, falls short of Kabir's reality or it is to present Kabir, in the words of a subtitle of a recently published book, as "the apostle of Hindu-Muslim unity."[9] Either way the crowd's response to his death serves as a prime example of the way people fail to hear the prophet's message that God is one.

Perhaps inevitably, Kabir's loving biographers have proven themselves not much better than the two bellicose crowds at accepting Kabir on his own terms. Priyadas, for example, makes a great point of Kabir's timidity, how shy he was before masses of people. But what we hear in the poet's own utterances seems to prove the opposite: he was pugilistic in the extreme, ever on the attack, and unwilling to let the opponent get a word in edgewise:

Pundit, how can you be so dumb?
You're going to drown, along with all your kin,
unless you start speaking of Ram.

Hey Qazi,
what's that book you're preaching from?
And reading, reading—how many days?
Still you haven't mastered one word.[10]

Priyadas also stresses the importance Kabir attached to being hospitable toward others in the *bhakti* community, but do these words sound hospitable?

Hey brother, why do you want me to talk?
Talk and talk and the real things get lost.[11]

If anything is credible in Priyadas's account of Kabir, perhaps it is the emphasis he lays on the saint's outlandish behavior and the embarrassment and grief it must have caused his mother. According to one story he dragged a prostitute around with him to keep away the pious throngs, and it is easy enough to imagine that he also scandalized his mother, if in somewhat less inflammatory ways.[12]

As for the incident of the flowers at Magahar, it too assumes an air of well-meaning unreality when one compares the story with what the poet himself had to say about Magahar. In poems that stand a good chance of being authentic, he makes it clear that it was hardly the urge to make peace between Hindus and Muslims that drew him to the town. He seems to have gone there strictly for Hindu—or rather, anti-Hindu—reasons, for he makes quite a point of setting Magahar on the same level as Benares. To the ears of any Hindu, that is a very demeaning comparison for Benares, and one strong tradition affirms that Kabir left the holy city deliberately lest he die there and appear to accept the notion that it had eternal benefits to confer.[13] There is little cause to doubt the unanimous testimony of tradition that Kabir decided to live his last years among the weavers of Magahar, and if he did, it was hardly a gesture of conciliation toward Hindus.

The irenic doctrine that Kabir was the great spokesman for Hindu-Muslim reconciliation is certainly a convenient article of faith in secular India, and one that finds eloquent expression in the identical twin buildings that have been constructed on his death site: a Hindu temple and a Muslim mausoleum. But the doctrine finds little support in the poetry itself. Nowhere in Kabir's sayings does he evince much of an attitude of acceptance toward the two great faiths of India. The only pronouncements that would lead one to believe that these religions are fundamentally the same are those in which they are denigrated in the same breath.

If the mosque is the place where God resides,
  then who owns the rest of the land?
Ram lives in images and holy locations?—
  Then why has no one ever found him there?

Hindus, Muslims—where did they come from?
  Who got them started down this road?

The Exemplar of *Nirguna* Religion

Kabir's uniform disdain for Hinduism and Islam reflects his most deeply held conviction: that God cannot be named, described, assumed, or bound. Kabir is sensitive to the many ways in which life's truth escapes the lazy hypocrisies in which we prefer to trade: it is often encountered only as a challenge to what we expect, only in conditions of extreme loneliness and death, only in silence or surprise, and with effort and cost. These are the themes that Kabir dwells on time and again, and they shape the way he expresses himself. He has no interest in becoming a new, "prophetic" version of the chattering, dogmatic *qazis* and pundits that he hears all around him, so he often speaks in feints and jabs. And when he goes on at greater length, it may be simply to confound listeners who come hoping to learn the sort of religious truth one can write down and file away. These confusing utterances are called Kabir's "upside-down speech" (*ulatbamsi*) because they defy comprehension:

Child of a childless woman,
  a fatherless son,
  someone without feet who climbs trees. . . .[15]

As for his other formulations, they have a tendency to be so short and trenchant, so earthy, that they scarcely qualify as "religious" discourse at all. From Kabir's point of view, that's fine.

The religion he knows—if religion it is—is of a totally different order from the admonitions and assurances that put bread and butter on the tables of *qazis* and pundits. His faith is the sort traditionally known as the "qualityless" or "formless" (*nirguna*) brand of *bhakti*. It lacks quality or form in two respects. First, its proponents insist that God is not the sort of reality that one can speak of and conceptualize, certainly not the sort one can see. God is not an object, but lies closer to us than our acts of language and symbolic organization permit us to view, and closer to life than the limitations of our own brief and flawed existences allow us to comprehend. If we come upon God, therefore, or God comes upon us, the moment is apt to have a simple, easy feel to it, at once empty and full—what Kabir calls, following a substantial tradition before him, "spontaneous" (*sahaj*).[16] Here is the experience in major and minor keys:

Kabir:
My mind was soothed
When I found the boundless knowledge,
And the fires
  that scorch the world
To me are water cool.

Kabir:
The instrument is still,
Its strings snapped.
What can the poor thing do?
Its player's no longer
  there.[17]

That brings us to the second sense in which *nirguna bhakti* is formless: in regard to the act of worship. *Nirguna bhakti* does not easily build institutions, and it is suspicious of the religious structures that exist in the world. From this point of view Islam is just as culpable as Hinduism, despite its very healthy admixture of *nirguna* theology. Islam has spawned a definite cultus and liturgy; certainly it has defined a judicial system sufficiently self-confident to punish any who stray from the written dictates of law and religion. Hinduism is just as bad, perhaps worse. Following an ancient urge toward form, and accepting the point of view that, initially at least, human beings can perceive in no other way but through the symbols that structure their consciousness, it has pictured God in a multitude of shapes and portrayed his actions in numerous events. This is *saguna* religion, the worship of a God who takes form to act and to be comprehended and loved, and its style of worship is similarly suffused with form and quality. To walk into a Hindu temple is to be surrounded by so many sights, sounds, and smells that inexperienced visitors often feel they have strayed into a religious jungle.

Kabir certainly thought so. He found the sacrifices that priests made to the goddess Kali hideous, and he thought it was the sheerest nonsense to picture God in a succession of animal and human avatars whose form could then be worshiped and adored and whose stories could spawn an industry of religious texts, complete with their Brahmin interpreters.[18] Even when the point of these stories was to demonstrate the unaccountably generous love of God, Kabir had his reservations. His experience of divine love seems to have been a sense of completeness that a story-telling mode, with its assigning of character roles and its necessary separation between subjects and objects, could not describe.[19]

But this did not leave Kabir without words or without the community that makes words meaningful. Traditional biographies supply Kabir with one kind of religious community; a close reading of his authentic poems suggests another. The traditional tales, such as the one composed by Priyadas, tell how Kabir sought out the spiritual guidance of Ramanand and became a member of his fold. The story goes that Kabir knew the great Brahmin would not accept as a pupil anyone whose caste was as low as his, so he resorted to trickery to earn the initiation he desired. He knew that Ramanand, like any good Hindu living in Benares, went down to the Ganges before dawn each morning to take his bath. The boy Kabir watched his habits carefully and one day rolled himself up on one of the steps leading down to the river, just where the holy man always trod.

As Kabir anticipated, Ramanand was unable to see him in the predawn darkness, so when his foot came to rest on a living being rather than the next step, he shouted an ejaculation of concern and surprise: "Ram!" That word is one of the great names for God in north India, referring both to one of the principal avatars of the high god Vishnu and to God in general; it is the cry that Gandhi emitted when he was shot. It is also present as the first element in Ramanand's own name. So when Ramanand shouted "Ram," Kabir chose to interpret it as an initiatory mantra being transferred from guru to disciple, a mantra accompanied by the laying on of hands—or, just as good, feet. Forever after, Kabir regarded Ramanand as his preceptor and participated in his coterie of disciples.[20]

As in the case of Ravidas, there is good reason to doubt the historical validity of this association between Kabir and Ramanand. Kabir never mentions his would-be guru in his poetry, and his use of the name Ram is only in the most exceptional instances what one would expect from a pupil of Ramanand. When Kabir speaks of Ram, as he often does, it is not in a *saguna* sense. He rarely makes a connection between the Ram he speaks of and any of the celebrated acts performed by the Ram who was a form of Vishnu. For Kabir, Ram is merely common coinage for the name of God,[21] and one major community to which he addresses himself and in which he seems to feel at home is of quite a different orientation from the Vaisnava religion Ramanand seems to have represented.[22]

This is a community of yogis, adepts belonging to the then influential sect that traces its lineage to a succession of masters (*naths*) that includes Gorakhnath, a teacher who probably lived sometime between the ninth and eleventh centuries. The Nath orientation is not to Vishnu or any of his avatars but to Siva, paradigm of yogis, whom the Nath Yogis regard as the first guru in their lineage.[23] The Nath Yogis of Kabir's day practiced a spiritual discipline involving *hatha yoga* that led to an immediate, spontaneous (*sahaj*) experience of truth in which the True Guru (*satguru*) revealed himself in the adept. Nath Yogis could be identified as a common sight in the streets by their characteristic emblems, including big, round earrings and a whistle made from the horn of a deer.[24] The peculiar thing about the Naths is that at a certain point in their history a whole segment of the order refused to accept the proposition that religious, even specifically yogic attainment requires celibacy; they married and become householders like their lay followers, who included many weavers.[25] There are persistent hints in Kabir's poetry that he had close ties with the Naths—sometimes friendly, sometimes adversarial—and that he was deeply indebted to them for his peculiarly interior understanding of what true religion was about. One of the important linkages between Kabir and the Naths was the matter of caste, for the Naths were particularly disdainful of the niceties of Hindu hierarchy, and many Untouchables and low-caste people had been admitted into their ranks. The *nirguna* vision of religious truth that they espoused was certainly a powerful antidote to the *saguna* institutions of image-worship and dietary precision that so often became the tutelary preserve of Brahmins. In a way *nirguna bhakti* was the natural haven for any who felt themselves shunned by Hindu society.

Kabir Versus Ravidas

For this reason it is curious to see what tradition has done to the natural bond between Kabir and Ravidas—both Benarsis, both low in the caste hierarchy, and both exponents of the *nirguna* persuasion. At first, of course, tradition affirmed this bond. The oldest stories portray Kabir and Ravidas as spiritual brothers by making them both pupils of Ramanand. There is a measure of theological cooptation in this, since through their teacher both become Vaisnavas—worshippers of Vishnu and his avatars Ram and Krishna—but the story supplies a link that recognizes how much they had in common. There have been other ways of doing the same thing. Contrary to what the *camars* of Sri Govardhanpur say, there is an important Benares tradition that makes Kabir and Ravidas brothers, as it were, from birth. Kabir's putative birthplace is located at Lahartara, on the western outskirts of the city, and Ravidas is said to have been born in the largely low-caste village of Maduadih not far away.[26]

Since the late seventeenth century, however, a document has been circulating that questions the comforting implications of such proximity and suggests that the two holy men were in fact opponents to some degree. This versified "Dialogue between Kabir and Ravidas" (*Kabir-Ravidas Samvad* or *Kabir-Ravidas Gosti*) was definitely composed by someone who saw Ravidas as an inferior to Kabir.[27] Throughout the discussion Ravidas addresses Kabir respectfully, first merely as his elder (*budhe*), but later as his master (*svami*), and by the time the dialogue is finished he has been entirely converted to Kabir's point of view. The issue that divides the two saints initially is the crucial one of *nirguna* versus *saguna* religion—whether God has form or not—and it is Kabir who is given the privilege of espousing the consistently *nirguna* position. To Ravidas is relegated the thankless task of defending *saguna bhakti*. He asserts that people need the kind of immediate, this-worldly salvation that Krishna and Ram provide, but Kabir always has a comeback. He bests Ravidas by pointing out, for instance, that the hell from which Krishna would save his followers is really an illusion,[28] or that the legend of Ram shows him capable of being deluded by the chimera of a deer. Can such a man be God?[29] Then Ravidas tries to argue the importance of a third member of the pantheon—the goddess Sakti or Durga—but Kabir scoffs at her dependence on sacrifices.[30] In the end, disabused of the notion that *saguna* and *nirguna* religion are essentially the same, even if his own teacher Ramanand had taught it, Ravidas asks Kabir what the truth of the matter is. Kabir explains that Gorakhnath is his guru and teaches Ravidas the truth of the God who has no shape (*nirakar*) and the Ram who is within (*atmaram*). Ravidas embraces this message gladly.[31]

It is no wonder that followers of Ravidas have sometimes resented this text, and they are able to point to others in which the outcome of the debate is depicted in a diametrically opposite way: Ravidas bests Kabir. Among these are a recent redaction of the *Bhavisya Purana* ("The History of the Future") and an equally recent *Ravidas Ramayana* ("The Epic of Ravidas"). The latter treats matters not only of doctrine but of practice, showing how Kabir at first refused to drink water offered him by Ravidas on the grounds that the *camar*'s touch had polluted it, then was made to see the error of his ways.[32] Such a vignette shows how theologically pliable such debates can be. Whereas the original *Kabir-Ravidas Samvad* scorns Ravidas for thinking that *nirguna* and *saguna* perspectives ultimately come to the same thing, this catholicity is held up as a mark of sophistication in the *Ravidas Ramayana;* and recent documents issued by Kabir's following have a tendency to say the same thing.[33]

The Kabir Panth

A Kabirian catholicity! How the man would have shuddered. But that would be nothing compared to the astonishment he might feel at seeing some of the ways in which his name lives on in modern-day

Benares. One of the great hubs of the city is called Kabir Square (*kabir caura*), and it is named not just for the man but for an institution: the Kabir monastary (*kabir math*) that lies hidden in the lanes not far away. It is built around the room where Kabir is said to have lived, and there one may view his relics: the wooden shoes he is said to have worn, the wooden pot from which he supposedly drank, the trident staff Gorakhnath is said to have given him, and the huge rope garland bestowed upon him by Ramanand in recognition of the teacher-student bond between them. But if one turns and faces the great courtyard, walks past the monks' cells, and peers into the shrine that dominates the great open space, one sees what is from the perspective of Kabir's own words much more remarkable: a great picture of Kabir himself. Here is the prophet of iconoclastic *nirguna* religion apparently enshrined in the enemy's sanctuary: to a certain degree he has become a figure in the pantheon of *saguna* Hinduism. Morning and evening, a lection of poems attributed to Kabir is recited in a fast-paced chant by the assembled monks and whatever lay adherents join their prayer. This ritualized reading is accompanied by a ceremony in which the likeness of Kabir is honored with an offering of lights—exactly the sort one expects to see waved before the images in any Hindu temple—and in one of the branches of the Kabir Panth, the Dharmadas sect, that likeness is in fact an image, a statue.[34]

In the evening service at Kabir Square it is made explicitly clear that these offerings of word and gesture are directed toward Kabir himself, and the way in which this is done, particularly at the end of the service, might have come as quite a shock to the master. Kabir tirelessly excoriated the Brahmins for pretending to have access to specialized religious knowledge, and the Sanskrit language was the chief medium that made this monopoly possible. Kabir is remembered as having ridiculed it as antiquated and stilted. One of his best known, if not best authenticated, verses contrasts its rhythms with those of the vernacular tongue by asking whether one would rather drink from the brackish waters of an old, little-used well or quench one's thirst at the side of a thriving, bubbling stream.[35] Yet at the close of the evening service performed at Kabir's shrine in Benares, the guru is held up as "the supreme Kabir" in no other language than Sanskrit, and on occasion the homily that follows the service also comes out in Sanskrit: the speaker of the day may simply read from a

Sanskrit commentary on Kabir's poems. One might think that such words would go over the heads of everyone in the audience, but this is not so, for the monastery actually boasts a school dedicated to teaching Sanskrit to the novitiates. Here as in other Kabir monasteries the residents and pupils are primarily lower-caste people, but they have cheerfully adopted the marks of brahminical religion in its ascetic mode. The abbot, who wears the same conical cap Kabir is supposed to have worn, is treated as deserving of the majesty one might accord to the head of any high-caste ascetic order.[36]

What has happened? Weber called similar transformations in the history of religion, "the routinization of charisma," a process whereby personal magnetism is transmuted into institutional authority.[37] But if the history of the Kabir Panth, the "path" that venerates him, is a history of routinization, it takes a particularly Hindu form, for not only have Kabir's teachings been codified and his spiritual lineage authorized, but at least in certain branches of the community Kabir is worshiped as a transcendent being, as God himself. In texts such as the *Anurag Sagar* ("Ocean of Love"), which appeared sometime in the eighteenth or nineteenth century, he is said to have been begotten by the Primal Being at the beginning of time to defend the cause of good against the ever-threatening forces of evil, which are under the command of an equally primordial demiurge called Niranjan ("Untainted") or Kal ("Death," "Time"). The struggle is great, especially after Kal emanates the Hindu pantheon to confuse and delude humankind, but Kabir is always more than able to hold his own, acting through various incarnations as ages pass. In the end, he favors the world with a direct expression of himself—the fifteenth-century Kabir whose words are treasured by devotees ever after—and the battle between good and evil is tipped decisively in the direction of good.[38]

The salty, skeptical Kabir we know from the poetry that is most likely to be authentic would doubtless have had unkind things to say about such cosmological and soteriological mysteries, even if they were flattering to him personally. And it is hard to imagine that he would find the services at his monastery in Benares much less bewildering than Jesus would find the extravagances displayed each Sunday morning at the Cathedral of St. John the Divine in New York City. But the institutions of Kabir have not silenced their "founder." Every merchant and milkman in Benares and indeed the whole of north India has a verse of Kabir to quote, and for all that they have been repeated in the last five hundred years, many retain the tart, true-to-life irreverance they must have had when the master first unleashed them on the world.

POEMS AND EPIGRAMS OF KABIR

Poems

Go naked if you want,
Put on animal skins.
  What does it matter till you see the inward Ram?

If the union yogis seek
Came from roaming about in the buff,
  every deer in the forest would be saved.

If shaving your head
Spelled spiritual success,
  heaven would be filled with sheep.

And brother, if holding back your seed
Earned you a place in paradise,
  eunuchs would be the first to arrive.

Kabir says: Listen brother,
Without the name of Ram
  who has ever won the spirit's prize?

[KG *pad* 174]

Pundit, how can you be so dumb?
You're going to drown, along with all your kin,
  unless you start speaking of Ram.

Vedas, Puranas—why read them?
  It's like loading an ass with sandalwood!
Unless you catch on and learn how Ram's name goes,
  how will you reach the end of the road?

You slaughter living beings and call it religion:
  hey brother, what would irreligion be?
"Great Saint"—that's how you love to greet each other:
  Who then would you call a murderer?

Your mind is blind. You've no knowledge of yourselves.
  Tell me, brother, how can you teach anyone else?
Wisdom is a thing you sell for worldly gain,
  so there goes your human birth—in vain.

You say: "It's Narad's command."
  "It's what Vyas says to do."
  "Go and ask Sukdev, the sage."
Kabir says: you'd better go and lose yourself in Ram
  for without him, brother, you drown.

[KG *pad* 191]

Hey Qazi,
  what's that book you're preaching from?
And reading, reading—how many days?
  Still you haven't mastered one word.
Drunk with power, you want to grab me;
  then comes the circumcision.
    Brother, what can I say?—
If God had wanted to make me a Muslim,
  why didn't he make the incision?
You cut away the foreskin, and then you have a Muslim;
  so what about your women?
    What are they?
Women, so they say, are only half-formed men:
  I guess they must stay Hindus to the end.
Hindus, Muslims—where did they come from?
  Who got them started down this road?
Search inside, search your heart and look:
  Who made heaven come to be?
Fool,
  Throw away that book, and sing of Ram.
    What you're doing has nothing to do with him.
Kabir has caught hold of Ram for his refrain,
  And the Qazi?
    He spends his life in vain.

[KG *pad* 178]

Kabir is done with stretching thread and weaving.
He's written on his frame the name of Ram.

His mother steals away and secretly weeps:
"O God, how will these children survive?"

Kabir says:
"Whenever I'd thread the weaver's shuttle
I'd forget to be a lover of Ram;

And listen, Mother, he's the king of all three worlds:
He is the one who provides."

[KG *pad* 12]

Tell me, Ram: what will happen to me?
I haven't shown much wit: I've abandoned Benares

Like a fish who leaves the water and finds himself outside,
I'm stripped of any merit earned in former lives.

I squandered a life spent in Siva's city:
moved to Magahar when my time was ripe–

Penance in Kashi year after year
And here I am in Magahar to die.

Kashi, Magahar: they seem the same.
Which can rectify a life of little faith?

In Kashi, they say, you can cry to Siva when you die.
And Kabir? Dead already.
He's enjoying life with Ram.

[KG *pad* 46]

If caste was what the Creator had in mind,
 why wasn't anyone born
 with Siva's three-lined sign?

If you're a Brahmin,
 from a Brahmin woman born,
 why didn't you come out some special way?

And if you're a Muslim,
 from a Muslim woman born,
 why weren't you circumcised inside?

Says Kabir: No one is lowly born.
 The only lowly are those
 who never talk of Ram.

[KG *pad* 182]

Why be so proud of this useless, used-up body?
One moment dead, and it's gone.

How nicely you adorn it with sugar and butter and milk:
Once the breath goes out, it's fit to burn.

That head with its turban so artfully arranged
Will soon be adorned with the jabbing beaks of crows.

Bones: they burn like tinder.
Hair: it burns like hay.

And still, says Kabir, people won't wake up—
Not until they feel death's club
 inside their skulls.

[KG *pad* 62]

Hey brother, why do you want me to talk?
Talk and talk and the real things get lost.

Talk and talk and things get out of hand.
Why not stop talking and think?

If you meet someone good, listen a little, speak;
If you meet someone bad, clench up like a fist.

Talking with a wise man is a great reward.
Talking with a fool? A waste.

Kabir says: A pot makes noise if it's half full,
But fill it to the brim—no sound.

[KG *pad* 61]

That master weaver, whose skills
  are beyond our knowing,
  has stretched his warp
    through the world.
He has fastened his loom
  between earth and sky,
  where the shuttlecocks are the sun
    and moon.
He fills the shuttle with the thread
  of easy spontaneity,
  and weaves and weaves
    an endless pattern.
But now, says Kabir, that weaver!
  He breaks apart his loom
  and tangles the thread
    in thread.

[KG *pad* 150]

That thief has gone thieving, careening around the world,
And he didn't say a word when he left.

Remember? You were my childhood friend.
Why did you run away so far?

You are my man, I am your woman,
and your going weighs heavier than a stone.

The body is dust, the body is air,
And this thief brings Kabir, his servant,
nothing but fear.

[KG *pad* 139]

Pundit, so well-read, go ask God
  who his teacher is
  and who he's taught.
He alone knows what shape he has
  and he keeps it to himself,
  alone.
Child of a childless woman,
  a fatherless son,
  someone without feet who climbs trees,
A soldier without weaponry,
  no elephant, no horse,
  charging into battle with no sword,
A sprout without a seed,
  a tree without a trunk,
  blossoms on a tree without a branch,
A woman without beauty,
  a scent without a flower,
  a tank filled to the top without water,
A temple without a god,
  worship without leaves,
  a lazy bee that has no wings.
You have to be a hero to reach that highest state;
  the rest, like insects,
  burn like moths in the flame—
A flame without a lamp,
  a lamp without a flame,
  an unsounded sound that sounds without end.
Those who comprehend it,
  let them comprehend.
  Kabir has gone off into God.

[KG *pad* 119]

Epigrams

So I'm born a weaver,
so what?
I've got the Lord in my heart.
Kabir:
Secure in the arms of Ram,
free from every snare.

[AG *sakhi* 82]

The true Master—
what can he do
When the pupil is inept?
Trying to awaken him is just
so much air
Blown through an unfingered flute.

[KG *sakhi* 1.5]

Kabir:
Even worthless bushes
Are invaded by a nearby
sandal tree.
Its fragrance
makes everything around it
A likeness of itself.

[KG *sakhi* 4.1]

Your chance of human birth
Doesn't come time and again.
Once the ripe fruit falls
You can't stick it back
on the branch.

[KG *sakhi* 15.5]

The lean doe
Avoids the greens
Beside this pond.
Numberless hunters,
Only one life.
How many arrows
  can she dodge?

[KG *sakhi* 16.3]

Scorched by the forest fire,
The wood still stands
  and wails:
"Don't let me fall to the smith!
Don't let me burn again!"

[KG *sakhi* 16.2]

They burn:
The bones like tinder,
  hair like straw.
And seeing the world
  in flames, Kabir
  turns away.

[KG *sakhi* 15.7]

Kabir:
My mind was soothed
When I found the boundless knowledge,
And the fires
  that scorch the world
To me are water cool.

[KG *sakhi* 17.1]

The sense of separation:
A snake inside the body
that no snakecharmer's sounds
can control.
And separation from Ram:
that's loss of life—
or worse, of mind.

[KG *sakhi* 2.1]

God is the jewel,
His follower the jeweler
hawking him through the bazaar.
Only when a discriminating
Customer comes along
will the jewel ever sell.

[KG *sakhi* 18.1]

I'm dead—
dead of bad company,
A banana plant near a tree of thorns.
With every breeze, that tree
tears the leaves.
If you're living near goddess-worshipers,
move!

[KG *sakhi* 24.2]

Kabir:
The hut was made of sticks
And all ten sides caught fire;
Pundits, pundits—
they burned inside
While the fools ran out
and saved their lives.

[KG *sakhi* 21.11]

The pundits have taken
A highway that takes them
   away,
   and they're gone.
Kabir has climbed to
The impossible pass
   of Ram,
   and stayed.

[KG *sakhi* 20.4]

Kabir:
The instrument is still,
Its strings snapped.
What can the poor thing do?
Its player's no longer
   there.

[KG *sakhi* 16.1]

THREE

Nanak

The guru is the lake, the sea,
The guru is the ship,
the guru is the place to ford the stream.

Of all the singer-saints of north India, it is Nanak whose name is most closely tied to a particular religious community. So closely, in fact, that the community has recast the name: Nanak is almost never referred to simply as Nanak. Instead he is Guru Nanak—Nanak the Teacher, Nanak the Preceptor—and so in a way takes his identity from those who are his pupils. These are the Sikhs, and their name means exactly that: "pupils."

Nanak and the Sikhs

The Sikhs are a colorful and energetic group. Their distinctive turbans, high and tightly tied, make them stand out in any Indian crowd, and they are even more noticeable in an international setting. Indeed, many Sikhs have settled abroad. In the early decades of this century tens of thousands migrated to farms in California and British Columbia from their home territory of the Punjab, in northwest India, and in more recent years a large influx of Sikh traders, professionals, and industrial workers have made their homes in Britain.[1] Within India, too, the Sikhs have fanned out from their native Punjab and are often seen driving trucks and taxis, running businesses, and serving as an important component in the Indian armed services, much as they did during the British Raj. They are an active, aggressive community, and their military heritage is by no means incidental to who they are.

The Sikh community was quick to form. Within several decades after the death of Nanak in 1539 they had established specific rituals and festival days, identified a place of pilgrimage all their own (Goindval; later the focus shifted to Amritsar, where the Golden Temple was built), and defined a body of sacred writings (later expanded into the *Adi Granth* or "Primal Book") they took to be authoritative. Before the sixteenth century was over, their ranks had swollen with great numbers of adherents from the Jat caste, a group of hefty Punjabi farmers whose skills at warfare brought Sikhs into increasing conflict with the Mughal rulers of the period, who were Muslims. These tensions deepened in the seventeenth century, until the Sikh leadership withdrew from the plains into the foothills of the Himalayas for safety. Sikh memory has it that there, in 1699, the tenth guru in the lineage that started with Nanak tested the fealty of his followers against the standard of life itself. Guru Gobind Singh announced that he required five men as sacrifices to his sword, but when the brave ones came forward he decapitated goats instead and made the men the nucleus of a Sikh brotherhood (*khalsa*) that he constituted along military lines. As signs of their new identity they agreed, among other things, always to carry a sword, wear a steel bracelet, and keep their hair uncut; and as if to consolidate their kinship with Gobind Singh, they each took his surname, meaning "lion," as their own.[2]

The struggles of Sikhs to maintain their identity in the face of Mughal hostility did not last forever, but a vigorous pride in the community's ability to survive and thrive became a permanent legacy of the period. It was expressed in one of the most widely used emblems in the Sikh heritage, a double-edged sword that has played a significant role in Sikh history ever since.

One series of events is recent history indeed. In 1984 a number of

FIGURE 1. Sword emblem

FIGURE 2. *1 Omkar* emblem

armed Sikhs barricaded themselves inside the Golden Temple, and the Indian government sent troops against them. In response, two Sikhs in Prime Minister Indira Gandhi's bodyguard succeeded in assassinating her, and not long afterward expatriate Sikhs were implicated in terrorist actions throughout the world. Meanwhile, hundreds of Sikhs were massacred in retributory riots that followed Mrs. Gandhi's assassination; in the current climate of world opinion, however, Sikhs are much more readily pictured as bloodthirsty avengers than as bloodied victims.

The roots of Sikh militancy are deep, but probably not deep enough to have sprung up in Nanak's soil. The sword of Sikhism takes one back to the seventeenth century, but to reach all the way back to Nanak one must seek out another Sikh emblem, one seemingly very different in tone. It is the diagram that emerges when the first two words of the *Adi Granth*—words attributed to Nanak—are written together in Punjabi script. The words are *ek omkar*—"1 *Omkar*" or simply "1 OM"—and they are almost always interpreted as meaning that God, who is signified by the mysterious syllable OM, is one. Sikhs regard this as the greatest message of their faith, so one finds *ek omkar* emblazoned in the insignia of political parties, on homes and places of worship, on bumpers and dashboards, and tattooed on the wrists of countless individual Sikhs. Universalistic doctrine may be no guarantee against sectarian narrowness in practice, but anyone who has ever gotten into a conversation with a turbaned taxi driver or bus passenger will attest that most Sikhs understand the affirmation "God is one" to be inclusive in spirit. Clearly this was Nanak's intention—so much so that one might even wonder whether the term "God" is too personal and therefore too restrictive to capture his meaning. Militant communalism plays no part in such a broad vision.

A second aspect of Nanak's teaching that fits ill with the violent streak in Sikh history is his evident quietism. Of all the *bhakti* poets of his era, Nanak is one who places the greatest emphasis on the need to wait for divine truth, to be silent before it. His poems breathe a deep tranquillity that makes him perhaps the least belligerent of all his *bhakti* compeers. He speaks time and again of the value of pondering and listening, as in this much-repeated refrain:

From listening,
  sin and sorrow
  disappear.[3]

The typical picture of Nanak among Sikhs has kept this sense of quiet interiority very much in view. In the poster art that is so ubiquitous in modern India he is almost always shown as a motionless white-bearded figure whose eyes roll up as if to survey an inward source of light. Inspiration comes to him in the form of a glistening "1 *Omkar*" mantra, and the luminosity it gives to his face testifies that his contact with the truth is direct and unmediated. He is a mystic.[4]

Yet Nanak was more than a mystic. If anything in his poetry suggests how he might have become the progenitor of a community with such a definite, defiant sense of itself, it is the sober integration of his thought. This may well have contributed a core of logical coherency around which a well defined social form could coalesce. In his attention to sustained theological discourse, as against the often episodic and metaphorical insights of *bhakti* poetry, Nanak stands out from forebears such as Kabir and contemporaries such as Ravidas. His poems often group themselves naturally as extended meditations on a single idea. Often a sequence of poems will serve to elaborate a central phrase: "by order," "if you ponder it," "beyond number," and so forth. And within individual poems Nanak has a tendency to adumbrate multitiered metaphysical visions, something no other *bhakti* poet of his period cares to do.[5]

Like Kabir, Nanak preached the overarching truth of God and the inadequacy of any human institution to capture it, but he also had a tendency to emphasize the sense of sovereignty and order that flows from such a transcendent state, whereas Kabir leaves its operations a mystery. It is true that Nanak's zealous followers have sometimes spent themselves in the cause of channeling and perhaps limiting such transcendent power, but the connection between him and them is not entirely absent. The systematic strain in Nanak's teaching seems to have provided them with a unified perception of divine power, and of themselves perhaps as its instruments. Hence Nanak's intellectual architecture has strengthened the hand of those in Sikh history who were concerned with institutional edifices, and Nanak himself may have been the first among them.

Nanak in History and Legend

Unfortunately, it is almost as difficult to piece together an accurate sense of Nanak's life and of the events that followed his death as it is to reconstruct accurate biographies for any of the other *bhakti* saints. Yet one can accept a minimal shell as biographically accurate, for the sometimes divergent accounts of Nanak's life agree in a number of details so mundane that it is hard to imagine any reason for fabricating them.[6]

Nanak was born in the town of Rai Bhoi di Talvandi, forty miles southwest of Lahore, in 1469. Nowadays the town is called Nankana Sahib in his honor. His father was a *bedi khatri,* that is, a member of a merchant caste. Some reports specify that he was the man who kept the town land records for the regional ruler, Daulat Khan Lodi, but this is not to be taken as definite. It does seem likely that the family was literate in some measure, since the reports agree that Nanak's brother-in-law was able to obtain a clerical position for him in the court of Daulat Khan. Nanak married and became the father of two sons, Lakhmi Das and Sricand, but family responsibilities seem not to have deterred him from undertaking a certain amount of travel; how much and where is not clear. At some point he settled in the town of Kartarpur, on the bank of the Ravi River, and there he died in 1539 or perhaps the year before. There is little reason to doubt that before his death he designated one of his followers, Angad, to be his successor—the second guru—and it is significant that he did not choose either of his sons for the role. A story preserved by the Udasi order of ascetics, whose history intersects that of the Sikh community at a number of points, states that Sricand, Nanak's younger son, was unhappy with his father's decision as to who should succeed him in heading up his community of devotees, but more of that later.

There is much more to be learned about Nanak than this pale shell provides, and a voluminous set of Sikh biographies stands ready to help in the task. The problem is, of course, that they tell us less about who the historical Nanak was than about who his followers wanted him to be. But in this regard several motifs are of particular interest. First, there is the quietism to which we have already referred. Although one or two legends depict Nanak as the stringent, demanding sort of individual who might well serve as a precursor of Gobind Singh,[7] it is at least as strong a theme in these hagiographies that Nanak's native preference was to withdraw from the world rather than engage it. He is said to have experienced recurrent periods of silence, inactivity, and somnolence that he subsequently explained as being caused by a profound suspicion of what passes for life and learning in this world, and he resisted taking up any of the occupations his family proposed for him, electing to keep to himself instead.[8]

According to his hagiographies, Nanak's moment of blinding insight came one day as he bathed in the river Vein near the town of Sultanpur. His response was characteristic: he immediately left the job he had finally accepted as a clerk in the court of the prince who ruled the area and set out to wander, as any Hindu ascetic or Muslim *faqir* might do. The legends say he persuaded a bard called Mardana to go along with him, and the two of them headed for the wilderness, the bard surviving on what he could scrounge and beg, while Nanak nourished himself on nothing more than air. The bulk of what is written about Nanak's life recounts what happened in various encounters after these two renunciants emerged again into contact with humanity, traveling far and wide. These were remarkable occurrences indeed. Animals were restored from death to life; Nath Yogis were bested in a debate that took place on mythical Mount Sumeru, at the center of the world; and when Nanak died, his body turned to vapor and two piles of flowers remained in its place—one for Hindus and the other for Muslims, much as at the death of Kabir.[9] We have, then, a picture of an extraordinary being active in the world, but it is clearly implied that he derived his powers from his primary devotion to the introverted life of the archetypal mystic.

A second motif in hagiographies of Nanak that attracts special attention is the emphasis they place on the relation they perceive to exist between Nanak and the other saints and potentates of his era. In particular, the authors of Nanak's life stories are eager to establish

Nanak's superiority over the Nath Yogis. He encounters them on a number of occasions, and often miracles occur that make it clear that Nanak is in possession of magical powers that exceed those the Naths and other yogis so carefully cultivate.[10] For example, when Nanak sits down beneath a withered banyan tree where Naths typically gather, it springs to verdant life. And when Nanak flies through the air, he is able to go three times as fast as his Nath counterparts.[11] An essential element in this comparison is that such powers are merely reflexes to Nanak: he does not desire them for their own sake. In one telling episode, Nanak actually has to break a pot that fills with jewels every time he tries, at the Naths' request, to fill it with water; then he reconstitutes it for his own purposes. Evidently he prefers the simplicity of water and the satisfaction of a request fulfilled to great riches.[12]

Nanak's indifference to his unusual powers is underscored in other ways, too. In one episode he is made to converse with the great Sufi saint Sheikh Farid in a land whose king has recently died and been cremated. The king's skull refuses to explode and thereby release the soul inside, because, as astrologers have determined, the king once told a lie. They divine that the skull will break once a *sadhu,* a true holy person, enters the kingdom. Sheikh Farid bows to Nanak on this score, feeling it should be Nanak who walks into the kingdom first, and when he does, the skull instantly pops open.[13] Thus Nanak is given pride of rank not only by the greatest Hindu adepts, the Naths, but by the most exalted Muslim saints as well, and in neither case at his own insistence.

This is the third arresting motif in stories of Nanak: the effort devoted to interposing him between Hindus and Muslims. In fact, this is made out to be the keynote for his whole ministry, the formula with which he is baptized. The story goes that once, after singing devotional songs, Nanak bathed in the river Vein at Sultanpur and was transported by divine messengers into the heavenly court. There he was given a cup of the liquid of immortality (*amrt*); it was the divine Name. Nanak was commanded to drink it and then preach it. Once back on earth he spent a day in silence, but when he began to interpret the Word he had imbibed, it was with the following utterance: "There is neither Hindu nor Muslim."[14]

The reader of Nanak's holy biographies learns this lesson many times over. The very first encounter Nanak has after he emerges from the wilderness after his "baptism" is with a certain Sheikh Sajjan, who has been waylaying, robbing, and killing members of the two communities by trapping them, each to his preference, in a temple or a mosque he has constructed to attract their religious attentions. This evil man, who thus stands apart from both Hindus and Muslims, becomes Nanak's first convert.[15] The sense is that Nanak's message represents an edifice more fundamental than either temple or mosque; Nanak shows a way not to destroy their respective worshipers but to give them new life. The same point is made visually in the garb Nanak is said to have worn. It combines the saffron-colored robes, wooden sandals, bone necklace, and forehead mark that characterize the Hindu ascetic with the white caftan, the slippers, the waistcloth, and the ascetic's hat worn by the Sufi *faqir*.[16] Nanak, we learn, is neither and both.

For all their evenhandedness in representing Nanak as equally Hindu and Muslim, it is understandable that Nanak's hagiographers should have been particularly eager to show his superiority to the religious group they evidently recognized as their most threatening opponent: the Muslims. This comes out at a number of points, but never so vividly as on the occasions when Nanak is said to have traveled to Mecca, the sacred center of Islam, and to Baghdad, the seat of its earthly power during the Abbasid caliphate. During his sojourn in Mecca, one account says, or on the way to Mecca or even in Medina, as others have it, Nanak entered a mosque and fell asleep with his feet pointing in the direction of the holy city and its central monument, the *ka'ba*. When this offense was discovered by an irate *qazi*, he rotated Nanak so that his feet would point the opposite direction and his head would honor the focal point of Muslim ritual, but to his amazement the niche in the mosque that indicates the direction of Mecca rotated along with Nanak's feet. It was clear who was honoring whom.[17]

Events at Baghdad were not quite so startling, but they make the same point. Nanak is said to have ascended to heaven there and to have surveyed the entire created universe, much as Muhammad did on the celebrated night journey in which he rose from Jerusalem to heaven. The story ends with an appearance of the food considered sacramental to Sikhs (*karah prasad*), suggesting which religion bears the stamp of true universality: Sikhism, not Islam. By the same token Muhammad is demoted to second place among the world's great prophets.[18]

Hagiography and Doctrine

While it seems unlikely that these stories correspond very closely to any real events in Nanak's life, there is a definite tie between what they teach in narrative form and what Nanak taught through the medium of poetry. Several of the themes found in the nine-hundred-odd compositions attributed to him in the *Adi Granth* do provide a basis in doctrine for tales such as these. Again, three are particularly worthy of mention: his connection to the Naths; his position somewhere between Hindus and Muslims; and his preoccupation with the Word, or Name, of God.

In Nanak's biographies it is reported that he had discussions with the most important progenitors of the Nath order, all the way back to the sage Gorakhnath and even the god Siva.[19] Nanak's poetry does not quite provide a script for these discussions, but one does find there several passages that he evidently addressed to individual members of the Nath community, and the issue of defining the at times genuinely close relation between his teaching and theirs comes quickly to the fore.[20] Both, for instance, cultivate an awareness of the "unstruck sound" (*anahad sabd*) that lies at the heart of the Creation, but they do so in different ways. For the Naths this means a specific regimen of *hatha yoga,* whereas Nanak recommends a more encompassing approach that involves every aspect of life and requires no special yogic preparation.[21] It is noteworthy that the vocabulary is the same, however, and the doctrinal difference does correspond to the sense of inveterate, generalized receptivity that Nanak's biographers take as distinguishing him from the industrious but uninspired Naths. Whether they are just in attributing a preoccupation with the cultivation of magical power per se to Nanak's Nath interlocutors is less clear.

The situation is much the same in regard to the relation between Hindus and Muslims. Here again Nanak has definite things to say, but they are characteristically in the same mode as Kabir's utterances. That is, Nanak is less concerned to make himself a broker between Hindu and Muslim ideas than to make clear how it is that both religions fall short of the truth. Nanak's hagiographers do capture something of this sense when they report him as saying, after his initiation, "There is neither Hindu nor Muslim."[22] But after that the stories of Nanak's life take a decisive turn. They are not content merely to show how Nanak cancels both Hindu and Muslim versions of religion; they also suggest that he encompasses them, thus transcending them not just in the negative sense but in a positive one, too.

With Kabir, whose death story Nanak shares, this would simply be wrong, but there is some justification for it where Nanak is concerned. His approach is more systematic than Kabir's: he describes a divine order (*hukam*) that not only transcends all earthly forms but dictates what they are. This is "order" in both senses of the word—something coherent and something demanded—and the sense of "design" perhaps mediates between the two meanings.[23]

This is quite different from the sort of transcendence that Kabir represents. As his "upside down" poems show, the truth he reveals ultimately contradicts human logic; with Nanak, by contrast, the True Guru's truth supplies the logic that gives the world the meaning it genuinely has. It is perhaps no accident that the term Nanak uses to describe that order, *hukam,* is drawn from an Islamic vocabulary. It is unusual in that virtually every other key term in Nanak's theological lexicon comes from the Hindu side—but even that one departure, a significant one, makes him more "Muslim" than Kabir and gives some rationale for the popular conception that he was a bridge between the two camps.

The leap to associating Nanak as guru with this transcendent order is one that the biographer-devotee makes, not Nanak himself, but here too Nanak paves the way. As the spokesman for this order he becomes more than a poet (and therefore, some might say, less); he almost attains the status of systematic theologian, something to which Kabir never aspires. There is a cerebral majesty in Nanak's depiction of divine truth that lends itself to being read not just as undermining the half-truths and mistaken practices of Islam and Hinduism, but as arching above them. He seems to establish a greater reality of which they are partial derivatives. Nanak may not quite say this himself—certainly he does not say anything like that *about* himself—but the jump from what he says to what his biographers conclude is not vast. In fact, there may be a specific point of transition, for in describing the five stages in the soul's spiritual ascent—something characteristically Nanak-like and totally at variance with most of Kabir—he begins with *dharam* (*dharma,* i.e., "religion," "religious order") as the lowest rung.[24] The highest rung, *sac* (*satya,* i.e., "truth"), is of course what he himself proclaims.

Finally, there is a connection between the hagiographers' description of the power of Nanak's "baptism" and commissioning at the river Vein, and what Nanak himself has to say about the divine Name, its focus and substance. The story of Nanak's initiation is phrased in the language of Hindu worship (*puja*): Nanak comes before the divine throne as if before an altar, and receives a substance that transmits divine grace (*prasad*) before he goes away. When Hindus come into temples, the two essential features of their worship are eye contact with the image of the deity (this is called *darsan*, "seeing") and receiving some item of food or drink that has first been ingested (symbolically, many Hindus concede) and therefore blessed by the god: *prasad*, or "grace."

According to Nanak's biographers, he goes through both these essential steps, but in a strikingly different mode. The temple into which he is ushered is the heavenly court, and in Nanak's case this carries the clear implication that it is a temple without form. His visual experience of the divine is translated into an aural one, and the "grace" that he receives to take home with him is similarly invisible: the divine Name. As the idiom of the ear is substituted for that of the eye and tongue, an interior experience of religion is substituted for one with a visible, external component.

This much is secondhand report, but Nanak effects just such a transformation of familiar Hindu notions in his own theology. Listening becomes the central sacrament, for according to Nanak the Word itself (*sabd*)—the revealing of the Name—is the true guru and the dispenser of blessing and order.[25] When he exalts the guru, he takes over a term familiarly used by the Naths and speaks of the *satguru*, the "True Guru"; like the Naths, he conceives this guru as an interior power, one that can be known specifically in the medium of sound. The effect of this Word-made-Guru or Guru-made-Word corresponds exactly to the benefits of Hindu *prasad*. On the one hand it unites the partakers, the hearers, with what is given, and on the other it purifies the recipients so that they are progressively less preoccupied with and less polluted by the sounds and substances they themselves generate. Nanak identifies these negative realities as products of self-centeredness (*haumai*)[26] and says that they can only be diluted by a growing sensitivity to the full dimensions of the order that God has decreed for the world. The remembrance, love, and above all repetition of the divine Name make that possible.

Hence one has in Nanak's utterances a high degree of repetition, whose effect is to make Sikhs experience the Word, the Name, as transforming over time. Gradually his pupils thus approach what Nanak is said to have experienced in a flash at the outset of his ministry: a pure, all-encompassing infusion of the Name.

That Name is an ocean, Nanak says, and he loves to emphasize the point by making clear that it has an oceanic breadth. He describes the divine as being motionless and immovable (*acal*), beginningless (*anadi*), timeless (*akal*), colorless (*anil*), spotless (*niranjan*), unborn (*ayoni*), intangible (*achut*), undecaying (*avinasi*), indestructible (*anahat*), unformed (*nirankar*), and much more. The nameless names are "numberless" (*asankh*) and without end (*ant na*).[27] Though the Name is singular and denotes a reality that is unique, one sees immediately that its meaning is by the same token boundless. Hence the first word of the foundational "*Omkar*" mantra (and therefore of the whole *Adi Granth*) is precisely the number one, and the rest of that mantra is a dense litany of boundless adjectives, several of which we have just listed.

The same can be said for the person who speaks such a Word or words. The guru is described as the singular bridge (or, alternatively, the raft) that makes salvation across the ocean of existence possible, but at the same time he is an ocean himself, containing nothing but the all-comprehending Word.[28] Nanak says one must bathe in that oceanic Guru—the archetypal Hindu act of purification—and his own initiation is also an act of bathing.

Of course, when Nanak says this about the guru, he means the inner guru, the True Guru, God Himself. But Sikh hagiography makes it clear that Nanak's disciples have also experienced the guru in external form, as Nanak. In a theological system that identifies the experience of the divine so totally with Name and Word, it is no surprise that the guru, who purveys the Word and reveals the Name, attains an almost divine status in the eyes of the believer. The situation is something like the one described in a familiar couplet attributed to Kabir. In it a believer finds himself simultaneously in the presence of God and his guru: which should he bow to first? The believer solves the predicament by saying that he should first show reverence to his guru since the guru points him, in turn, to God.

To outsiders it sometimes seems that Nanak's pupils, his Sikhs, have come close to making the same choice. But if there is an element of Nanak-olatry in the Sikh community, it is not the simple-minded apotheosizing of a particular man. When one looks at the Sikh scriptures one finds that the name Nanak denotes not just one man but a class: all the gurus in his lineage who composed poetry that was collected in the *Adi Granth*. They all sign their poems, as is characteristic in the *pad* genre that is the backbone of the *Adi Granth* and most medieval north Indian devotional poetry, and remarkably, they all sign their poems with a single name—Nanak's. (Divisions in the text indicate which "Nanak" is which.) So Nanak, the guru, is not just a person but a principle. Hence it is fitting that the Book itself be understood as tantamount to the Guru, and that, indeed, is what Sikhs do. It is said that Gobind Singh, the tenth guru, was responsible for declaring that after him the lineage of gurus was at an end; in its place would be the guidance provided directly by the *Granth*.

It is the Word, the uttering of the Name, that makes Nanak Nanak for Sikhs, and it is at least in part for that reason that no Sikh house of worship contains an image of Nanak, an individual human being. The Book, which contains the words of other "Nanaks" and the words of other saints such as Kabir and Ravidas, is honored with all the ceremony that would attend his image if it were there: offerings of flowers and food, great fannings and circumambulations, and the placing of a canopy overhead. Readers of the Book (*granthis*) even perform the traditional priestly role of collecting food that, when blessed by the presence of the Book, will become *prasad* to be eaten by devotees. Here the aural transposition of Hindu practice is complete. The Word, the Book, is the ultimate guru, and when Sikhs insist on calling the house of worship that holds it a *gurudvara* ("door to the guru") rather than a temple, they mean that the Book is there.

This exaltation of word and book is not, however, universal among all who profess themselves followers of Nanak. There are communities inspired by Nanak that do not quite fit inside normative Sikhism. Important among them are the Udasi ascetics—their name says they are "withdrawers"—who trace their lineage back to Nanak through his second son, Sricand. Sricand, they believe, considered himself to be his father's rightful successor and resigned himself to the ascetic life when he was passed over in favor of someone outside the family. For some time a close tie apparently persisted between those who followed Sricand and those who embraced the succession of gurus claimed by the Sikhs, and through the early decades of the twentieth century the Udasis remained the custodians of many of the major Sikh shrines.[29]

In Udasi monasteries, quite by contrast to Sikh *gurudvaras,* a tradition of image veneration is preserved: an icon of Sricand, the founding guru, is found in each and is the object of devotional attention. This does not place the Udasis outside the Nanak Panth or even altogether outside the community of Sikhs. The *Japji,* a collection of poems by Nanak that begins the *Adi Granth* and is daily recited by observant Sikhs, provides the verses used in the initiation of Udasi novices.[30] And a good proportion of those novices are recruited from families of the Jat caste, the same that forms such an important part of the Sikh community.

Still, there is a difference, and it is not just the obvious difference between celibacy among the Udasis and householdership among the Sikhs. To walk into an Udasi monastery is to enter a world not too dissimilar from that of the Kabir Panth; there is even the oddity that a fair emphasis is placed on instruction in Sanskrit, despite the fact that the great words of the tradition are in the vernacular.[31] To walk into a Sikh *gurudvara* is something else altogether. Here the religion of the Word—the vernacular Word—is absolutely paramount. People come in the early morning hours of every day to hear the reading of the Book, and they come at intervals, if time and inclination permit, until evening.

They may have to come and go quickly, and if they do, they reduce the ritual to its core. They prostrate before the Book, make an offering before it, circumambulate it, receive from in front of it the food of grace (*prasad,* which in Sikh *gurudvaras* is a mixture of flour, clarified butter, and sugar), and depart. But for the Book that serves as its axis, this sequence would seem an entirely Hindu pattern: every step replicates the worship that normally surrounds Hindu images. Yet the context makes it different. There is an air of quiet that really does remind one more of a mosque than of a temple, and the strongly congregational feeling that obtains in the room where such a ritual takes place reinforces the impression. People who can stay awhile spread themselves around the room to think, to listen together, to sing. As the "reader" (*granthi*) cares for the Book, three "cantors" (*ragis*) lead the crowd in singing poems from the *Adi Granth,* and anyone who knows the lines is welcome to join. "By listening," Nanak says, come a host of benefits, and "by pondering" and "by singing" too.

On the face of it, it seems improbable that some of the same people who intone these admonitions to listen, sense God's order, and submit, could then pledge themselves to acts of terrorism and violence. But every religion has its varying textures—and fringes—and there is a seriousness of purpose and sense of deep belonging in Sikh worship that serves as a resource for the whole community when it feels threatened. This conviction lends itself to the dedicated defense of order when that order is perceived as good, and it fuels the fires of destruction if the prevailing order is judged defective, damaging, or unfair.

POEMS OF NANAK

1
Omkar
True name
Person who creates
Beyond fear and opposition
A form beyond time
Unborn, self-born
The guru's grace.

Repeat this.

The ancient truth, ageless truth
Is also, now, truth.
And Nanak says,
It will always be truth.

[Ek Omkar, the root mantra]

By order
  shapes take shape—
An order
  that cannot be uttered—
By order
  creatures live;
By order
  each finds its status;
By order
  high or low;

By written order
  joy or sadness.
By order
  some are given alms;
By order
  others ever wander.
Under that order
  is all that is;
Beyond that order,
  nothing.
Nanak says,
  to understand that order
Is to say goodbye to
  "I".

[Japji 2]

From listening,
  Siddhas, Pirs, Gods, Naths—
  the spiritually adept;

From listening,
  the earth, its white foundation,
  and the sky;

From listening,
  continents, worlds, hells;

From listening,
  death cannot approach.

Nanak says,
  those who hear
    flower forever.

From listening,
  sin and sorrow
  disappear.

[Japji 8]

From listening,
  Siva, Brahma, Indra—
  the gods;

From listening,
  great leadership:
  dullards become worthy of praise.

From listening,
  the yogic yoke leads
  to secrets of the body;

From listening,
  Sastras and Smrti,
  Vedas—sacred words.

Nanak says,
  those who hear
    flower forever.

From listening,
  sin and sorrow
  disappear.

[Japji 9]

From listening,
  truth, fulfillment, knowledge;

From listening,
  the virtue of bathing
  in all the holy places;

From listening,
  effortlessly
  one gains a sense of worth;

From listening,
  spontaneously
  meditation arises.

Nanak says,
  those who hear
    flower forever.

From listening,
  sin and sorrow
  disappear.

[Japji 10]

From listening,
  a depth, a well of virtues;

From listening,
  Sheikh, Pir, Badshah—
  those revered as masters;

From listening,
  the blind find the way;

From listening,
  the endless ocean
  in the measure of a hand;

Nanak says,
  those who hear
    flower forever.

From listening,
  sin and sorrow
  disappear.

[Japji 11]

The way one ponders it
   cannot be described;

Those who try
   should recant, apologize.

No paper, no pen, no scribe

Can capture or comprehend
   the magnificence of pondering it.

That name—
   so immaculately clear—
   only the mind that ponders it
                     can truly be aware.

[Japji 12]

If you ponder it,
   there is mindfulness, wisdom of mind;

If you ponder it,
   the whole of the universe is known;

If you ponder it,
   you will never face harm;

If you ponder it,
   you will never walk the way of death.

That name—
   so immaculately clear—
   only the mind that ponders it
                     can truly be aware.

[Japji 13]

If you ponder it,
  no obstacle blocks your path;

If you ponder it,
  you openly show your honor;

If you ponder it,
  you will walk life's way with zeal;

If you ponder it,
  to the righteous life you'll be bound.

That name—
  so immaculately clear—
  only the mind that ponders it
    can truly be aware.

[Japji 14]

If you ponder it,
  you find the door of deliverance;

If you ponder it,
  the family prospers;

If you ponder it,
  you are transformed,
  and can teach transformation;

If you ponder it,
  Nanak says, you never stand in need.

That name—
  so immaculately clear—
  only the mind that ponders it
    can truly be aware.

[Japji 15]

Beyond number
  are the fools, who simply cannot see;
Beyond number
  are the thieves, thriving on deceit;
Beyond number
  are the tyrants, the ones who rule by force;
Beyond number
  are the murderers who kill by cutting throats;
Beyond number
  are the sinners: sin is all they do;
Beyond number
  are the liars, spreading worthless trash;
Beyond number
  are the barbarians: they eat filth for food;
Beyond number
  are those who slander: the weight their heads must bear!
So says Nanak, the lowly—
  These thoughts I've uttered
  though I've yet to sacrifice
      myself to you.
The things that please you—
  these things go well.
  You are evermore,
    secure,
      and beyond all form.

[Japji 18]

The guru is the stepping stone,
The guru is the boat,
  the guru is the raft of Hari's name.

The guru is the lake, the sea,
The guru is the ship,
  the guru is the place to ford the stream.

Would you like to glisten
  in the lake that's made of truth?
  Go then and bathe in that name.

[Siri ragu 9.3]

If the True Guru is gracious
  trust becomes complete.
If the True Guru is gracious
  no one ever wastes away.
If the True Guru is gracious
  trouble is a thing unknown.
If the True Guru is gracious
  one is painted with God's hue.
If the True Guru is gracious
  how could there be fear of death?
If the True Guru is gracious
  one is given instant joy.
If the True Guru is gracious
  one finds life's nine great jewels.
If the True Guru is gracious
  one mingles with the Truth.

[Var majh, pauri 25]

Nights, seasons, dates, times,
  air, water, fire, hell:
In the midst of this is the earth,
  a place to rest from travel and practice religion,
And in it there are manifold lives—
  names without number, names without end—
They act. And when they act, notice is taken
  by Someone who is true, whose court rules true,
Whose council of just ones radiates light
  as the Vigilant One sets his mark on our deeds.
Well done or ill done—the verdict is found.
  So says Nanak in chant and song.

[Japji 34]

That was the religion of the realm of religion,
  but now the realm of wisdom:
How many forces—air, water, fire?
  How many Krishnas and Sivas are there?
How many Brahmas have shaped what's been shaped
  in all its color and form?
How many worlds? How many Mount Merus?
  How many sermons to Dhruv?
How many Indras? Suns and moons?
  How many regions and lands?
How many Siddhas? Buddhas? Naths?
  And how many kinds of goddess?
How many gods and demons? Sages?
  How many jewels in how many seas?
How many continents? How many languages?
  How many masters and kings?
How many who worship, how many who serve?
  Nanak says:
    no end, no end.

[Japji 35]

In the realm of wisdom, wisdom reigns
  with resonance, pleasure, festivity, and joy,
But the sound of the realm of effort is form—
  beautiful shapes are shaped there,
    quite beyond compare.
No words can describe it,
  and those who try will repent.
Attentiveness, insight, thought, and mind
  are also given shape; and there is shaped
    the purity of sages and gods.

[Japji 36]

In the realm of action the sound is pure force:
  there, there is nothing, nothing else.
There, there are warriors with heroic strength,
  whose being is suffused with Ram;
There, there are Sitas—Sitas in majesty,
  whose beauty is more than can be told.
Since Ram dwells inside, they are never robbed
  or deceived; they never die.
There dwell worlds of lovers of God,
  whose actions brings happiness; truth is in their minds.

The realm of truth: there dwells the Formless One.
  He makes, and seeing what is made, is pleased.
There, there are universes, regions, realms,
  and to try to speak of them—no end, no end.
There are worlds and worlds, worlds and shapes,
  and whatever he commands, they do.
He looks on them, thrives on them, gives them his thought.
  Nanak says, to tell it is as hard as iron.

[Japji 37]

Discipline is the workshop;
patience, the goldsmith;
the anvil, one's thinking;
wisdom, the hammer;
Fear, the bellows;
austerities, the fire;
and feeling, the vessel
where the deathless liquid is poured.
In such a true mint
is forged the Word,
and those on whom He looks
do their rightful deeds.
Nanak says:
the One who sees,
sees.
He observes.

[Japji 38]

FOUR

Surdas

For who has ever recognized the brilliance of the sun
but by seeing it through eyes gone blind?

THE POETS we have spoken of so far—Ravidas, Kabir, and Nanak—belong to a single branch of the family tree of medieval Indian devotional saints: the *nirguna* branch. They insist that God, more than any other reality, exceeds the shapes by means of which human senses interpret the world, and hold therefore that to move in the direction of truth is to leave those senses behind, particularly those that are most successful in convincing us that the world is solid, definite, and real. Among such senses are taste and touch, but the standard-bearer is sight. In the realm of faith, as in ordinary perception, seeing is an enormous part of believing—particularly in Hinduism, with its powerful iconic thrust—and it was just this illusion that the *nirguna* poets tried to combat. For if one trusted God to the senses, especially to sight, one objectified him, one saw him "out there" rather than grasping the truth that the only real access is from the inside, through one's heart and soul. So interior is Nanak's conception of faith, indeed, that the very word God—or rather Ram, its closest equivalent in medieval north India—almost never occurs in what he says. In poem after poem he tries to guide us toward recognizing the deepest truth by encouraging us to put aside the eyes with which we are accustomed to see.

The *Saguna* Saints

The other side of the *bhakti* family tree features saints of a markedly different persuasion. They are the *saguna* group, who affirm that what makes for illusion in this world has less to do with our senses as such than with the uses to which we put them: we construct our fantasies and delusions from the inside out, driven by appetite and desire. Given this derangement of the inner person, in fact, one of the ways in which God acts to restore proportion and direction is to assume a sensory manifestation, particularly one that can be seen and visualized. It is a miracle of the religious life, *saguna* poets and theologians say, that what people see can have a permanently steadying effect on them, as corresponding images are formed within. The Hindu temple, with its array of icons, encourages this miracle to happen as worshipers come to have "sight" (*darsan*) of the divinities housed there. The *saguna* perspective maintains that a central feature of divine grace is God's consent to become available to human perception "with attributes" in this way, not just in temple images but in full self-manifestations that have rescued and inspired history from age to age. No one denies that God exceeds what humans can imagine, but insofar as the remedying of our error and misery is concerned, *saguna* thinkers find it more important and more remarkable that God meets us in the world we actually inhabit, stretching our sense of what is possible.

The three singer-saints we are about to explore—Surdas, Mirabai, and Tulsidas (or Sur, Mira, and Tulsi for short)—are *saguna* poets, devotees identified with one of the personal forms of God. For Sur and Mira this is Krishna, the god whose playful childhood is proverbial in India and whose amorous youth and maturity exert a sweet fascination. Krishna has a heroic side too: as an infant he was capable of miraculous feats against threatening demons; as a young man he defeated the evil king who had usurped the throne of Mathura, the city at the heart of Braj, not far south of Delhi; and as a mature figure he played a critical advisory role in the world-scale battle that is the subject of India's great epic, the *Mahabharata*. But Krishna's heroic aspect, though historically the more venerable portion of his mythology, serves only as background for the major concerns of Sur and Mira. It is Krishna's playful, amorous side that draws them.

Tulsidas too is a *saguna* poet, but he is primarily a worshiper of another divine personality: Ram. This Ram is not just the supreme divinity of which the *nirguna* poets speak, but the storied hero-god of the same name who relinquished the throne that was rightfully his to fulfill a commitment his father had unwittingly made, who wandered in the jungle for fourteen long years, fought the powerful demon Ravan, and only then returned to his kingdom to receive the tumultuous welcome of his subjects. The very model of good behavior, Ram exerts a strikingly different kind of attraction than does Krishna, who lures by means of pranks, play, and loving abandon. Tradition has depicted these two as something like brothers—avatars of the venerable god Vishnu, who maintains through them a distant but sustaining presence in north Indian religion. Fittingly, Ram, the sober one, is the older of the pair, and Krishna, who has no cares, is the younger. (Each of them has a real brother too, but again Ram is the elder and Krishna the younger.) They are normally calculated as being the seventh and eighth avatars of Vishnu, but their devotees insist that they are not just expressions of divinity, but God himself, in his full form.

Sur and Tulsi, the two males in our *saguna* trio, are often pictured in the annals of Hindi literature as a pair of distant brothers, like Krishna and Ram themselves. Sur is the great poet of Krishna, and Tulsi, similarly, of Ram. A well-known epigram styles them the sun and moon in the firmament of Hindi poetry;[1] and although both poets did dedicate compositions to both gods, their chief loyalties color their personalities fundamentally. Moreover, just as an ardent *nirguni* such as Kabir sometimes adopts a typically *saguna* mood by longing for God as a woman might for her lost lover,[2] so Sur and Tulsi on occasion move outside their accustomed *saguna* world and strike a *nirguna* note. This happens when they seem to speak directly out of their own experience rather than projecting themselves into the world of dramatic potential created by the sojourns of their favorite gods on earth. But once again the emphasis is clear: Sur and Tulsi are far more likely to tell the tales of Krishna and Ram than to make an independent appeal to their listeners.

Mirabai, the third poet in the *saguna* group, is a somewhat special case in that she herself has become the focus of a latter-day version of the lovestruck milkmaids who surround him—a *gopi* ever longing for her Lord. Tradition and legend have evidently seized on the fact that she is the only woman among the important *bhakti* poets of north India, and have bound her so closely to Krishna that it is hard to imagine what voice she might have beyond his thrall. She is left, then, with no experience of the profane world that could serve as a basis for the down-to-earth critiques we find in *nirgunis* such as Kabir and Ravidas; equally, her inner experience is appropriated into the *saguna* realm. So with the same stroke she becomes the least historical, the least individual of the *bhakti* poets, and yet the one who most closely approximates an ideal *saguna* type. As she says in her own words, she is altogether "colored with the color of my Lord."

But Sur, in a different way, is scarcely less so. Indeed, he is sometimes thought of as the *saguna* poet par excellence, since his depictions of Krishna are the most acute in their visual detail. It is Sur who is remembered for having captured every smile and pout of Krishna's childhood, every glance and gesture of his youth. Tradition affirms that Sur was blind, a condition that gave him a uniquely privileged access to the divine world: he was never in danger of having his vision of Krishna polluted by what he saw on the earthly plane.

The Blind Poet

The standard account of Sur's life is the one recorded in the *Caurasi Vaisnavan ki Varta,* "Conversations with Eighty-four Vaisnavas," a work whose original compilation is attributed to Gokulnath (traditional dates, A.D. 1551–1640). The commentary that almost always accompanies it comes from the hand of Hariray, a man customarily assigned an impressive lifespan extending from A.D. 1590 to 1715. The *Varta* is a sectarian work, for Gokulnath and Hariray were important figures in the lineage of the sixteenth-century theologian Vallabhacarya (or Vallabha, for short), who is revered as the founder of the rich and influential Vallabha Sampraday, a devotional community whose membership extends west from Braj across Rajasthan and all the way to Gujarat and Maharashtra, on the shores of the Arabian Sea.[3]

There is good reason to believe that sectarianism has left a deep mark on the biography of Sur. One of the main objectives in the *Varta*'s account of Sur's life is to show how Sur became a pupil of

Vallabha and then subsequently of his son Vitthalnath, who assumed the leadership of the community when his father died. The reader is told in many ways what a profound effect this spiritual parentage had on Sur. Yet it is plain to an outsider's eye that the *Varta*'s efforts to fashion Sur's poetry in the image of his supposed masters are but precious fabrications designed to cover up the fact that nowhere in the massive collection of verse attributed to Sur—the *Sur Sagar,* "Sur's Ocean"—is mention made of Vallabha or the theology of his sect.

In fact, things went the other way. The nascent Vallabha community made much use of Sur's "ocean" in its devotional life, and increasingly gave him a prominent, formal place in its liturgical system. This created the need to make Sur a pupil of Vallabha after the fact, and the general outline of Sur's life as reported in the *Varta* develops under that impetus. According to Hariray, the first great event in the poet's life was his submission to the wisdom of Vallabha, who met Sur when he was a morose figure constantly preoccupied with the painful distance between himself and Krishna. The songs he sang to the considerable following that had gathered around him all complained of Krishna's refusal to requite his affections. When Vallabha expounded his theology, however, it opened Sur's inner eyes. Henceforth he celebrated the Lord's presence at every turn and did whatever his teacher commanded, singing regularly in the great Vallabhite temple atop Mount Govardhan in the heart of the Braj country and making occasional forays to the Vallabhite temple in the little town of Gokul, where Krishna is said to have been born. Sur's involvement in the life of the sect was total, to hear the *Varta* recount it. He admonished the faithful, drew in the faithless, inspired other poets, and refused to let himself die until he received the last blessing of the reigning guru at the time, Vitthalnath.

The artificiality of this picture—or should we say its theological artistry?—is plain at a number of points, beginning with the meeting between Sur and Vallabha. If indeed this encounter took place, Sur was not likely to have instigated the visit. The theologian arrived from the east; Sur had been there all along, ensconced on the banks of the Jumna.[4] In similar fashion the *Varta* is shaped to show how Sur's life created natural occasions for him to compose his poems in just the order in which the Sampraday had collected them. By the time the *Varta* was written, in fact, the Vallabhite sect was maintaining that the *Sur Sagar* was in essence a vernacular rendition of the *Bhagavata Purana*, a Sanskrit work devoted primarily to Krishna on which Vallabha wrote a major commentary, the very one that he is supposed to have exposited to Sur at his initiation. The problem is that none of the old manuscripts of the *Sur Sagar* display this order, for none of them—a significant fact in its own right—was preserved in the Vallabhite milieu. The division between Sur's poems of personal lament and his evocations of life in Krishna's world is far more blurred in the old manuscripts than the sectarian biography would lead one to believe. To the extent that this bifurcation is valid, furthermore, it is backward: the poems of complaint tend to be placed after those describing events in Krishna's life, not before.

What, then, remains of the *Varta*'s account after one has subtracted the elements that owe their origin to a sectarian impetus? Two tantalizing motifs, chiefly, and neither has much to do with Vallabha. The first depicts an encounter between Sur and the sympathetic, syncretizing Mughal emperor Akbar. Sur is not the only poet said to have met Akbar—Mira shares that honor—and the tale of a meeting between the servant of God and the ruler of this world, whoever he may be, is one that runs through numerous hagiographies of the period. We have seen it already in stories of Kabir and Ravidas, always conveying the message that religion has no need to bow before temporal power. But this encounter has a new twist: Akbar was supposed to have been such an aficionado of Sur's poetry that he offered handsome sums for any poem that could be found bearing the poet's genuine signature. When an avaricious poet named Kavisvar ("Lord of Poets") attempted to pass off one of his own inferior compositions under Sur's name and thereby reap the reward, the emperor smelled a rat. He ordered that the poem be set alongside one of indubitable authenticity and that both be immersed in a bowl of water. The result was that the forgery got soaked immediately, while the genuine Surdas poem emerged from its bath undampened. Evidently Sur's name was already sufficiently famous at the time this story was told that people were aware that not everything signed "Sur" was worth the title.[5]

The second motif is of even greater importance than the first, for it concerns the poet's blindness, traditionally his most notable personal feature. In fact, when Hariray appends his commentary to the *Varta* he feels obliged to add a whole battery of stories about the poet's childhood blindness that had been omitted from the earlier account—perhaps because the stories did not seem to touch on a specifically Vallabhite theme. We learn from Hariray that as a young blind boy Sur was cursed by his own parents for being a drain on the family finances, but that he subsequently proved to have clairvoyant powers that would more than make up for the loss. On one almost dire occasion he was able to divine where mice had hidden two valuable coins in the thatch of the family's house, but was only willing to direct his parents to the place if they promised him they would let him leave home and wander with full freedom to sing of his only true concern, Krishna. Reluctantly, they consented. Once launched on his travels, the young poet had to ward off people's desire to avail themselves of the material benefits of his powers of miraculous vision rather than reap the spiritual ones.[6]

There is no question about the hagiographical value of stories concerning Sur's blindness, but their relation to historical fact often seems distant. This has caused some scholars to turn to poems included in the *Sur Sagar* itself as evidence that the author of this collection was a blind man. Such efforts are not very convincing. The poems cited are either among those added to this ever-growing corpus long after the poet's death, a fact that has only recently been known with clarity,[7] or of such formulaic nature that they seem plainly to refer to the maladies of old age in general, rather than to blindness specifically. And while a couple of poems may be read to suggest that Sur became blind as an old man, there is no evidence at all to support the traditional belief that Sur was blind from the day he was born.[8]

The truth is, we know nothing for sure about the poet's life. We know even less about Sur than we know about Kabir or Ravidas. We can be confident that Benares played an important role in the lives of the latter two, but with Sur even geography is unclear. The traditional accounts place him in Braj, which is certainly possible, even likely; but it is nowhere demonstrable. Accounts of Sur's infancy disagree about the village in which he was born (the one Hariray accepted is Sihi, immediately south of Delhi), and the *Sur Sagar*'s close acquaintance with the landscape of Braj says very little about the poet's provenance. The places of which Sur's poetry speak are Krishna's places, for Braj is where Krishna is said to have spent his early life in the unassuming role of a cowherd, and as such they were famous throughout the subcontinent.

Even the language in which Sur composed, Braj Bhasa ("the language of Braj"), is no certain indication of where he lived. The boundaries of literary dialects were not as well defined in the sixteenth century as they later became, and there is a fair amount of overlap between the language of poems attributed to Sur and that of poems appearing under the signature of Nanak or even Kabir.[9] Furthermore, Braj Bhasa was more than a local dialect. Its association with romantic Krishna caused it to be revered as the lyrical dialect of Hindi par excellence, so it was regularly adopted by poets living far from the Braj region. Nor are the historical records of Sur's time very helpful. Although a number of scholars have made valiant attempts to wrest information about Sur from the nonhagiographical documents of his period, principally those written in the Mughal court at Agra, all have failed.[10] We are left with only the words of the poet himself to gain an accurate impression of who Surdas was.

Major Themes in Sur's Poetry

Fortunately an abundance of old manuscripts recording Sur's poetry makes a study of this kind both possible and fruitful. One manuscript recently made accessible apparently draws together three earlier collections and is even older than the *Adi Granth,* though not nearly so massive. It bears the date V.S. 1639 (A.D. 1582) and may have been written during the lifetime of the poet himself.[11] An examination of other manuscripts from diverse locations makes it possible to discover other poems belonging to roughly the same period.[12] These reveal a rather different Sur from the one that current generations feel they know.

For some years now Sur has been praised most highly for his minute, clever, sometimes almost fawning descriptions of the infant Krishna. These compositions are said to make him the exemplary poet of *vatsalya bhava,* the tender, all-giving emotion that parents and especially mothers feel toward their children, a feeling that is epitomized by the attitude of a cow toward her calf (*vatsa*). The "cows" involved here are usually the *gopis,* the milkmaids of Braj, through whose experience Sur speaks; occasionally one can hear him speaking for himself more directly, too. Some poems of this parental ilk do emerge in the older reaches of the *Sur Sagar,* but they are surprisingly few—so few, in fact, that one of the scholars first allowed to see the 1582 manuscript in this century concluded that it could not be authentic.[13]

More numerous than the childhood poems in old manuscripts of Sur are poems having to do with Krishna's amorous adventures. These are traditionally grouped under the heading *madhurya bhava* and are poems having to do with the sweet, literally "honeyed" emotions that lovers feel. Here again Sur projects himself into the persona of a *gopi* lost in love for Krishna, or perhaps he assumes the role of an observer or go-between. Nowadays these *madhurya* poems are not thought to be Sur's trademark, since many other poets also explore amorous themes. Yet there they are: a central aspect of the old *Sur Sagar,* insofar as we can reconstruct it.[14]

Even more important is a genre closely related to the *madhurya* poems. Rather than celebrating the joyful liaisons between Krishna and his cowherding mistresses, poems of this genre serve as a forum for expressing the distress the *gopis* feel when the great lover is absent. Sometimes Krishna's departure is inexplicable, but all too often it is easily enough understood: he has taken up with another woman in his vast, informal harem. These poems are attractive love poems in their own right, but they are at the same time piercing expressions of the painful emotions experienced by human beings when for all their devotion, the God to whom they have dedicated themselves seems unavailable. The experience is called *viraha,* a word that refers to the separation of lovers and the tortured feelings of longing and anger that it provokes.[15]

Not unrelated to these poems of the *gopis*' separation from Krishna is a final major genre. These are traditionally called the *vinaya* poems—poems of humble supplication—and they are explicitly voiced on the occasion of a devotee's feeling deserted by his or her Lord. Sometimes, like *viraha* poems, these are poems of great sadness. Sometimes, again like *viraha* poems, they record their author's remonstrations with himself. But other poems in the group are expressions of complaint and anger (here too one can think of analogues from the lips of the *gopis*), and they are scarcely as humble as the title *vinaya* would lead one to expect. On the contrary, they are often argumentative, pugilistic, and even insulting to the Krishna whom they address. Undoubtedly it was these tart poems as well as the morose and self-denigrating ones that the writer of the *Varta* hoped to discredit by relegating them to an era in the poet's life before he met Vallabha and saw the light. The *vinaya* group, however, is well represented in old manuscripts of the *Sur Sagar,* and in a few of the oldest manuscripts they are even more numerous than poems of *viraha,* which otherwise compose the largest category.[16]

Saguna and *Nirguna* in Sur

Each of the genres mentioned above is notable and important in its own right, but as an introduction to the *saguna* sensibility one can hardly do better than focus on a subgroup within Sur's *viraha* poetry that has made him particularly famous. In these poems he takes on the role of the poor jilted *gopis* that Krishna has left behind. In many *viraha* poems, as in a host of miniature paintings from the same general region and period, one of the *gopis* wakes to find that she has been deserted by the very lover whom she risked everything to join, and raises her plaint. Or she may merely smart from the longing that attends unfulfilled love: Krishna has broken down her defenses and stolen in like a thief, but just as deftly he has stolen away.[17] In this particular group of poems, however, the separation that the *gopis* suffer is permanent. Krishna has left them all, departing from their idyllic pastoral world to lead an adult life as the ruler of urban Mathura.

As we learn from these poems and from many other expressions of devotion to Krishna, the moment of his departure is touched with great sadness and foreboding.[18] After a youth spent herding the cows, trysting with the *gopis,* and stealing butter throughout the village, he is called to a life of a different kind. A messenger comes from Kamsa, the wicked king of Mathura who has been aware of the potentially threatening presence of this unusual child since his birth, and announces that Krishna and his brother Balaram are invited to participate in a tournament the king has arranged. Krishna's foster parents, Nanda and Yasoda, beg him not to go, for they know that Kamsa's intentions are anything but honorable; as subsequent events prove, he plans to crush the boys under the feet of a mad elephant before they can ever engage the brawny, unscrupulous wrestlers he has set against them. No matter: the boys have miraculous powers that will carry the day, but Nanda and Yasoda have no way of knowing.

It is if anything even worse for the *gopis* to see their beloved go—especially Radha, Krishna's favorite. Powerless to make him stay, they watch the carriage disappear down the seemingly endless road to Mathura and into a world that is foreign and unapproachable to them. Time passes. The nights go slowly and the days are spent scanning the horizon to see if, as promised, he might return. But there is nothing, and again nothing, until one day a yogic adept, a philosophical sort called Udho, appears and announces that he has been sent by Krishna, now king of Mathura, to comfort the girls with a message that will transform their condition. It is the message of *nirguna* religion, as it happens, a perspective on life that Udho says will be the answer to all the girls' problems. If they will but recognize that the real Krishna is not the outward, fleshly being they think they know but rather an interior, spiritual presence they can cultivate through austerity and meditation, they will see that there is no reason to speak of separation at all: they have the true Krishna, the formless *nirguna* Krishna, at hand wherever they are.[19]

This message proves less successful at dousing the fires in the *gopis'* breasts than Udho had any reason to believe. It is an inherently comic situation, for cowherd girls are not usually the audience that itinerant philosopher-yogis choose for their sermons. And indeed there is more than a touch of humor when the *gopis* reply to Udho in such a way as to display the ridiculousness of his position. But there is a serious message as well: the rarefied abstractions that the *gopis* take as characterizing the *nirguna* position simply do not cut to the heart of life, which is *saguna* not just in its sheath but in its essence. These poems attest that it's love that makes the world go round—real bonds between people—rather than some hidden level of reality that one must close one's eyes and bury one's emotions to find. More than that, those who love with all their hearts turn out to be already the perfect exemplars of the life that the yogi would foist upon them. He and his ilk must undertake extraordinary exertions to remain ever wakeful, to sit still, to generate a store of interior heat, and to focus their eyes and thoughts on a single object of attention. But these *gopis,* overcome with the love of Krishna, are yogis whether they like it or not. Fully *saguna* in their perspective, they manifest the state of perfect concentration for which *nirguna* yogis eternally and unsuccessfully strive. In their distress they even manifest the yogi's external appearance, with loose, tangled hair and a total inattention to dress.

Sur has a wonderful time demonstrating this in a type of *viraha* poem that has come to be called *bhramargit,* meaning "songs of the bee."[20] The name derives from the fact that the *gopis,* in their state of single-minded delusion, respond at first not to Udho but to a passing bee, whose black coloring makes them think that it, not he, is the messenger from Krishna, whose name means "black." Ever afterward they address Udho as Krishna's bee, and the word *bharmargit* might more accurately be interpreted as songs to the bee rather than as songs of the bee, since Udho can scarcely get a word in edgewise. In the end all he can do is admit defeat and recognize the startling strength of the *gopis' saguna* devotion. As many poems show, their love has made them truer yogis than he.[21]

One might think from all this that we have a total and unreconstructed *saguna* poet in Sur, but the case is not quite so simple as that. Notice that the figures who serve as Sur's paradigmatic devotees do so precisely in the absence of the Lord they seek—the worldly Lord, full of qualities. But for their vivid memory, he would be for them as unmanifest, unmoving, timeless, unyielding, and intangible as anything the *nirguna* poets ever imagined. And in fact, that is precisely the reality that they complain of, so in a way they are as much examples of *nirguna* religion as of *saguna.* They show what it is to be devoted to a God who is in some fundamental way not a part of the world they know and inhabit, and they show how tenacious such an attachment can be.

One sees something similar in the poems in which Sur appears to speak for himself, lamenting the absence of his Lord. Here, too, it is a *saguna* divinity for whom he longs; indeed, he often lists the great acts of mercy that Krishna has done in the past and recites the many titles he has earned as a result—but always in accusation. By refusing to come to the rescue of the poet who speaks, Sur's Lord seemingly falsifies everything that everyone has ever said about him, including the poet himself. These qualities now seem absent—a *nirguna* situation—and it is this that forces the poet to cry out in protest. Admittedly this is a very different sort of formlessness or qualitylessness from the transcendent but ultimately benevolent negativity that *nirguna* poets praise, yet Sur's devotion is as undistracted as anything they have ever produced. And indeed, when Sur speaks from his own experience of loss, he draws on the *vinaya* genre, so well known in *nirguna* literature. Sur's poems of lament and complaint are more combative than those we typically hear from a *nirguna* poet such as Kabir, but their spirit is ultimately the same, and they even draw on a common store of images and figures of speech.[22]

Sur's Legacy

One should not conclude from similarities such as these, however, that Sur and his *saguna* comrades are remembered and recited in just the same ways that the *nirguna* poets tend to be. For one thing, the poems of the *saguna* poets contributed naturally to the worship of groups that already had a focus for their devotion—Krishna worshipers in Sur's case—so they were a bit less apt to become the devotional focus of communities of their own. And perhaps in part because they spoke less than did their *nirguna* counterparts about the importance of the True Guru, they were less likely to be perceived in that role themselves. Furthermore, of course, they named the gods they worshiped and distinguished them from themselves with a clarity that tended to keep themselves—human devotees—from being apotheosized.

But that does not mean a poet such as Sur has been forgotten. One hears his songs not just in temples of the Vallabha sect but in almost every Krishna temple of north India, and in countless homes as well. When Krishna's birthday comes around, one finds for sale in the bazaars not only little clay images of the child Krishna but little statues of the blind bard as well; with one hand he clangs his cymbals and with the other he plucks his one-stringed instrument, the *ektar*. And to travel in Braj in the rainy season—Krishna's favorite, since love is in the air as at no other time—is to hear Sur's lyrics everywhere, for they more than any others fill the musical dramas (*ras lilas*) that celebrate all the magical and poignant moments that Krishna shared with the *gopis* and his family and friends in Braj. Several famous plays, for instance, depict the great debate between Udho and the *gopis,* and in a significant measure Sur provides the text.[23] In Delhi, where large-scale innovation is more palatable than in rural Braj, people have gone so far as to design musical dramas that make use not only of Sur's words but of his person. They depict his life story, and include a little ballet.[24]

The greater legacy of Sur, however, is far from the glittering stages of modern Delhi. Sur may be found begging beneath trees on lonely roads, inching apologetically through the crowds on railway platforms, or walking down the street with his hand on someone else's shoulder. For in Hindi parlance every blind person is a version of Surdas, whose poems are felt to have ennobled not just himself but the whole class to which he is believed to have belonged. Many blind people sing, today as when Sur was alive, and an unfailingly polite way to address a blind man, whether he sings or not, is to call him Surdas. The blind readily adopt the name for themselves, too, and the large number of sightless people who have wandered about north India from Sur's time until our own may have had much to do with expanding the *Sur Sagar* from the relatively modest lake it was in the sixteenth century—a body of several hundred poems—to the ocean of thousands it is today.

POEMS OF SURDAS

"If you drink the milk of the black cow, Gopal,
  you'll see your black braid grow.
Little son, listen, among all the little boys
  you'll be the finest, most splendid one.
Look at the other lads in Braj and see:
  it's milk that brought them their strength.
So drink: the fires daily burn in the bellies
  of your foes—Kans and Kesi and the crane."
He takes a little bit and tugs his hair a little bit
  to see if his mother's telling lies.
Sur says, Yasoda looks at his face and laughs
  when he tries to coax his curls beyond his ear.

[NPS 792]

"Far off and furtive, Gopal's in the butter.
Look, my friend, what a bright shimmer streams
  from the dusk-toned body of Syam,
With drop after drop that was churned from curd
  trickling down his face to his chest
As if the far ambrosial moon
  rained beams on loves below.
His hand lends grace to the face beside it
  and flashes forth as if
The lotus had dropped its feud with the moon
  and come forth bearing gifts.
Look how he's risen to peer from his lair,
  to look around on every side;

With wary eye he scans the scene and then
  he cheerfully feeds his friends."
Seeing Sur's Lord in his boyish fun,
  the maidens start, love-struck and weakened,
Until their hearts are lost to speech
  in thought after thought after thought.

[NPS 901]

Look, my friend, look at Hari's nimble eyes.
How could the shimmer of lotuses and fish,
  even of darting wagtails,
    compare in charm with this?
When for a brilliant blink of time his hands
  and face and eyes bow down to the flute—
    they all become as one—
It seems the lotus no longer wars with the moon:
  together they sound a note to soothe
    those lunar steeds, the deer.
Look at that beauty: slender, mind-entrancing curls,
  how they ramble uncontrolled
    over eyebrows just below
And startle the deer, it seems: they flee their chariot
  till the moon with a tremor of worry
    moves to tighten its reins, the brows.
Hari is a mirroring, the image of all desire;
  for him the women of Braj are offering
    their wealth—that is, their life.
They look with loss and longing at the face of Sur's Dark Lord.
  With him to fill their thoughts, their minds
    have nowhere else to roam.

[NPS 2415]

She's found him, she has, but Radha disbelieves
That it's true, what she sees when her eyes behold
her master's moonlike face.
Her gaze is fixed, but her mind is glazed;
her eyes refuse to close;
And her intellect wages a raging debate:
Is it a dream? Or is this her true Lord?
Her eyes fill and fill with beauty's high pleasure,
then hide it away in her breast:
Like bees driven wild by any distance from honey
they dart back and forth from the hoard to the source.
Sometimes she musters her thoughts; she wonders:
"Who does he love? Who can this Hari be?"
For love, says Sur, is an awkward thing.
It ripples the mind with waves.

[NPS 2741]

Radha is lost to the onslaught of love.
She weeps from tree to tree and finally succumbs,
searching through the forests and groves.
Her braid—a peacock grasps it, thinking it a snake;
her lotus feet attract the bees;
The honey of her voice makes the crow in the *kadamb* tree
caw, caw to mimic its cuckoo;
Her hands—the tender leaves of blossom-bringing Spring:
the parrot, when he sees, comes near to taste;
And the full moon in her face inspires the *cakor* bird
to drink the water washing from her eyes.
Her despair, her desperation—the Joy of the Yadus sees it
and appears at her side just in time;
Surdas's Lord takes that seedbud of new birth
and cradles it, a newborn in his arms.

[NPS 1744]

With love there's never a thought that one might die.
With love the moth can be drawn into the flame
  and never flinch from the fire.
With love the turtle dove will mount the skies
  and dive to earth with no care for its life.
With love the deer lusts for sound, and draws so near
  it's doomed to the hunter's arrow.
The thirsty cuckoo, in the rainy month of *sravan,*
  coos love, coos love—she shouts it out,
For what, says Surdas, does she have to fear?
  A lonely woman speaks for herself.

[NPS 3908]

Black storm clouds have risen in the sky
  and herons in an eerie row.
Please, Kanh, look: a rainbow—such beauty!—
  bearer of all colors,
    bow for the arrows of the gods.
Lightning flashes forth and strikes here and there
  like an eager, restless woman
Whose husband, the rogue, is at every other house:
  now she has the chance to range about herself,
    ignited by the God of Love.
Peacocks and cuckoos cry out in the woods
  and trees dispatch their messenger girls—the vines—
To find their loves, but it seems love's longing
  has so impassioned the vines and angered them
    that they break their vows, what they promised to do,
And mate with every tree they meet
  in a network of darkened groves.
Kama, the expert, awakens to the wish
  of Sur's dark Syam: he lifts his own hand
    to decorate a bower as a home.

[NPS 1806]

Gopal has slipped in and stolen my heart, friend.
He stole through my eyes and invaded my breast
  simply by looking—who knows how he did it?—
Even though parents and husband and all
  crowded the courtyard and filled my world.
The door was protected by all that was proper;
  not a corner, nothing, was left without a guard.
Decency, prudence, respect for the family—
  these three were locks and I hid the keys.
The sturdiest doors were my eyelid gates—
  to enter through them was a passage impossible—
And secure in my heart, a mountainous treasure:
  insight, intelligence, fortitude, wit.
And then, says Sur, he'd stolen it—
  with a thought and a laugh and a look—
    and my body was scorched with remorse.

[NPS 2490]

Thoughts of him stalk me, even in my dreams,
Now that he has gone; and oh, my friend, it hurts
  as hard as on the day that Nandanandan left.
Last night, in fact, that cowherd came to my house:
  he laughed his laugh and grasped me by the arm.
What am I to do? The night is now my foe.
  Will I ever know another wink of sleep?
I've become like a sheldrake who sees her own reflection,
  takes it as the gladdening image of her mate,
And then, says Sur, that menacing Creator
  masquerades as wind and brings ripples to the lake.

[NPS 3886]

Lord of Braj, the memory of my passion remains:
How stubbornly I acted, how silent and hurt
  as I played with you so happily—we two.
You saw you were lost, but your penitence I spurned
  as you laughed and touched your hand to my feet.
Then you feigned sleep. You turned your face away.
  You curled up and covered your face with your shawl.
But love's a restless thing. You couldn't stay away
  when you saw the night was passing fruitlessly—
That great long night. And then
  I found that it had cheated me of you,
    Sur's Syam, as I recalled it all at dawn.

[NPS 3821]

Away! Go back to where you spent the night!
Manmohan, what clues are you trying to erase?
  Signs of tight embraces are not so quickly hid.
A necklace, now stringless, is etched into your chest:
  what clever girl was pressed against your sleeping heart?
Her hair is on your clothes, and your jewels are askew:
  they were tangled in a bout with her lust-hardened breasts.
Teethmarks, nailmarks: oh what you've endured
  to have your fill of passion in that other woman's lair.
Surdas says, your honey lips have lost their sheen
  and your sleepless eyes bear the weight of lethargy.

[NPS 3122]

Ever since your name has entered Hari's ear
It's been "Radha, oh Radha," an infinite mantra,
  a formula chanted to a secret string of beads.
Nightly he sits by the Jumna, in a grove
  far from his friends and his happiness and home.
He yearns for you. He has turned into a yogi:
  constantly wakeful, whatever the hour.
Sometimes he spreads himself a bed of tender leaves;
  sometimes he recites your treasurehouse of fames;
Sometimes he pledges silence: he closes his eyes
  and meditates on every pleasure of your frame—
His eyes the invocation, his heart the oblation,
  his mutterings the food to feed
    the priests who tend the fire.
So has Syam's whole body wasted away.
  Says Sur, let him see you. Fulfill his desire.

[NPS 3399]

Having seen Hari's face, our eyes are opened wide.
Forgetting to blink, our pupils are naked
  like those who are clad with the sky.
They've shaved their Brahmin braids—their in-laws' teachings,
  burned up the sacred thread of decorum,
And left their veils—their homes—to mumble exposed
  through the forests, day and night, down the roads
In simple concentration—their ascetic's death:
  beauty makes them vow their eyes will never waver,
And anyone who tries to hinder them—husbands,
  cousins, fathers—fails.
So Udho, though your words touch our hearts
  and we understand them all, says Sur,
What are we to do? Our eyes are fixed.
  They refuse to be moved by what we say.

[NPS 4184]

Those Mathura people, they're rife with vice,
My friend: they've taken our beautiful Syam
  and the fine technique they've taught him!
Udho, they say, has arrived in our midst
  to peddle his yoga to poor young maidens;
His postures, dispassion, his eyes turned within—
  friend, how can they shorten our distance from Syam?
Of course, we're just herders, so how should we know
  the pleasures of mating with a hunchback girl?
But what kind of doctor, says Sur, can this be
  who hands out prescriptions
    when he doesn't know the disease?

[NPS 4208]

Hari has fashioned an offering of lights
Created in so utterly unusual a way
  that language can hardly give it measure.
A tortoise provides him with a throne unexcelled,
  while Sesa the snake makes a long, hooded handle
For its vessel, Island Earth; the seven seas are the butter-oil;
  and the wick is as thick as a mountain.
The sun and the moon fill the world with their flame,
  vanquishing the darkness of night,
And sparks fly up like stars, undarkened by a sky
  spread black with the collyrium of clouds.
Siva and Brahma, Sanak, Prajapati
  and all the host of gods and antigods and men—
They rise and dance their dance of many parts,
  each in a rhythm of its own.
The times, the deeds, the character
  of those who love the Lord
    are creatures of his wisdom and will,
For Surdas's Lord has fashioned it all—
  substance and artifice—
    an offering unexcelled.

[NPS 371]

I, only I, am best at being worst, Lord.
It's me! The others are powerless to match me.
  I set the pace, forging onward, alone.
All those others are a flock of amateurs,
  but I have practiced every day since birth,
And look: you've abandoned me, rescuing the rest!
  How can I cause life's stabbing pain to cease?
You've favored the vulture, the hunter, tyrant, whore,
  and cast me aside, the most worthless of them all.
Quick, save me, says Sur, I'm dying of shame:
  who ever was finer at failure than I?

[NPS 138]

Madhav, even those who haven't a shred of worth
  are hesitant to come to you for aid:
Even though they lack all trace of strength or grandeur
  they shrink from relying on your grace.
A dumb blade of grass: if someone swept down a river
  reaches out a hand and grasps,
That grass holds as fast to its roots as it can
  and surrenders its tortured self if it must.
You, Lord, you're unbested, untamed, you rule the world,
  while I am unlettered and unwise:
Nothing can ever hinder you, nothing can impinge,
  and think of this poor inundated soul!
Night and day I have to bear the barbs of ridicule,
  and that's why I have come to you to ask,
Says Surdas: Who, after singing of the mercies
  that stream forth from your feet, was ever saved?

[NPS 181]

Madhav, please, control that cow.
Night and day she wanders over paths that aren't paths,
  too elusive to be caught,
And hungry, so hungry—why can nothing fill her?
  She's stripped the Veda-tree of all its leaves.
From the eighteen vases she's drunk Purana-water
  and still there's no slaking her thirst.
Place the six kinds of taste before her
  and she'll sniff around for more,
Eating what's unhealthy, food she shouldn't touch,
  things the tongue can scarcely describe.
Oceans, mountains, forests, heaven and earth—
  she forages through them all. They're not enough.
So every day she tramples down the fields of fourteen worlds
  and even there she cannot be contained.
Her hoofs are dark blue; her belly, brilliant red;
  her horns, a satisfying white;
So when she does battle with the three-colored world
  this threefold beast has nothing to fear:
She subjugates the demons with the power of hooves and heart
  and she tosses the gods off the top of her head,
Whose face and eyebrows are artfully shaped:
  as she roams about she captivates the mind.
Narad and the rest, and Sanak, Suk, and so forth—
  they've wearied themselves to no avail,
So tell me, says Sur, how a bumbling fool like me
  can ever hope to herd someone like her?

[NPS 56]

Life has stumbled, stumbled, unraveled,
Roped to politics and salary and sons.
  Without my even noticing, my life has ambled off
And gotten tangled in a snare of illusion so foolproof
  that now I cannot break it or loosen its grip.
Songs of the Lord, gatherings of the good—
  I left myself hanging in air without either
Like an overeager acrobat who does just one more trick
  because he cannot bear to close the show.
What splendor, says Sur, can you find in flaunting wealth
  when your husband, your lover, has gone?

[NPS 292]

Until you wake up to what you really are
You'll be like the man who searches the whole jungle
  for a jewel that hangs at his throat.
Oil, wick, and fire: until they mingle in a cruse
  they scarcely produce any light,
So how can you expect to dissipate the darkness
  simply by talking about lamps?
You're the sort of fool who sees your face
  in a mirror, befouled by inky filth,
And proceeds to try to erase the blackness
  by cleaning the reflection to a shine.
Surdas says, it's only now the mind can see—
  now that so countless many days are lost and gone—
For who has ever recognized the brilliance of the sun
  but by seeing it through eyes gone blind?

[NPS 368]

Now I am blind; I've shunned Hari's name.
My hair has turned white with illusions and delusions
  that have wrung me through till nothing makes sense.
Skin shriveled, posture bent, teeth gone;
    my eyes emit a stream of tears;
      my friends, a stream of blame.
Those eyes once ranged as free as a cat's,
    but failed to measure the play of Time
Like a false-eyed scarecrow failing to scatter
    the deer from the field of the mind.
Surdas says, to carry on without a song for God
    is courting Death: his club stands poised
      above your waiting head.

[Jodhpur 1359/14]

FIVE

Mirabai

I'm colored with the color of dusk, oh Rana,
colored with the color of my Lord.

WE COME AT LAST to a saint who is a woman, but this is hardly the first time we have heard a woman speak. Many of Kabir's songs of longing are voiced as if by a woman waiting for her faraway lover, and the same is true of Sur's. By assuming the female role, these male poets cultivated the capacity for the intense emotion that they and their culture supposed to be the particular province of women, and also the sense of homebound captivity that produced it. They understood a woman's gift for feeling to be a *bhakti* virtue and willingly stripped themselves of the status that went with their male rank to learn what true feeling meant. The sense of confinement, even helplessness before the larger world, that is the lot of many Indian women seemed a natural metaphor for much of what human beings experience in relation to God: a mood of loss and bewilderment in the face of a beloved being who is freer and more powerful than we. To be sure, India has developed images of womanhood that contrast broadly to this one—it applies the title Power (*sakti*) to many of its goddesses and it recognizes that human women can be far more threatening to the men in their lives than their position in society would imply—but the image of the tenacious woman whose strength is learned in love and suffering was the one that seemed most relevant to the religious needs of male figures in the *bhakti* world.

The female persona through which these poets spoke was always just that, however: a persona. Tradition might protest that the womanly voice these poets adopted was the true one, the sound of the inner self, but the plain fact remains that the poets were men. They had to go through all the work of "becoming" women to experience God as husband and lover. With Mirabai, by contrast, no sexual transformation was necessary, and the consequences of that fact were many.

Mira's Fame

In the first place, she attained enormous celebrity. Just as Antal, the only woman among the Alvar poet-saints of south India, is the one whose verse and life story are best known of all the Alvars', so Mira's poems are probably the most often quoted of any north Indian saint, and her biography the most familiar. More than any other saint with the possible exception of Kabir, she has become a pan-Indian figure. Her songs are sung all the way to the southernmost tip of the subcontinent by people who otherwise have little command of Hindi, and in fact some of the most popular renditions in recent times have been made by a south Indian vocal performer, M. S. Subbalaxmi. Subbalaxmi is a woman, and her recording of selections from Mira is intense and personal; it is one of the most influential discs of Hindu religious music ever produced.[1] For sheer numbers of copies sold, of course, it has plenty of competitors in the music that emerges from India's huge film industry, but there too Mira has made her mark. Not that she is the only *bhakti* saint to have become the subject of a feature-length movie—one could say the same for every poet in this book—but Mira's story has been enacted ten times on the screen, in a succession of films that goes back to the earliest days of sound cinematography in India.[2] Once M. S. Subbalaxmi herself played the leading role.[3]

There are other signs of Mira's popularity. In Pune, in the western state of Maharashtra, an institution called St. Mira's School has developed a whole philosophy of education that sets it apart from most Indian schools. Founded in 1933 in Hyderabad, in present-day Pakistan, by a visionary named T. L. Vaswani, the Mira Movement in Education called for the sort of training Vaswani believed would make sense for girls. He insisted that one must educate the whole person, not just the mind, so he attempted to inculcate not just formal learning but purity, prayer, simplicity, and service—virtues that he saw exemplified in "the queen saint" Mirabai, whom he held up as a beacon to his young charges.[4] Every day, beneath huge portraits of him and of Mira, and before little dioramas that illustrate what it means to be kind to brother dog and mother cow, hundreds of neatly uniformed girls assemble for the school's "sanctuary" hour. There in flawless unison they recite a chapter from the *Bhagavad Gita*, sing the songs of the saints—often Mira's songs—and reaffirm their dedication to God, school, and world in the words of their school song, "I Would Be Simple."[5] In St. Mira's College for Girls, a glistening campus some distance away, older girls celebrate Mira's birthday with a solemn ceremony that begins at 5:00 A.M. each June 4th. An hour of Mira's songs serves as the centerpiece for readings from the world's great scriptures on that day, and at other points in the school year—for instance, on the occasion of Krishna's birthday some months later—students enact incidents from Mira's life.[6]

If one goes to Brindavan, the town in Braj that serves as the principal pilgrimage center for devotees of Krishna, one finds another memento of Mira. It is in the form of a temple dedicated to her, which was established in the middle of the nineteenth century by one of the chief ministers of the state of Bikaner, in Mira's native region, Rajasthan. It is a lovely little temple built around a courtyard draped with dense green foliage, and it has become a regular stop on the pilgrim route. This temple is not just memorial in nature, but sacramental. The central deity is Krishna, of course, and to his left is an image of Radha, his favorite consort. To his right, however, stands another female figure—apparently another consort, a counterpart to Radha. This is Mira herself, and not a few people think of her in just this way.[7]

Nowhere is this sentiment more evident than in Rajasthan, the region of deserts, rocks, and fortresslike princely kingdoms to the west of Delhi that is said to have been Mira's home. There in Merta, the town that claims her birth, a huge, gaily lit temple proclaims her fame, and during the summer rainy season pilgrims pack themselves so densely inside that when they join together to sing her songs the sound is deafening. Once again, the temple is formally dedicated to Krishna, Mira's chosen Lord, but an auxiliary shrine is devoted to her, and it is there that most of the music and dancing takes place. The building is supposed to commemorate the site where Mira herself prayed as a little girl in her grandfather's house, and its compound also includes the place where she was married. All over Rajasthan bards, traveling singers, and ordinary people sing of "the one from Merta," and though there is a characteristic tone of affection that goes with knowing she is one of their own, there is also a tendency to suggest that she was somehow more than human.

Mira's special, even divine, status among *bhakti* saints has directly to do with her sex. For her, womanhood before God was no religious conceit, but a total identity. So those who treasure Mira's songs often feel that her words have an authenticity that no male poet can match. It transports her to a different level in the eyes of those who look upon her legends and sing her songs. For them, and to a large extent for the poet as well, the distinction between Mira and the *gopis* who form Kirshna's inner circle is blurred. Owing to her sex, she belongs with them in a way that Sur never can, and the thin membrane that separates her world from theirs seems often to disappear.[8] When the voice is Mira's, the audience frequently cannot tell whether Mira is speaking for herself or through the voice of one of the *gopis*. Either both things are true and Mira speaks on two levels, or one has to assume that Mira herself has become a member of the charmed circle. And if this is the case, it raises the question of whether she really has her feet planted on this earth at all.

History and Hagiography

The question is an important one, for not only do we lack a reliable historical frame to associate with Mira's life, we also lack a corpus of poetry that can convincingly be associated with a historical person. Only five poems bearing Mira's signature can be found in documents whose date can be accepted as coming before the beginning of the eighteenth century. For a sixteenth-century poet, this is serious. One of these poems occurs in the *Adi Granth*, so we know that Mira must have had a fair reputation at the beginning of the seventeenth century when it was compiled, and Nabhadas's *Bhaktamal,* the oldest extant hagiographical statement concerning Mira, dates from the same period. But where are the rest of the poems?[9]

At present it is hard to give a satisfying answer. One possibility is that as a woman Mira was excluded from the devotional anthologies that began to take shape around the turn of the seventeenth century. But if sex was the obstacle, one wonders how Mira gained such widespread acceptance a century or two later. Another possibility is that her poetry, which is definitely closer to the folk idiom than any other we have explored, was regarded as insufficiently "poetic" to be preserved in writing. In that case it would have been the preserve of bardic groups and circles of female singers, who were not literate. Evidently her life story would also have been told—and also, often, in verse—by these same groups, for the legend of Mira colors her poetry more than is the case with any of the other *bhakti* poets. And that raises a final possibility: perhaps the large quantity of poetry now bearing Mira's signature grew up, in the course of time, as a response to the existence of her well-known legend.

Whichever explanation we choose, we seem to be left with a group of poems whose date of composition is so late that they can scarcely provide a check on the accuracy of Mira's biography. They must have been written by other "Miras" than the original one, if ever indeed she existed at all. In such a situation all we can do is listen critically to what the legends say, and for that purpose the oldest is probably the best. It is Nabhadas's brief sketch:

> Mira unraveled the fetters of family;
> she sundered the chains of shame to sing
> of her mountain-lifting Lover and Lord.
> Like a latter-day *gopi,* she showed the meaning
> of devotion in our devastated age.
> She had no fear. Her impervious tongue
> intoned the triumphs of her artful Lord.
> Villains thought it vile. They set out to kill her,
> but not even a hair on her head was harmed,
> For the poison she took turned elixir in her throat.
> She cringed before none: she beat love's drum.
> Mira unraveled the fetters of family;
> she sundered the chains of shame to sing
> of her mountain-lifting Lover and Lord.[10]

Although several major themes make their appearance here, one needs the extended commentary of Priyadas (A.D. 1712) before Mira's hagiography really becomes clear. Priyadas's life of Mira is the oldest full narration that has come down to us, and it is one of the liveliest in his large anthology. His central focus, like that of Nabhadas, is on a woman ever at loggerheads with the segment of society that matters most to an Indian woman: her family. It was not her natal family that presented the problem but the family into which she married. Yet since north Indian custom decrees that marriage—particularly a girl's marriage—take place at an early age, and since the girl is ever after expected to regard her husband's family as her own, Mira's struggles with her husband and his family essentially occupied her entire life.

As the story goes, the problem was desperately simple. Ever since she was a little girl, Mira knew perfectly well whom she wanted to have for a husband—Krishna—and no earthly man could compete. The form of the deity that had particularly won her affection was Krishna Giridhar, the "Lifter of the Mountain," and this title recurs in countless poems attributed to her. It is a youthful, heroic, protective aspect of Krishna, and one very widely worshiped in Rajasthan.[11] The story it commemorates is one in which Krishna as a young man held aloft Mount Govardhan, the symbolic center of Braj, to shield the cattle and cowherds of the region from the wrath of the rain-god Indra. It was Krishna who had provoked Indra to anger in the first place, by urging the Braj people to turn their devotional attentions away from the quixotic sky-god, captain of the old Vedic pantheon, and toward the mountain itself, which symbolized the nourishment and prosperity that were already in their midst. The mountain, as it turned out, was a form of Krishna. When Indra rained down his resentment for seven days and nights, Krishna countered by raising his mountainous umbrella above the heads of those he loved. Priyadas reports that Mira had a personal image of Krishna in this mountain-lifting guise, and that she repaired to him for protection herself.

Such protection was necessary because, as she saw it, to be devoted to Krishna meant that no other devotion was possible. Given her own preference she would have eschewed marriage, but she had no control over such matters. In Rajasthan, today as in the sixteenth century, marriages are arranged; and she had no choice but to go through with it. So she converted the marriage to her own purposes. When her Rajput family, the rulers of Merta, betrothed her to the son of a princely family from another Rajput state, she merely went through the motions. She followed her youthful husband around the marriage fire as tradition dictated she must, but the mantras she said in her heart as she did so tied her for life to a different youth, the one she called the Mountain Lifter. When it came time for her to depart for her new home, similarly, she was uninterested in taking along the requisite dowry. All she wanted to have at her side was her image of Krishna.

What she did when she arrived at the palace of her new family was even more appalling to them: she refused to bow her head to her mother-in-law when the older woman greeted her at the threshold, and she refused to bow to the goddess who was the family's chosen deity. To have done so, she felt, would have compromised her fealty to Krishna. These acts caused humiliation to her mother-in-law, shame to her father-in-law and her husband, and discredit to her own father's lineage as well.

Never content with the family that marriage had given her, Princess Mira proceeded to replace it with another, "the company of the saints" (*sadhu sang*) who were "attached to the will of Syam," that is, Krishna.[12] Her sisters-in-law tried to dissuade her from associating with wandering mendicants and religious enthusiasts—hardly the proper involvement for a woman sheltered inside the palace—but to no avail, and before long the *rana* took action by dispatching to Mira a cup of poison intended to bring an end to such disgraceful behavior. Whether Priyadas means Mira's husband or her father-in-law when he uses the term *rana* ("king" or "ruler") is not entirely certain, but the latter may be more likely, since Mira's father-in-law would have been head of the house.[13] More recent versions of the story have seen it the other way around, however, attributing this heinous act to Mira's husband, or blaming it on an evil brother-in-law.

Whoever it was, the action failed. The poison was sent in the guise of a liquid offering (*caranamrt*) to the feet of Krishna, Mira's deity, with the foreknowledge that Mira would be bound by Hindu practice to consume whatever was left over from the table of her divine Lord as *prasad*. But as she dutifully drank it, the poison became *caranamrt* indeed: "immortal liquid from his feet." Not only did she emerge unscathed from the wicked draft, she glowed with an even greater health and happiness than she had before.

This is the central event in Mira's life story and the one to which everyone from Nabhadas on makes reference. Other events tend to be patterned after it. Some later versions of Mira's biography have the *rana* sending her a snake when the cup of poison failed, but again to no avail: the asp transformed itself into a rock holy to Krishna (*salagram*) that Mira honored on her altar. According to another story, this one told by Priyadas himself, Mira was overheard one day as she whispered affectionately to Krishna behind her closed door. Her in-laws quickly concluded that some secret liaison had been detected, and the *rana* (again, the ambiguity between husband and father-in-law persists) raced to the door to avenge the family honor. Sword in hand, he demanded to be admitted to Mira's chamber and see the man with whom she had been conversing so sweetly. She opened the door and replied that the man with whom he desired to speak was standing directly in front of him—Krishna, her image—and that he was never one to shy away from a confrontation, at which point the *rana*, flustered and angry, froze "like a picture on the wall." Thus the gross reality paled in strength before the subtle: the living *rana* turned to stone while Krishna was shown to be much more than an image, more than "real life" itself.[14]

In time, Mira escaped the confines of her earthly family to join the larger family she had embraced. She traveled to Brindavan to join the "company of saints" gathered around Krishna there, but again a confrontation ensued. This time her opponent was none other than the great Krishnaite theologian Jiv Gosvami, with whom she wished to speak about matters of faith.[15] Jiv refused. He had undertaken a vow to think only of Krishna and never, therefore, to have concourse with a woman, since that would be apt to distract him from his holy thoughts. Mira was incensed at this attitude and let it be known that as far as she could see there was only one male in all of Brindavan, and it wasn't Jiv. Before Krishna, she implied, the rest of the world is female. Jiv saw the point and relented, and Mira stayed some time in Brindavan as the focus of a large circle of devotees who gathered around her in song.

The final journey in Mira's life took her in the opposite direction from her native Rajasthan—west to the great temple of Krishna in Dvaraka, on the shores of the Arabian Sea, to serve her Lord once again. When she had been gone for some time the *rana* finally missed her. He recognized that she was the very "personification of love," and sent a delegation of Brahmins to bid her return.[16] She resisted, of course, and the Brahmins found themselves driven to extremes in their effort to carry out their mission: they went on a hunger strike. This did indeed earn Mira's sympathy, and she prepared to go home, but as she did so, Krishna intervened. One day, as she worshiped in the temple, he drew her into his own image, and she was never seen again. Although Mira herself was at last willing to explore the possible coexistence of earthly propriety and heavenly devotion, her Lord could not bear to see her try.

This, then, is the outline of Mira's story, but because of the fascination it exerts throughout north India there have been a number of expansions and modifications since Priyadas's time. First and most important, there has been a tendency to specify that the family into which Mira married was the ruling house of Cittor, a city in southwestern Rajasthan known for its defiantly proud Rajput heritage. More than that, she has been given a historical husband. Apparently the first choice was Rana Kumbha, one of the great heroes and builders of Cittor, but when it was realized that his dates preceded those of the man in Merta whom tradition had come to recognize as Mira's father, a later prince of Cittor received the honor, a sixteenth-century figure named Bhojraj.[17]

Once such an honorable historical marriage had been arranged, it became necessary to extricate the groom from the opprobrium he would have earned as a would-be murderer of his wife. For this purpose Bhojraj was perfect, since in fact he soon disappeared from history. It was proposed that his marriage to Mira occurred shortly before he died, and that one of his younger brothers was responsible for the attempts on Mira's life. In several versions of Mira's life, including the one that has become standard comic-book fare in the Amar Chitra Katha series, this has a most desirable effect. Mira can be said to be "an ideal Hindu wife" with respect to Bhojraj[18]—an astonishing reversal of Priyadas's picture—and still retain the enmity she expresses in so many poems toward the *rana* who tried to poison her.

Another alteration that may have been made to improve Mira's image as a wife may be seen in Priyadas's report that Mira was once set upon by a man who pretended to be a wandering ascetic come to sing Krishna's praises in Mira's devotional group, but who actually had less elevated matters on his mind. One day he confronted Mira with amorous advances and claimed that the Mountain Lifter had commanded she submit. Fearlessly Mira complied, offering the man food and preparing a bed for them to use; but this she laid out in the presence of the worshiping company before she urged her forward guest to have a good time. Faced with so many eyes, it was not she but he who blanched with shame. He lost all desire for corporeal contact and begged Mira to help him attain the godly devotion she displayed.

The story has an uplifting ending, but it must have seemed risky to subsequent generations, because it has been omitted from many accounts of Mira's life. As Mira became a symbol of devoted womanhood in general—both religious and secular, or domestic—she lost some of the latitude she once had in demonstrating how freely one might respond when the intensity of *bhakti* led to situations that offended ordinary morality. Such offense was minimized. One particularly instructive page in the comic-book version of Mira's life, in fact, shows that her extraordinary faith could be altogether reconciled with an exemplary home life. In the foreground and in color we see Mira tending dutifully to the needs of her husband; only when these have been fulfilled does she slip away into the background frame, into the shadows of black and white, to serve her other Mate.[19] No mention is made, of course, of Mira's resistance to the idea of sharing Bhojraj's bed—this is a publication intended for young minds.

But this portrait is an extreme. The drama of Mira's defiance of the expectations of ordinary womanhood is still at the core of her legend as usually told, and no one has ever dared to suggest that she was anything but a virgin. Motherhood and Mira don't mix. Most changes in the myth of Mira have been in the nature of elaboration rather than revision, and many serve merely to associate motifs in her story with places people can visit today. Temples once dedicated to other divinities have been converted to Mira shrines in Cittor and the neighboring city of Udaipur,[20] and in the Mira temple in Brindavan one can now view the very *salagram* stone that once appeared before her in a much more threatening form.[21] As the sign there says, in Hindi and in capital letters in English,

> THIS TEMPLE IS BUILT ON THE RESIDENC OF THE TOPMOST SAINT MEERA BAI, BY THAKUR RAM NARAYAN SINGH. RAJDIVAN OF BIKANER ON 1842. IN THE MIDDLE SHRI KRISHNA, LEFT SHRI RADHA, RIGHT SHREE MEERA. MOVE-

ABLE RADHA KRISHNA IS ON THE LOWER THORNE AND TO RIGHT THEM IS THE SHALIGRAM FOR WHOM IT IS FAMOUS THAT IT IS THE VERY SHALIGRAM, CONVERTED FROM THE SNAKE SENT BY RANA, TO BITE MEERA. THE MANAGEMENT OF THIS TEMPLE DEPENDS UPON YOU. THEREFORE TO MAKE THIS PEACEFUL, CALM AND CHARMING ATMOSPHEPHERE ETERNAL DONATE YOUR DONATION IN THE DONATION BOX AND OBEY THE ORDER GIVEN BY SHRI KRISHNA IN GEETA (CHAPTER-XVII VERSE-20).

The relevant verse in the *Bhagavad Gita* assures visitors who wish to consult it that Krishna values any gift that is offered purely out of the sense that one ought to give, rather than with the expectation of getting something in return. And on Krishna's behalf, indeed, the priests at Mira's temple are willing to accept gifts of any order. But they do have definite ideas about how the urge to generosity will normally manifest itself among different classes of people, and are not reluctant to say so.

Themes in the Poetry

Many of the themes and emphases in poetry attributed to Mira correspond closely to what we have in the compositions of the other *bhakti* saints. Mira speaks of the importance of the name of God;[22] she praises the True Guru;[23] she uses nautical imagery to characterize what it is to cross "the sea of existence;"[24] she underscores the importance of sharing the company of other worshipers (*sants, sadhus, bhaktas*);[25] and there are times when she indulges in the sort of self-denigration that points by contrast to the greater glory of God.[26]

But there are strains in Mira's poetry that would seem distinctly out of place if one encountered them in the poems of Kabir, say, or Sur. One such strain is the close resemblance in style between many poems that bear Mira's signature and the often anonymous folk compositions sung by women in Rajasthan and elsewhere. These are generally simple in format, involving a great deal of repetition, as one might expect in a round or a refrain, and they take up themes that belong typically to women. Mira's poetry too tends to be simple, with ample repetition, and it often mentions family tensions, or the emotions a bride might feel, or festivals confined to women.[27] One also finds in her work such typically female genres of poetry as songs depicting the various characteristics of the twelve months and songs describing the coming of the rains, when one's man is not yet home and the roads become impassible.[28] These moods and genres are not entirely absent from poems composed by men and put into the mouths of women, but in Mira they are particularly pronounced. Considering our inability to isolate a body of poetry composed by a historical Mirabai or even by close associates in a "school" that might have grown up around her, this osmosis between "Mira" on the one hand and folk poetry on the other is easy to understand.

Another distinctive tendency in poems attributed to Mira concerns the line separating Mira from Krishna's *gopis*. There are poems in the Mira corpus in which this separation is carefully maintained. The poet may even assign herself the status of a maidservant (*manjari*) and watch from the sidelines as love develops between Krishna and Radha, paramount among the *gopis*, as is theologically correct.[29] But when Radha is absent from the scene, as is frequently the case, it is much harder to tell who is speaking, and there are times when it is almost impossible not to conclude that Mira understands herself as a *gopi*. She concludes one poem, for instance, with the following line:

> Let Mira, your servant, safely cross over,
> a cowherding Gokul girl.[30]

It is often much harder with Mira than it is with Sur (to choose a parallel *saguna* case) to subtract the poet's signature from the poem and still have it make sense. The line between the internal drama of Braj—the *gopis'* world—and what Mira experiences is not fixed, and grammar often forces the hearer to assume a close link between the two. This is not so with the poets we have studied so far. In poems of Ravidas and Kabir the signature is often cordoned off from the body of the poem by means of the verb "says," a word that appears directly in the text. Or it may just be understood, as is typical in many instances involving Nanak and Sur: only the poet's name appears, and the hearer supplies an implicit "says." With Sur the formal bond between the poet and the world he describes sometimes becomes stronger, in phrases such as "Sur's Lord" (*sur prabhu*). It is the Lord who acts in the poem, but the poet's presence is suggested indirectly through the use of the genitive. Yet the genitive meaning is only one possibility; usually one can also divide such a phrase so that the "Lord" participates in the drama and the "Sur" merely speaks it. All the hearer needs to do is supply the verb "says" and the poet becomes a mere narrator, formally distinct from the world he describes.

With Mira, however, one often has no choice but to pull the poet directly into the poem. We have already quoted one concluding verse in which this is required, and by far the most frequent formula for ending a Mirabai poem has equal force. In such a poem the whole first half of the final line enters as an indissoluble unit—"Mira's Lord is the clever Mountain Lifter"—and the presence of the genitive marker *re* in "Mira's Lord" (*mira re prabhu,* or *mira ke prabhu,* depending on the dialect) makes it impossible to factor her name out of the direct action of the poem by understanding it as the subject of the unexpressed verb "says." It is as if the whole phrase becomes Mira's signature, pulling her, via her Lord, into the world of the poem, which is most often the *gopis'* world. Often other things she says suggest that she is there anyway, not merely in the persona of a *gopi* but as a woman of Rajasthan, someone the *rana* tried to poison; but this clinches the case. And the repeated mention of Krishna in a particular role, as the one who lifts Mount Govardhan, has the effect of further attracting the action described toward Mira herself. The image of Krishna as the Mountain Lifter is the one she holds most dear.[31]

One often has the feeling that because Mira's own biography is of such vivid importance in north India, whoever composed the Mira poems was eager to draw in as much of Mira herself as possible. Clearly this happened when episodes from her own life such as the incident of the cup of poison or the snake made their way into poems she is said to have composed, but it may even be true when the only autobiographical fragment is an expanded version of her signature—something like "Mira's Lord is the clever Mountain Lifter." What happened, of course, was that the signature itself, like the rest of the poem, became something to be composed. In the absence of a historical Mira, she too had to be created.

A third distinctive emphasis in poems attributed to Mira has to do with this same set of issues. It is the particular view Mira takes of marriage and yoga in relation to Krishna, a view that is somewhat deviant when measured against much that is standard in Krishnaite doctrine. *Saguna* theology has some pointed things to say about these institutions. Typically it rejects the view that Krishna was married to the *gopis,* reserving that sacrament for a much later stage in his life, when he has assumed the throne of Dvaraka. The *gopis* are his paramours, not his wives, and theirs is therefore a costly, dangerous liaison: they risk the opprobrium of all society, and perhaps worse than opprobrium at the hands of their husbands if their trysts are discovered. With equal vehemence, *saguna* theology rejects the idea that Krishna was in any way an ascetic, a yogi. When Krishna recommends this pose to the *gopis* through Udho, it is in large measure a joke on Udho. No one who fools around as much as Krishna does can possibly hope to build a reputation as a yogi, and the *gopis* are quick to say so. For that reason we suspect that it is only a daring metaphor when a go-between reports to Radha that Krishna yearns for her with such unbroken concentration that he has begun to act like a yogi. Or worse: perhaps it's just a ploy to break down her resistance.[32]

In the poems of Mira both these sacred cows—marriage and asceticism—are defiled. Not only does Mira have a tendency to portray herself as wed to Krishna, a theme familiar from her hagiography, but she often depicts her betrothed as a yogi. Whether this marriage actually transpired is another matter. In one much-quoted poem, Mira seems convinced that the wedding happened in a dream in which Krishna appeared to her; in others she longs for the union to take place and describes her bridal readiness.[33] As for Krishna's identity as a yogi, it seems to have much to do with the fact that he is so distant, wandering as if he were an ascetic. Indeed, Rajasthani women's folk poetry sometimes touches on this theme in depicting an absent husband or lover. But here more is involved: Mira is ready to take up the yogi's life herself in order to go where he is.[34] Strangest of all, she imagines this liaison not just as one between a male and female yogi who are fellow travelers, but as an actual marriage between the two—a marriage of yogis, something whose possibility is simply disallowed by basic categories of Hindu thought.[35] To become a yogi is to leave behind one's marriage and everything that goes with it—family, home, and all. Mira, however, would seem to create a new institution to answer her urges. In doing so, she once again confuses the realms that others hold apart, and once again her audacity seems to have to do with her gender.[36]

Bhakti is a force that propels a person beyond the confines of ordinary life. In a man's case such a departure may take the form of imagining one's way into the lives of women, and specifically women who themselves abrogate social norms. This is what happens when Sur takes on the voice of a *gopi*. But if the poet is a woman, the landscape necessarily changes, so a woman who imagines her religious involvements as transgressing the boundaries of ordinary life may well do so in different ways. Rather than accepting the loving profligacy that official *saguna* theology designates as the appropriate avenue of escape from mundane, domestic involvements—a theology, of course, designed by men—she may try something new. She may attempt to forge categories that give new bite to *bhakti* from a woman's point of view. This is what Mira did in demanding for herself a marriage with the world's most eligible and unmarriageable bachelor and in imagining this marriage as taking a form the world regards as impossible: the coupling of two yogis. In Hindu terms a female yogi is already an oddity, since women are so closely identified with home and family. But to compound this aberration with marriage to a yogi whose personality seems to contradict the spirit of yoga in every way is to hatch an act of madness.

Mira says that the world did indeed call her mad—mad with love—and no wonder.[37] Whoever she was, whether a historical individual, a collective, mythical projection, or some combination of the two, she fired the imagination with her fearless defiance. In one respect she is revered as Krishna's spiritual wife, as quiet and humble and self-sacrificing as any woman could be expected to be in relation to her "husband-god" (*patidev*), but in another sense she is celebrated as the kind of person who shattered complacencies wherever she went, particularly by making it clear that the world's conception of a woman's place is not always a place one wants to be. In both these aspects, and as the only one of her gender to have earned a place on the honor roll of north Indian *bhakti* saints, she exerts a fascination that none of her male counterparts can match.

POEMS OF MIRABAI

I'm colored with the color of dusk, oh *rana,*
    colored with the color of my Lord.
Drumming out the rhythm on the drums, I danced,
  dancing in the presence of the saints,
    colored with the color of my Lord.
They thought me mad for the Maddening One,
  raw for my dear dark love,
    colored with the color of my Lord.
The *rana* sent me a poison cup:
  I didn't look, I drank it up,
    colored with the color of my Lord.
The clever Mountain Lifter is the lord of Mira.
  Life after life he's true—
    colored with the color of my Lord.

[Caturvedi, no. 37]

Life without Hari is no life, friend,
And though my mother-in-law fights,
  my sister-in-law teases,
  the *rana* is angered,
A guard is stationed on a stool outside,
  and a lock is mounted on the door,
How can I abandon the love I have loved
  in life after life?
Mira's Lord is the clever Mountain Lifter:
  Why would I want anyone else?

[Caturvedi, no. 42]

Today your Hari is coming,
  my friend,
  to play the game of Spring.
The harbinger crow in the courtyard speaks,
  my friend,
  an omen of good times ahead.
All the cowherds have gathered in the garden,
  my friend,
  where the basil grows:
I hear the sound of tambourines and drums,
  my friend.
  Why sleep? Wake up and go!
There's water and betel-leaf, mats and sheets,
  my friend.
  Go greet him: touch his feet.
Mira's Lord is the clever Mountain Lifter,
  my friend,
  the best blessing you could have.

[Sekhavat, no. 76]

I saw the dark clouds burst,
                dark Lord,
Saw the clouds and tumbling down
In black and yellow streams
                they thicken,
Rain and rain two hours long.
See—
  my eyes see only rain and water,
  watering the thirsty earth green.
Me—
  my love's in a distant land
  and wet, I stubbornly stand at the door,
For Hari is indelibly green,
                Mira's Lord,
And he has invited a standing,
                stubborn love.

[Caturvedi, no. 82]

Hey love bird, crying cuckoo,
    don't make your crying coos,
  for I who am crying, cut off from my love,
    will cut off your crying beak
  and twist off your flying wings
    and pour black salt in the wounds.

Hey, I am my love's and my love is mine.
    How do you dare cry love?
  But if my love were restored today
    your love call would be a joy.
  I would gild your crying beak with gold
    and you would be my crown.

Hey, I'll write my love a note,
    crying crow, now take it away
  and tell him that his separated love
    can't eat a single grain.
  His servant Mira's mind's in a mess.
    She wastes her time crying coos.

Come quick, my Lord,
  the one who sees inside;
    without you nothing remains.

[Caturvedi, no. 84]

Murali sounds on the banks of the Jumna,
Murali snatches away my mind;
My senses cut loose from their moorings—
Dark waters, dark garments, dark Lord.
I listen close to the sounds of Murali
And my body withers away—
Lost thoughts, lost even the power to think.
  Mira's Lord, clever Mountain Lifter,
  Come quick, and snatch away my pain.

[Caturvedi, no. 166]

The Bhil woman tasted them, plum after plum,
  and finally found one she could offer him.
What kind of genteel breeding was this?
  And hers was no ravishing beauty.
Her family was poor, her caste quite low,
  her clothes a matter of rags,
Yet Ram took that fruit—that touched, spoiled fruit—
  for he knew that it stood for her love.
This was a woman who loved the taste of love,
  and Ram knows no high, no low.
What sort of Veda could she ever have learned?
  But quick as a flash she mounted a chariot
And sped to heaven to swing on a swing,
  tied by love to God.
You are the Lord who cares for the fallen;
  rescue whoever loves as she did:
Let Mira, your servant, safely cross over,
  a cowherding Gokul girl.

[Caturvedi, no. 186]

Sister, I had a dream that I wed
  the Lord of those who live in need:
Five hundred sixty thousand people came
  and the Lord of Braj was the groom.
    In dream they set up a wedding arch;
    in dream he grasped my hand;
    in dream he led me around the wedding fire
    and I became unshakably his bride.
Mira's been granted her mountain-lifting Lord:
  from living past lives, a prize.

[Caturvedi, no. 27]

I have talked to you, talked,
  dark Lifter of Mountains,
About this old love,
  from birth after birth.
Don't go, don't,
  Lifter of Mountains,
Let me offer a sacrifice—myself—
  beloved,
    to your beautiful face.
Come, here in the courtyard,
  dark Lord,
The women are singing auspicious wedding songs;
My eyes have fashioned
  an altar of pearl tears,
And here is my sacrifice:
  the body and mind
Of Mira,
  the servant who clings to your feet,
    through life after life,
      a virginal harvest for you to reap.

[Caturvedi, no. 51]

Go to where my loved one lives,
  go where he lives and tell him
    if he says so, I'll color my sari red;
    if he says so, I'll wear the godly yellow garb;
    if he says so, I'll drape the part in my hair with pearls;
    if he says so, I'll let my hair grow wild.
Mira's Lord is the clever Mountain Lifter:
  listen to the praises of that king.

[Caturvedi, no. 153]

Oh, the yogi—
my friend, that clever one
whose mind is on Siva and the Snake,
that all-knowing yogi—tell him this:

"I'm not staying here, not staying where
the land's grown strange without you, my dear,
But coming home, coming to where your place is;
take me, guard me with your guardian mercy,
please.
I'll take up your yogic garb—
your prayer beads,
earrings,
begging-bowl skull,
tattered yogic cloth—
I'll take them all
And search through the world as a yogi does
with you—yogi and yogini, side by side.

"My loved one, the rains have come,
and you promised that when they did, you'd come too.
And now the days are gone: I've counted them
one by one on the folds of my fingers
till the lines at the joints have blurred
And my love has left me pale,
my youth grown yellow as with age.
Singing of Ram,
your servant Mira
has offered you an offering:
her body and her mind."

[Caturvedi, no. 117]

Let us go to a realm beyond going,
Where death is afraid to go,
Where the high-flying birds alight and play,
Afloat in the full lake of love.
There they gather—the good, the true—
To strengthen an inner regimen,
To focus on the dark form of the Lord
And refine their minds like fire.
Garbed in goodness—their ankle bells—
They dance the dance of contentment
And deck themselves with the sixteen signs
Of beauty, and a golden crown—
There where the love of the Dark One comes first
And everything else is last.

[Caturvedi, no. 193]

श्री राम

SIX

Tulsidas

Say Ram, say Ram, say Ram,
you fool!
That name is your raft
on the awful sea of life.

WE BEGAN the first chapter of this book on the outskirts of Benares, in the poor village of Sri Govardhanpur where Ravidas is venerated, and we start this last chapter, which concerns his *bhakti* cousin Tulsidas, just across the Ganges. The Maharaja of Benares lives there, in a palace that rises like a fortress from the bluff and affords him a lonely, imperial view of the city he once ruled. His isolation is certainly splendid, but for a full month every year he gives it up and surrounds himself with the masses.

This is the month of *ram lila,* "The Play of Ram," which comes early in the fall, after the rains have spent their force. All month long people arrive in boatful after groaning boatful to see the god-king Ram, played by a Brahmin boy, abandon the throne that is rightfully his, wander through the forests of India in fourteen years of exile, and return at last to be crowned in glory. Sometimes he is accompanied only by his courageous, beautiful wife Sita and his fiercely loyal younger brother Laksman—roles also taken by Brahmin youths. At other times, however, he is surrounded by an army of monkey warriors led by his greatest devotee, the monkey general Hanuman. With the help of these animal allies he is able to defeat the demon king Ravan in his island fastness. Ravan's thirty-foot-high bamboo-and-paper form bursts into a tower of fire as Ram's forces set the torch to his capital and thereby free Sita from her captivity. Then, on the last day of the cycle, Ram returns to be crowned in his native Ayodhya, where another brother, Bharat, has been guarding his throne all the time he has been away.

Crowds of up to a hundred thousand relive the story of this divine king as pilgrims from all over India join the faithful from Benares. As the scenes change, the entourage of devotees lumbers from one part of the Ramnagar plateau to another, and pushes to get a closer look at these gods in human form whenever they pose in tableaus illuminated against the night by flares. Every afternoon the crowd reassembles for the next episode in the story, and as night succeeds night everyone from the maharaja on his elephant right down to the poorest villager and weirdest ascetic takes part in the struggle that ritually reestablishes the just hegemony of Ram on earth.[1]

The classic tale of Ram, the *Ramayana,* was framed in Sanskrit by the poet Valmiki some two thousand years ago. Sanskrit, however, is a language for gods and Brahmins, not for the rank and file; so the tale ordinary people hear is a vernacular one instead. Their poet is Tulsidas, who in the latter half of the sixteenth century composed his *Ramcaritmanas,* a verse epic in the eastern Hindi dialect of Avadhi that plumbs the depths of what its title calls "The Spiritual Lake of the Acts of Ram." At Ramnagar, Tulsi's *Manas* (as the *Ramcaritmanas* is often called for short) is chanted by a dozen carefully chosen Brahmins while portions are excerpted and magnified for performance so that the boys who play Ram and his company may act out the events and emotions before the crowd. With the maharaja as patron and Brahmins as the chief performers, this is a ritual that in an obvious way solidifies the solemn bonds of the status quo, and Tulsidas' role in it has played no small part in making him the establishment saint of Benares and indeed of all north Indian culture. Almost universally assumed to have been a Brahmin, he is the scholar saint, the Jerome of north India, for he had evidently digested Valmiki's *Ramayana* and several other relevant Sanskrit texts before embarking on a Vulgate of his own composition. Yet Tulsi is a *bhakti* saint too—a poet whose language and concerns tied him to people of all castes—and in the tension between his brahminhood and his *bhakti* lies the power he has wielded ever since he began chanting the *Manas* some four hundred years ago.

The Poet's Life

Modern accounts of Tulsidas crown him the greatest of Hindi poets, and since the late eighteenth century rulers have vied with one another to serve as his posthumous patron,[2] yet the fragments of biographical detail that we can glean from Tulsi's poetry indicate that life seemed much more embattled to Tulsi himself. Some of this embattlement had to do with the common events of his age. Benares suffered a round of devastating disease in the early years of the seventeenth century, and Tulsi reacted to it in some of the final compositions of his *Kavitavali* ("A Garland of Verse").[3] He attributed it to a terrible conjunction of Pisces and Saturn,[4] and to the unexplained wrath of Siva against the city he is supposed to hold dear;[5] he prayed that the name of Ram could bring relief from distress as it had so often in the past. An example Tulsi sometimes cited was his own childhood. He says on more than one occasion that he was born into poverty, and implies that his parents had despaired of feeding another mouth when they cast him into the streets to survive on "scraps thrown out for dogs."[6] All that, however, was merely the "before." By the intervention of the name of Ram he became someone the world celebrated so heartily as to call him a "great sage." Perhaps they were comparing him with Valmiki himself.[7] The petitionary *vinaya* genre in which Tulsi says these things requires a litany of ills, so his subsequent celebrity—not something the genre would demand—is at least as noteworthy as his former degradation. Still, the fact that several times he calls to mind a childhood of abandonment suggests it may have been more real than invented.

One other adversity also deserves our notice. In beginning the *Manas,* Tulsi makes the customary obeisance at the feet of his guru, whom he calls Nararupahari, a name that means Hari—Vishnu—in the form of a man.[8] Next, in a second gesture recommended by tradition, he honors "the company of the saints," the good people in whom the name of Ram flourishes. Then comes a passage that is startling in its novelty. Tulsi bows his head not just to the good people in his world but to the evil ones as well, those who are predisposed to be critical and unappreciative, who hate any helpful act, and—more to the point—who are apt to laugh contemptuously at the faults of the poem Tulsi is about to begin.[9] It is hard to know quite what prompted this last bow. One may take it at face value and see it as an indication of how tentative Tulsi felt about the venture upon which he had embarked, and how evenhanded he was in soliciting response: he professes to believe that one can benefit as much by criticism as praise.[10] Or one may read these lines as an effort to defuse criticism before it could build: the poet's disclaimers about his poetic ability are elegant poetry indeed. In any case one gets the sense that there may have been strong resistance among conservative Brahmins to the idea of rendering the *Ramayana* in a vernacular language. To do so was to popularize it and take it a step beyond the confines of traditional brahminical control.[11]

History shows that Tulsi overcame all these adversities. Unhappy childhood? If homelessness was part of his own past, it gave him greater insight into the difficulties Ram experienced when he was separated from his kith and kin. Pestilence? If it was a resurgence of the Benares plague that finally claimed Tulsi's life, still it was only at a ripe old age—eighty, or even ninety, long after he had completed his epic to Ram and the several anthologies to follow. Priestly opposition? Today there is no more famous Brahmin name in all Benares than that of the renegade who dared to compose a *Ramayana* in a language people could understand.

Already in Tulsidas's own day Nabhadas was saying that he was a veritable Valmiki come to rescue the present, degenerate world-age from its crooked ways.[12] This became common coinage. Writing a hagiographical anthology in western India in the eighteenth century, the Marathi poet Mahipati expanded on the theme by reporting a dialogue in which Vishnu, lying on his great serpent in the midst of the timeless Milk Ocean, literally commissions Valmiki to reenter the world as Tulsidas. So Tulsi is Valmiki's explicit avatar—a rubric Mahipati used to relate other poet-saints to divine antetypes as well—and such an important avatar, indeed, that he all but heads the list.[13] Yet for all this enthusiasm about a Brahmin who earned success by turning to *bhakti,* one can still detect traces of a perceived tension between Tulsi and other Brahmins in the legends recorded about him in our earliest narrative hagiography, Priyadas's expanded version of the *Bhaktamal.* One story that touches on this theme seems to have been inspired by a phrase Nabhadas used in characterizing the glory of Tulsi's work. He said that a single syllable from Tulsi's great poem was sufficient "to redeem a person accustomed to such deeds as killing Brahmins." Priyadas then recounts the tale of a Brahmin-murderer who did indeed receive grace at Tulsi's hands, much to the consternation of his Brahmin castefellows.[14]

The medium of grace was the name of Ram. This is what the murderer shouted as he went from one holy place to another begging alms, and when the sound reached Tulsi's ears, his heart melted. He gave the man food—*prasad,* food that had been blessed by being offered first to God—and "sang him clean," as the text says, as if he were his own "dear one."[15] At that a committee of Brahmins was assembled and Tulsi was commanded to explain how he could have disregarded the sin of someone who had been treated as an outcaste for his deeds, and remitted it by sharing food with him. Tulsi retorted that his colleagues had evidently read their sacred books without allowing anything of the content to touch their hearts. Their thinking was deformed, he said: nothing of Ram's grace had yet penetrated their mental darkness.

The Brahmins were taken aback and did indeed return to their scriptures to learn of the wonder-working power of the name of Ram. Still disturbed at the notion of reinstating a murderer to full status in the community, however, they proposed that he be tested by seeing whether Siva's bull Nandi would consume food offered to him by the criminal. Tulsidas accepted this challenge and prayed to Nandi on the murderer's behalf, reminding him of the glory of Ram's name. Soon the offering was consumed. Thus the *prasad,* the sacred food, went full circle—from God via Tulsi to a sinner, and via Tulsi back to God again—truly earning its name, which means "grace."[16]

Another episode suggests a continuing tension between the "reformed brahminism" for which Tulsi stood and the usual patterns of brahminical practice. This time things develop from a faux pas committed by the saint himself. Tulsi is out one day when he meets a Brahmin woman he knows, accompanied by a group of people. She acknowledges him from a distance with a respectful greeting, and without exactly sizing up the situation he answers with a similarly formulaic response: *suhagavati!*[17] This is a salutation one can address to a woman, with the meaning, "May fortune be yours." It also carries the connotation, "May your husband have long life," since a woman's fortune is assumed to follow from the presence of her spouse. That was the problem. Although this woman's spouse was indeed present, it was in the form of a corpse—this was his funeral cortege—and Tulsi's failure to grasp this reality faced the woman with an agonizing necessity. She was forced to explain to the absent-minded poet that her husband was no more and that she was on her way to commit suttee at his side. As soon as she did so, however, she was filled with remorse, for to announce her intent before acting it out was to guarantee that it would have no effect: she could no longer hope to be reunited with her husband on the other side of death. Tulsi's enthusiastic inadvertence had ruined her resolve and transgressed the sanctity of a cherished Brahmin institution.

Fortunately the story does not end there. Because Tulsi's aim was not to destroy what Brahmins value, but to translate it to another level of truth, he took matters into his own hands and declared that if the widow and her company would truly embrace Ram, he could raise the dead man to life again. They did so, and so did he, and with that the whole entourage abandoned the "disease" that separated them from what Priyadas calls "the abode of Syam" (*syam dham*), which in this context must mean not only the home that Krishna (Syam) provides but the refuge that is Ram. The story records a victory of *bhakti* over a brahminhood too narrowly conceived, and the victory comes in the form of possibilities not even imagined by those imprisoned in old and rigid patterns.[18]

Yet the Brahmins who surrounded Tulsidas were not the only ones unable to see as far as they should. Early in his career Tulsi himself is portrayed as a man of limited vision, and the tale that tells of his liberation has to do with another Brahmin wife—his own. He loved her exceedingly, and when one time he returned from a trip to find that she had gone to her parents' home, as is the Hindu custom for young brides at certain times of the year, he nearly went out of his mind. Immediately he raced off to find her.

In later, more romanticized versions of the story he is made to cross a rain-swollen river by appropriating a floating corpse as a raft, and to climb up to her window on a huge snake he mistakes for a rope hanging from her balcony: both are mementi mori.[19] In the more parsimonious story that Priyadas tells, the reality of death is brought to the scene in a more muted way. When Tulsi is face to face with his wife again, she sees his ardor and greets it with a certain chagrin. She feels compelled to remind him of the evanescence of earthly love by observing that "this body is just bones covered with skin," whereas "the love of Ram stays new."[20] Tulsi is shocked into a recognition of the truth and forthwith leaves home and family to take up a life of godly austerity in Benares.

The tale goes on. He may no longer thirst for the sight of his wife, but he thirsts desperately for the sight of Ram. A series of episodes follow that remind one vaguely of the events reported in Tulsi's own *Vinaya Patrika,* in which he takes to Ram a petition to be freed from the ills of this dark age, but is able to reach him only after first working his way past the many other divine figures who stand as intermediaries between human beings and this utmost expression of holiness. In the *Vinaya Patrika* the poet seems to move at his own urging, with a momentum that he generates himself, though Hanuman is ever his guide. In the *Bhaktamal,* by contrast, even the measured determination of a Tulsidas is sufficient to force the Lord's hand. The general pattern is the same—he begins at the outskirts and closes in on his goal—but in the *Bhaktamal* he requires the help of a presence hidden to himself before he can even get started; and when he reaches the grail and is granted a vision of Ram, he does not even know he has done so until the moment has passed. In Priyadas's story, then, the poet is always learning to open his eyes.

The first unseen spirit who comes to Tulsi's aid is a ghost that inhabits the place where he performs his toilet functions every morning—by tradition, a spot across water and beyond the confines of Benares, where Tulsi went to avoid defiling either the Ganges or the city built on its banks. In Priyadas's day the water Tulsi crossed was probably understood to be the little Assi River, which flows into the Ganges near his house, but nowadays, since Benares has spread well beyond the Assi, people sometimes think Tulsi boated all the way to the far shore of the Ganges to answer the needs of his body.

The ghost he met there was at first an unsavory creature, but in time it was purified by the Ganges water that Tulsi brought to wash himself with, and when it began to speak it was able to tell the poet where to look for Ram's devotee Hanuman, who could direct him further. Tulsi's improbable informant tells him that he can recognize Hanuman as the first person to arrive at any recitation of Ram's deeds[21] and the last to leave when it is done. Sure enough, when Tulsi next sings a segment from his *Manas,* he notices that there is a shabby old man who comes early and leaves late, and he insists so unshakably on this man's true identity as Hanuman that the monkey hero at length relents and reveals his native form. He asks, furthermore, what boon the poet wants, and Tulsi responds by asking for the sight of Ram. Compliantly Hanuman tells him of a day when Ram and Laksman will come riding by on horseback, and Tulsi waits eagerly for them to appear. When they do, however, he is unable to distinguish them from others they are with, so when Hanuman returns and asks if Tulsi has seen them, he can only say, "What? I didn't see anything!"[22]

The episode is left at that, but a later stanza takes up the theme, and with a similarly enigmatic approach. This time the scene is night, and robbers are trying to make a raid on Tulsi's house. They make a number of forays, but each time they are frightened off by a dark-skinned youth who guards the premises with a bow and arrow. When morning comes, the thieves are sufficiently confounded that they go to Tulsi and ask who this guard is. From their description he knows instantly that it was Ram, but he is so overcome at the thought that he cannot speak: all he can do is weep. The story ends with Tulsi giving up all his possessions, for he is moved by shame at the thought that Ram should be troubled to guard such paltry things, and the thieves are converted too.

So Ram is in the wings everywhere, but never quite visible to the eye of the poet. Priyadas seems to resolve this mystery only at the end of his section on Tulsi, and in a way that suits his own theological predilections. Tulsi has been to Delhi, where he has demonstrated the superiority of his Lord over anything that can be conjured up by the Mughal emperor,[23] and he decides to pass through Brindavan, where Krishna reigns, on his way home. There he meets none other than Nabhadas. In a way it is a strange place for a rendezvous, since Nabhadas, like Tulsi, is a man who leans to Ram: the verses at the beginning of the *Bhaktamal* say as much. By placing Nabhadas in Brindavan, however, his commentator Priyadas makes him in some measure a devotee of Krishna, and he does the same to Tulsidas. But only in a measure: after Tulsi meets Nabha, he proceeds to the temple of Madan Gopal, where he explains to the deity, Krishna, that the form of God he has chosen for his own worship is Ram. Would he manifest himself in that form?

In a flash the deed is done—a splendid, incomparable vision—so one has the oddity that the only time Priyadas reports Tulsi as seeing his Lord directly is an occasion on which he gazes at him by means of an image of Krishna. Perhaps this is merely another motif in the series that shows Tulsi seeking Ram's sanctum from whatever distance and angle he can, as in the *Vinaya Patrika,* and perhaps the swiftness with which the vision is reported by Priyadas indicates that he thinks of Tulsi as having had other visions of Ram, though he does not report them. But it seems significant that Priyadas puts the final touches on his portrait of Tulsi by placing him against the background of the sectarian affiliation that was his own. Priyadas was a follower of the Bengali ecstatic Caitanya, whose devotion to Krishna stimulated the settlement of Brindavan as a place of pilgrimage; the temple of Madan Gopal was a Caitanyite temple.[24]

The story Priyadas reports stops short, however, of making Tulsi into something he was not. We learn that when Tulsi entered the sacred precincts and made his request, an onlooker threw out the challenge that Ram was really just a portion of God while Krishna was divinity entire. Priyadas neither denies nor endorses this point of view. He merely has Tulsi say that if what the man says is true, it only increases his devotion to Ram, for at that moment he is indeed granted a vision of his Lord and he reports that the "portion" he sees is already so beautiful as to exceed any possible term of comparison. Tulsi's devotion, then, transforms a sectarian jab into yet another occasion for the increase of faith, and the question of who is greater than whom is simply left in abeyance. The connection between Krishna and Ram is made; that seems enough.[25]

A Magisterial Theology

It would be a mistake to see this story as merely serving Priyadas's own sectarian ends. It illustrates something genuine and significant about Tulsidas, something that emerges from his own writings: his ecumenicity. In a more considered way than any of the other poets we have surveyed, Tulsi was a theological bridge-builder, someone interested in spanning the gaps between several of the important religious communities of his day and, in the course of doing so, between the gods themselves.

One can see this at many places in the oeuvre that Tulsidas has bequeathed to us. To begin with, there is the fact that Tulsi departed from his overwhelming orientation toward Ram to dedicate a small collection of verse to Krishna, as if he really had visited Brindavan, as Priyadas claims.[26] Hints of the mythology of Krishna's childhood creep into the *Manas* too, as the unseen backdrop for his descriptions of the infancy of Ram. Other members of the pantheon are also present. We have alluded already to the structure of the *Vinaya Patrika,* which has a long roll call of poems to various divinities before Tulsi presents his petition to Ram. He begins with the other four deities a Smarta Brahmin should worship—Ganesa, Surya, Siva, and the Goddess; passes on to the river goddesses Ganges and Jumna and the holy cities Benares and Citrakut; and finally concentrates his attention on members of Ram's inner circle—Hanuman, Ram's three brothers, and Sita—before addressing Ram himself. This latter group plays a role again at the very end by joining in the chorus that proclaims Tulsi's petition to have been favorably received. Ram is the last to add his voice.[27]

This is not just godly name-dropping on Tulsi's part. He is serious in his ecumenical intent, as we can see plainly in the way he shapes the *Manas*. Other versions of the *Ramayana* begin, naturally enough, with Ram, and earlier versions of Tulsi's own poem evidently began the same way.[28] But the final form is different altogether. There, a discussion between Siva and his wife Parvati stimulates the telling of the story of Ram. Parvati asks her husband how Ram can be the impersonal Absolute and yet moan on earth at the captivity of his dear Sita. Indeed, she wonders, why did he take on human form at all? In answering, Siva plays the philosopher. He insists that there is no true difference between *nirguna* and *saguna* aspects of reality, the seemingly unconditioned and the seemingly conditioned. To see such a disparity is to project the delusory limitations of mortal perception upon the divine. But Siva goes further. He acknowledges that he himself, though god and philosopher, can only partly penetrate the mystery of the drama he has been interpreting. He too must rely on formulas he has been taught—the creed that from time to time God enters the world to pull it back from the brink of chaos and hurt, and the individual stories of how that has transpired—for in the end he too is only a devotee of Ram.[29] In the city of Benares, where Siva reigns supreme, this is important news, and it is no accident that Tulsidas buttresses it by introducing an account of the marriage of Siva and Parvati into the fabric of the epic itself.

Interestingly, the matter surfaces a second time as well. This time it is at the end, when the great bird Garud, who has come to Ram's aid at a point in the story when the hero was trapped in the coils of a serpent, reflects on the matter and wonders why he should have had to do such a thing. If Ram is God omnipotent, there is no excuse for his becoming so debilitated. Tormented by his doubt, Garud goes from door to door in the pantheon, ultimately arriving in the presence of Siva, but Siva directs him onward to a higher authority who is, improbably, a crow by the name of Bhusundi.[30]

The humility and impurity of Bhusundi's status in life—crows eat anything—are significant. They symbolize how devotees should perceive themselves in relation to Ram, for Bhusundi has come to know his god with a clarity of perception that is vouchsafed to few. It turns out that Bhusundi first encountered Ram when the latter was but a tiny infant. The child tried to reach out to the crow, and when the bird retreated Ram began to cry. Bhusundi himself was perplexed to see the Lord of all power reduced to tears, but not for long. Ram lunged after him, and wherever he flew to escape—even as high as Brahma's heaven—his captor would always confront him two fingers' breadth before his eyes. Before long Bhusundi had to close his eyes to save his sanity, but at that point he fell into the mouth of the child and watched endless eons pass as the pantheon emerged and Ram again manifested himself as a child on earth. Then as the child in his vision laughed, he was disgorged from the mouth of this other child—but the same one, really—and begged from him, in wonder and terror, the boon of faith. It was granted, and that is how Bhusundi came to have the privilege of singing Ram's praises eternally, incarnation after incarnation, on the banks of the holy lake at Mount Pravarsan, which is located far above the valley of illusion where the rest of us stumble about.

Garud is impressed by what he hears, and willingly concedes Bhusundi's claim that to understand God from the point of view of his formlessness—the *nirguna* side—is far easier than trying to comprehend what the *saguna* side can mean. To the mystery of God's manifestations, *bhakti* is the only adequate response. The confusing presence of God turns things inside out and upside down, so it is no anomaly that Siva, who stands at the pinnacle of the hierarchy of heaven and is acknowledged as the preceptor of Brahmins on earth, is himself the pupil of a crow, and that the crow is really someone Siva had once cursed as an upstart Untouchable in a former life. The humble crow knows only how to worship Ram, and to complete the circle there is a point in the epic where Ram acts as a worshiper of

Siva.[31] But the main point of emphasis is that Siva, the symbol of a barely understood ultimacy, turns to Ram in wonder. Ram is yet more ultimate, if that is possible. His descent to earth to establish a kingdom of righteousness—seemingly such a straightforward act—is in reality a mystery that not even Siva can comprehend.

This, then, is ecumenism with a point, and we meet it in a somewhat different guise in several of the poems that are translated below. Here Ram's incomprehensible trustworthiness is represented in the form of his name.[32] As in its use by Kabir—one even sees analogies in Nanak's view of God's name—the name Ram is a vocable without syntax or grammar, and therefore *nirguna* in its import. Yet it is not just that with Tulsi, but *saguna* as well, for its meaning is also related to the Ram of the *Ramayana*—the syntactical, storied Ram. So Tulsi is perhaps in a better position than any of his *bhakti* confreres to give us a sense of how the divine name, and with it the ultimate truth about God, can succeed in being both *saguna* and *nirguna* at the same time. Like Kabir, he affirms that God's story is ultimately untellable,[33] but at some level of truth he is able to go on telling it anyway.

Just what level that is has troubled some of Tulsidas's interpreters. The *nirguna* message has often been preached by people whose position in society is marginal and embattled—the outsiders, the oppressed—and they have sometimes bristled at the *saguna* side of Tulsidas. This is the part that enables him to affirm the traditional structures of Hindu society out of the sense that God's "qualities" are somehow encoded, protected, and accessible in the world we know. This is the Tulsi who is quoted with approval by such groups as the Ram Rajya Parisad, a political party established not long after India's independence with the intent of restoring the country to a long-lost Hindu order of righteousness and prosperity symbolized by Ram's rule (*ram rajya*).[34] It is also the Tulsi who in extreme moments apparently insists on the value of the brahminical status quo, no matter what its faults. At one point in the epic he goes so far as to have Ram say:

> Though a Brahmin curse you, beat you, or speak cruel words,
> He should be worshiped. So sing the saints.
> Worship a Brahmin, though he lack kindness and virtue.
> Don't worship a Sudra, though he possess all virtue,
> Skill, and wisdom.[35]

A passage such as this is odious to the ears of many who hear it chanted,[36] but they have only to wait a few verses before hearing Ram give voice to almost exactly the opposite sentiments:

> I recognize
> Only one relationship: devotion. Caste, kinship,
> Lineage, piety, power, wealth, strength, connections,
> Virtue, achievements—a man with all these but without
> Devotion is like a cloud without water.[37]

Here the "reformed brahminism" that Priyadas's stories so often associate with the power of the name of Ram is fully in evidence. No low-caste or woman saint could dissent, and in fact the episode in which it occurs, an incident in which Ram accepts food from the outcaste woman Sabari and grants her salvation, is also one celebrated by Mira in a poem we have already heard. Similarly, many other poems Tulsidas composed remind us of those attributed to other poet-saints, from Ravidas on up the social hierarchy. He bemoans the state of the world; he praises the transcendent power of the name of Ram; he cherishes the value of teachers, good company, and singing God's praise; he berates himself for falling as low as he has, pleads with God to rescue him, and describes himself as a poor and lowly servant of the Lord he beseeches for help.[38]

Such a message may be threatening to the orthoprax, but it does not actually defame them, and it may be that the difficulties Tulsi experienced with the Brahmins of Benares really had more to do with sectarian conflict than with social criticism. In a passage or two Tulsi implies that the people who troubled him were of Siva's camp,[39] and the length to which he goes in establishing the relation between Siva and Ram in the *Manas* and elsewhere may not have been without a social motive. In Tulsi's epoch Ram was integral to the established religion of Benares, as he is today, and the ecumenical devotion that Tulsi fostered seems to have played an important part in making possible the transition from then to now.[40]

A Saint Still Growing in Sainthood

To go to Benares today is to meet Tulsi in many places. The house in which he is said to have lived, once a relatively modest abode constructed by a wealthy admirer, has been expanded so that it rises magnificently above the river bank. Huge letters on a sheer wall nearby announce that the neighborhood is called Tulsi Ghat—"Tulsi's Landing"—and no boat plying the Ganges can miss them. The room where Tulsi lived is preserved, and his sandals, necklace of *tulsi* (basil-tree) beads, and shrine to Hanuman can still be glimpsed through the window. The family that lives there is headed by the man who runs the temple of Sankat Mocan ("Release from Extremity"), which is today one of the most crowded in the city. Significantly, it is not situated in the central area near the great temples to Siva and the goddess Annapurna, but on the outskirts of town. Evidently the deities it celebrates—Ram and Hanuman—are relative newcomers on the scene. But that does not deter the crowds. Every Tuesday and Saturday in particular, inauspicious days when God's protection is particularly needed, you can see foreheads all over Benares that have been touched with the bright orange mark showing that a person has received *prasad* at Sankat Mocan. And every day of the week—indeed, every day of the year—you can hear an exposition of a segment from the *Manas* on one of the temple verandahs in the hour that transforms afternoon to evening.[41]

Not far down the road is a temple that celebrates the faith of Tulsidas even more directly. A stunning marble structure built not long ago by one of the great Marwari merchant clans of Calcutta, it is called the Tulsi Manas Mandir, "the temple to Tulsi's *Manas*." Each year on Tulsi's birthday it is the source of a procession that takes the temple's message to the city at large. The procession has bagpipers, devotional groups with banners to Ram, blind boys from a school the temple supports, and a hundred and eight identically clad Brahmins, all chanting from the *Manas*. There are floats, too. One carries Brahmin boys clad as Ram and Sita, just as in the *ram lila;* another is surmounted by a boisterous, club-wielding Hanuman; others display pictures and effigies of Tulsidas chanting his epic; and, of course, there are episodes from the book itself. To top it all off, one can see mockups of the latest in Indian military hardware: a dashing cardboard tank and a large paper helicopter mounted precariously on a bicycle like some oversized mechanical insect.

This tilt toward the technological is replicated at the temple itself. Its inner walls are covered with verses from the *Manas,* all handsomely etched in marble, but in contrast to this more traditional display there are brightly lit dioramas with moving parts, such as the life-size Tulsidas who endlessly turns the pages of his masterpiece, welcoming each new page by intoning a deep, mysterious "Ram." On special days the place is jammed. The road out front is blocked and its traffic diverted elsewhere so that pilgrims with children on their hips and bundles on their heads can come in and gawk at each panel or explore the holy Disneyland that awaits them in the garden outside. There the Ganges descends from the Himalayas in an eternal cascade, a stony snake-charmer ever succeeds in rousing his metal cobra to excitement, and an elephant devotee is rescued from his plaster crocodile attacker. At the end of the series one comes to a sort of "saints' alley" where the most famous song attributed to Surdas, "I didn't eat the butter, Ma," is brought to life by a scene that shows the child Krishna, who makes this claim, doing just what he denies. In the booth next door Mirabai sings a tireless serenade. And last but not least the pilgrims meet two Lionel trains carrying the "Manas Mail" to needy post offices along a little oval track. Its ultimate message, the name of Ram itself, is proclaimed from the temple too, for on both sides of the door great Hanumans stand guard and rip their chests open to hearts on which the letters R-A-M are inscribed. Each time this happens, a gravelly voice from somewhere inside repeats the sacred name.

Such marvels of modernity are not really out of step with the cult of Tulsidas, which has undergone a swift development in the last hundred years. Halfway through the nineteenth century people seemed mainly aware of Priyadas's account of the saint's life. A few specialists could also quote stanzas from the *Tulsi Carit* or *Gosai Carit* ("Life of Tulsi"), which perhaps dates to sometime late in the eighteenth century, but no one seemed to have the text. Since then not only has a full version of the *Gosai Carit* been "discovered," but two other sources have appeared, to flesh out a picture of the poet's life. The more recent their appearance, the closer their dates of composition are said to have come to the life of the poet himself. This is suspicious, and one can hardly imagine how earlier generations could have been indifferent to such material if indeed it lay beneath their noses. Chances are that much of it was produced only in response to a need that has been forcefully felt since the nineteenth century.[42]

That need, apparently, was for details about a figure who could serve as the voice for a mainstream Hinduism that had not been diverted from its course by the challenge of the British.[43] The more Tulsidas became a full-blown "historical" figure, the more his counsel seemed adequate to meet Britishness and Christianity on their own terms. And though his candidacy for moral leadership had much to do with his conservative ecumenicity within the Hindu spectrum, as time passed, his progressive *bhakti* side also received its play. Today he is celebrated not only for having preached an image of an ideal society—the rule of Ram—that legitimates a program of Hindu self-reliance, but for doing so in a reformist spirit. Hence on the one hand ascetics of the conservative Saivite *dasnami* order are invited to participate in his birthday celebrations at the Tulsi Manas Temple, symbolizing the ancient message Tulsi is thought to have affirmed, and on the other hand the poet is praised in speeches uttered that day for his supposed opposition to caste inequities and the denigration of women.[44] Moreover, recent hagiographies forge explicit links between him and the other great lights of the *bhakti* movement, at least in its *saguna* expression. The *Mul Gosai Carit* ("An Essential Life of Tulsidas") has Sur come to Tulsi to ask his blessing on the *Sur Sagar,* and someone has composed a poem in which Sur states his gratitude once the blessing is given.[45] As for Mira, it is claimed that through an exchange of letters Tulsi urged on her the importance of giving up everything for God, and that was what it took to kindle in her the courage to declare a final break with her in-laws and leave home.[46] The example of Tulsi's own behavior in parting from his wife cannot have hurt.

This saint-for-all-sides is a perfect candidate to be honored at an institution such as the Tulsi Manas Temple, which was constructed with the money of Marwari merchants. The Marwaris were originally from Rajasthan, but since the late eighteenth century they have built a financial and industrial network that extends throughout most of the subcontinent: Marwaris operate a significant segment of the economic infrastructure that runs modern India. One Marwari family in particular, the Birlas, has devoted its largess to the building of a religious network that parallels the financial one. Birla temples can be found at key points all over India, encouraging a sort of national Hindu integration, and the Tulsi Manas Temple is built in a style that effectively adds it to the series. It is not just the inclusion of Sur and Mira at Tulsi's temple that gives it an air of Hindu ecumenicity, but the architecture itself. The Manas Temple shares with its Birla cousins an almost uniform design whose streamlined neotraditionalism says that Hinduism is not a thing of the past, and the carnival accoutrements announce the same message. Up-to-date Christians who like radio stations that set a Friend Jesus libretto to music that makes for "easy listening" can perhaps sympathize with the spirit that animates such an institution, for its specific religiosity goes only a step or two beyond the sort of clean family fun that makes the Disney establishments such attractive meccas for pilgrimage from all over the world.

Today Tulsidas is customarily accorded the title *gosvami,* which literally means "master of the senses" but has come to connote a sectarian leader in the Vaisnava tradition. To extend the title to Tulsidas, as has been done for two centuries now, is to recognize in this specifically nonsectarian figure a religious teacher at least as worthy of veneration as the Brahmins who earn the name hereditarily. It is, on the whole, a staid epithet. Although it groups Tulsi with the leaders of the great religious communities who define themselves by their *bhakti,* it does so in a way that bespeaks the value of tradition. The *gosvamis* of north India, though by no means as conservative as the Brahmins who lived in Benares before Tulsi came on the scene, have nonetheless exercised their religious influence for half a millennium now, and to a man they too are Brahmins.

If such "reformed brahminhood" can have true meaning, something beyond the cosmetic overlay of modernity that one confronts in the Manas Temple, it may well be exemplified by the man who is Tulsi's distant successor as the chief devotee to Hanuman at the temple of Sankat Mocan. Tulsi himself is supposed to have established this temple, and the man who superintends it has the hereditary right to occupy the house on the Ganges where the *gosvami* once lived. This is Veer Bhadra Mishra, who is not only the head of Sankat Mocan but a member of the faculty at Banaras Hindu University, and not only a theologian but a scientist: he teaches in the Department of Civil Engineering. In response to one facet of his interest he has made Sankat Mocan the center of a revival of traditional arts in which the recitation and proclaiming of the *Manas* play an important role. In response to the other side of his concern, however, he has established a Sankat Mocan Foundation whose purpose it is to find a way to purify the Ganges of the pollution that has made it in Mishra's opinion perhaps the greatest public health hazard in Benares. Mishra's campaign to clean up the Ganges—principally by fashioning an effective sewer system for the city—has attracted enough attention internationally to earn him coverage in *Time, Smithsonian,* and *National Geographic,*[47] but not everyone in Benares is so enthusiastic. There are the usual recalcitrant bureacrats, of course, but in addition Mishra is opposed by Brahmins who find it wildly heretical to suggest that the Ganges—goddess that she is and the agent of ultimate purification—can be anything but pure herself.

Faced with these considerable tensions and the almost unthinkable task of really changing anything in the city that epitomizes traditional Hinduism, Mishra remains patient, personable, and enthusiastic. And if one stops to think of it, he has a right to his optimism, for in a certain sense he has the weight of the past not only against him but on his side. It is hard not to see in him a modern-day version of his sixteenth-century preceptor, the man who is reported to have rowed to the other side of the river daily so as not to pollute her and who in consequence of that unusual discipline was ultimately granted a pathway to Ram.

It is said that when the Brahmins of Tulsi's day challenged his right to have composed a *Ramayana* in Hindi, it was decided to enlist Siva himself as an arbiter, so copies of the main sacred books of Hinduism, all written in Sanskrit, were piled on top of the *Manas* in the sanctum of that stronghold of Benares brahminism, the Visvanath temple at the center of the city. If Siva did nothing to alter the priorities that that pile implied, it would prove the Brahmins were right. But in fact the opposite occurred. The temple was locked for the night, and when the conservative priests returned in the morning they found the *Manas* sitting right on top.[48] Given the weight of tradition in Benares, it is hard to see how Mishra's struggle for the establishment of a new rule, at least in the realm of health, can quickly succeed. All those texts! All those customs and ties! But miracles do fill the lives of the saints, even one as methodical and hard-working as Tulsidas, and it would dishonor the spirit of *bhakti* to think that some sort of wonder cannot happen here too.

Can it extend to the social realm as well? Can the Untouchables of Sri Govardhanpur also be welcomed into a new era? That *would* be a miracle, but there is precedent among the saints of north India, and some say that it is already happening. For years a dispute has raged as to whether low-caste people ought to be allowed admission to the Visvanath temple, the religious hub of Benares, but at Sankat Mocan, where Tulsi's faith rules, they are welcome to petition Ram and Hanuman for release from their troubles just like anyone else. Their troubles may be greater than most people's—often true "extremities," as the name of the temple implies—but at least the spirit of *bhakti* enables them to address these ills in a language they share with the best-born Brahmin in the city.

POEMS OF TULSIDAS

The fire of my stomach has forced me
To grasp at the scraps of any caste—
My caste, high caste, low caste—
  and this in full public display.

I have done evil as if it were truth,
In thought and word and action—
I know they call me "servant of Ram,"
  but I'm treacherous even so.

Yet the force of the name of Ram is such,
The splendor of his feet so fine,
That the world has counted this Tulsi
  as great as some great sage.

Such a surprise. Pathetic are those
Who see this and hear of this
And do not love the feet of Ram.
  Such fools!

[Kavitavali 7.72]

I was born in a beggar family
And, hearing the sounds of celebration,
My mother and father felt anguish,
  felt pain.

From childhood on, poor thing that I was,
I went weeping, begging from door to door.
To me the four great goals of life
  were four little grains of food.

And that is the Tulsi who has become
The good servant of that worthy Lord:
When Fate, the great astrologer, hears,
  how cheated it feels.

Your name, O Ram:
Is it wise or mad?
It makes a weighty mountain
  from a tiny scrap of straw.

[Kavitavali 7.73]

It is said in ancient writings—
And the evidence is seen in the world—
That whatever is good rejoices
 because of the name of Ram.

Those who die in Benares
Are taught this by Lord Siva,
Who looked at countless ways of faith
 and rejected everything else.

Because of Ram's name, that gracious food,
Those who craved even the water
Left over from butter now spurn
 the cream of fragrant milk.

One hears that the reign of Ram
Is a time of proper rule
When, by your name, O Ram, the currency
 could be leather hides.

[Kavitavali 7.74]

A blind, mean-minded,
 dull-witted, withered-up
Old Muslim on the road
Got knocked down
 by a son of a pig.

As he fell, fear filled his heart.
"Oh God, Oh God! Unclean, unclean!
An unclean thing has killed me," he moaned
 and groaned as he fell
 into the jaws of death.

Tulsi says, his sorrows vanished
And he went straightaway
To the land of the lord of all worlds.
As everyone knows, it is because
  of the power of the name.

That very name of God
Is what people say with love.
So how can they say its grandeur places it
  where it's impossible to go?

[Kavitavali 7.76]

Say Ram, say Ram, say Ram,
  you fool!
That name is your raft
  on the awful sea of life.

It is the only way of gaining
  true gain and wealth,
For this sick age has swallowed ways
  that helped in ages past.

Whether good or bad,
  right-handed or left,
In the end the name of Ram
  works for everyone.

This world is a sky garden
  of flowers and fruits,
Towers that are only clouds—
  you should never forget.

Those who abandon Ram's name
  for something else, Tulsi says,
Leave the table set at home
  to beg for filthy scraps.

[Vinaya Patrika 66]

The name of King Ram: think of it with love.
It is provisions for those who journey empty-handed,
  and a friend for those who travel alone,
It is blessedness for the unblessed,
  good character for those with none,
A patron to purchase goods from the poor,
  and a benefactor to the abandoned.
It is a good family for those without one,
  they say—and the scriptures agree—
It is, to the crippled, hands and feet,
  and to the blind it is sight.
It is parents to those who are destitute,
  solid ground to the ungrounded,
A bridge that spans the sea of existence
  and the cause of the essence of joy.
Ram's name has no equal—
  Rescuer of the Fallen:
The thought of it makes fertile earth
  from Tulsi's barren soil.

[Vinaya Patrika 69]

Oh Siva, great giver,
  great god of great simplicity,
You have sent away the sadness
  of all who join their hands in prayer:
They serve and remember and worship you
  with a little rice, a few leaves,
But you have given the world horses and chariots,
  elephants—whatever pleases.
Oh left-handed god, while living in your town
  I haven't asked for a thing
But now your servants, these earthly trials,
  have come to block my path.
Quick, I beg you, speak:
  Restrain the evil actions
Of those scoundrels who'd surround
  this Tulsi tree with trees of thorns.

[Vinaya Patrika 8]

River of the gods, the act of recalling you
  snuffs out sin and the threefold fire.
You wend across the earth like a desire-fulfilling vine
  flowering with transports of gladness
And shine, filled with the fluid of undying life,
  like the white shining current of the moon.
Your waves, unsullied, glisten and shimmer
  like the deeds that are done by Raghuvar.
Oh Ganges, mother of the world, without you
  what in this age of destruction can be done?
And how can Tulsi ever cross life's ocean—
  that terrible, shoreless sea?

[Vinaya Patrika 19]

To those who look to Hanuman
The fulfillment of promises is certain,
  like a diamond-cut line in stone.

He makes the impossible possible, the possible impossible—
  no one else receives such praise.
Those who think on him, that joyful treasure,
  are freed from adversities and cares.

He is favored by the gods—Parvati, Siva,
  Laksman, Ram and Sita—
And Tulsi, the gracious gaze from that monkey
  is a mine of good fortune, a mother lode.

[Vinaya Patrika 30]

The flame offered to Ram
  extinguishes the flame of pain;
It burns up sin and sorrow,
  burns down to the root of lust.
In a lovely mist of incense,
  in a row of splendid lamps
Its ritual rhythm—the hand-claps—
  scares the bird of sin away.
It dissipates the darkness, the dumbness,
  from the house, the heart, of devotees;
  it casts wide the net of purest truth.
It is the frosty night that chills
  the lotuses of this dark age:
  the lurching, the drunkenness, the rage.
It is the messenger girl of liberation
  embodied in a flash of lightning,
The fingers of the moon spread out to catch
  and lift the lotuses of the night—
  the forest of those who flee for refuge.
It is the force of a multitude of Kalis
  pitted against the buffalo of Tulsi's pride.

[Vinaya Patrika 48]

You are the pitying, I the pitiful one,
  you the beneficent, I the one who begs;
I am notoriously fallen,
  and you dash away mountains of sin.
You are the father of those without fathers,
  and who could be more orphaned than I?
No one is so downtrodden—none more than I—
  and you are the one who lifts the heavy weight.
You are all life, I am one life;
  you are the master and I the servant;

You are mother and father, teacher and friend:
in every connection my lot is relieved.
We are bound by numerous ties, you and I,
so choose whichever you please.
Somehow, says Tulsi, oh you who send mercy,
let me find at your feet a refuge of peace.

[Vinaya Patrika 79]

Madhav, you'll find none duller than I.
The moth and the fish, though lacking in wit,
can scarcely approach my slow standard.
Transfixed by the shimmering shapes they meet,
they fail to discern the dangers of fire and hook,
But I, who can see the perils of fiery flesh
and still refuse to leave it, have wisdom even less.
I've drifted along in the grand and entrancing
river of ignorance, a stream that knows no shores,
And abandoned the rescue raft of Hari's lotus feet
to grasp after bubbles and foam
Like a dog so hungry that he lunges for a bone
grown ancient and marrowless; and bitten so tight,
The bone scrapes his mouth and draws blood—
his own blood—yet he tastes it with delight.
I too am trapped in jaws. The grip that clamps
is that of a merciless snake, this life,
And I yearn for relief, a frightened frog, but have spurned
the one chance I had: the bird that Hari rides.
Here and there other water creatures float;
we are snared together in a tightening net:
Watch them, how greedily they feed on one another,
and they never sense that next may be their turn.
The goddess of learning could count my sins
for countless ages and still not be done,
Yet Tulsidas places his trust in the One
who rescues the destitute, and in trusting hopes to live.

[Vinaya Patrika 92]

"Tomorrow, a body of youth.
Tomorrow, the wealth of the earth;
Tomorrow, victories in battle."
  So says he who goes in evil ways.

"Tomorrow, I'll finish my tasks;
Tomorrow, I'll join the regal throng."
And, mosquito that he is, he says,
  "My weight will make Mount Meru quake."

Many houses have collapsed;
Many houses are collapsing;
Many houses will collapse.
  Says Tulsi, this is a bad way to be—

To see this and hear this and know this
And not let it really sink in.
Not once do you hear him say,
  "Tomorrow, the time to die."

[Kavitavali 7.120]

It's as if you thought your body
was shielded with copper
and you didn't need the Lord,
But don't you know, lowly one,
that death is overhead?
Who hasn't surrounded himself
with land and house,
Wife and wealth,
sons and friends—
But whose have they become?
Can they go with you when you go?
They are reflections
of your own deceit, those loves.
Kings who conquered the world,
who bound up the ruler of the realm of death—
Those great kings: Death ate them for breakfast.
What, then, will he do with you?
Look, and think about what is true,
what the Vedas themselves have sung;
Even now, Tulsi, though you know,
you fail to praise the One
on whom even Siva has set his mind.

[Vinaya Patrika 200]

Who aside from you, King Ram,
  is my true patron?
No one.
I've thought it out, and will tell it
  to all, including you, my master.
If anyone knows anyone more special than you,
  let him lay it on the line.
Friends who are formed of body and soul
  are stitchwork badly done,
Or, as I think of it, they are like the false fruit
  in the heart of a banana tree; or cheap beads
That glisten only when jewels and gold
  are placed on either side.
This letter of petition from someone lowly—
  Father, please read it;
And what Tulsi has written
  from his heart—take it, correct it
By your good nature, and place it
  before the divine court.

[Vinaya Patrika 277]

This darkest of ages has destroyed
  the lines of caste, the stages of life:
All that is proper has been tossed aside
  like a bundle thrown to the ground.

Siva is angry:
  his anger is seen in the plague.
The Master is angry:
  daily poverty doubles.

They cry out, destitute men
  and women. No one hears.
Who are the gods who conspired to strike us
  with this thick, black-magic curse?

And then merciful Ram, remembered
  as protector of the terrified by Tulsi,
Praised for his fine compassion,
  gestured
    —he waved it all away.

[Kavitavali 7.183]

Notes

Chapter 1: Ravidās

1. The literature on Śrī Govardhanpur is principally confined to Julie Womack, "Ravidas and the Chamars of Banaras," an essay written for the Junior Year Abroad Program of the University of Wisconsin in Benares, 1983. Also relevant are B. R. Gherā, *Śrī Guru Ravidās jī kā Saṃkṣipt Itihās* (n.p.: All India Adi Dharm Mission, n.d.); Mark Juergensmeyer, *Religion as Social Vision: The Movement Against Untouchability in 20th-Century Punjab* (Berkeley: University of California Press, 1982), pp. 260–62; and R. S. Khare, *The Untouchable as Himself: Ideology, Identity, and Pragmatism Among the Lucknow Chamars* (Cambridge: Cambridge University Press, 1984), pp. 40–50, 94–104.
2. AG 38, translated in this chapter. This and most other citations of poems of Ravidās are drawn from the series recorded in the *Ādi Granth* [AG]. They have been sequentially numbered by Padam Gurcaran Siṃh, *Sant Ravidās: Vicārak aur Kavi* (Jullundur: Nav-Cintan Prakāśan, 1977), pp. 191–204.
3. AG 9.
4. AG 19, 27.
5. AG 13, translated in this chapter. Ravidās was not the first poet to voice this sentiment. For an earlier example from south India, see A. K. Ramanujan, *Speaking of Śiva* (Baltimore: Penguin, 1973), p. 90.
6. AG 28, 31.
7. AG 14, 35.
8. AG 19.
9. AG 11.4, 33.5.
10. AG 33.5.
11. AG 11.3, 33.5, 39.6.
12. Printed collections of poetry attributed to Ravidās are given a systematic listing in Darshan Singh, *A Study of Bhakta Ravidāsa* (Patiala: Punjabi University, 1981), pp. 3–4. To this list should be added the edition compiled by Candrikāprasād Jijñāsu, *Sant Pravar Raidās Sāhab* (Lucknow: Bahujan Kalyāṇ Prakāśan, rev. ed. 1969 [orig. publ. 1959]) and, notably, the two-hundred-odd poems assembled in B. P. Śarmā, *Sant Guru Ravidās-Vāṇī* (Delhi: Sūrya Prakāśan, 1978), pp. 66–142.

The most ample English translation is that of K. N. Upadhyaya, *Guru Ravidas: Life and Teachings* (Beas, Punjab: Radha Soami Satsang Beas, 1982), pp. 76–210. For information on manuscripts, see the "Texts" section in the notes accompanying Ravidās's poetry.

It is worth noting at this point that the Radhasoami community, one of whose branches is responsible for the publication of the last mentioned work, understands itself as the lineal descendent not just of Ravidās but of all the saints studied here. For that reason it has also played a role in publishing selections and translations of poems attributed to several among them. For information on the Radhasoami movement, one may consult Lawrence A. Babb, *Redemptive Encounters: Three Modern Styles in the Hindu Tradition* (Berkeley: University of California Press, 1987); Daniel Gold, *The Lord as Guru: Hindi* Sants *in the Northern Indian Tradition* (New York: Oxford University Press, 1987); and Mark Juergensmeyer, *Radhasoami Reality: The Logic of a Modern Faith* (forthcoming).

13. The version reported at Śrī Govardhanpur is that Nānak came to Guru Bāgh in quest of the meaning of spirituality. Ravidās satisfied him with a sermon on the subject, in consequence of which Nānak took initiation from Ravidās before departing. Kāśī Dās, interview, Varanasi, August 20, 1985.
14. The standard version of this text is that of Bakhsīdās, edited by Rājā Rām Miśra (Mathura: Śyām Kāśī Press, 1970); the Mīrābāī section occurs on pp. 67–81. An entirely revised and even more recent version is to be found in Girjāśaṃkar Miśra, *Raidās Rāmāyaṇa* (Mathura: Bhagavatī Prakāśan, 1981), pp. 92–98.
15. Bakhsīdās, *Ravidās Rāmāyaṇa*, pp. 81–82; Miśra, *Raidās Rāmāyaṇa*, pp. 98–102.
16. Nābhādās, *Śrī Bhaktamāl*, with the *Bhaktirasabodhinī* commentary of Priyādās (Lucknow: Tejkumār Press, 1969), pp. 282, 471–72, 480–81. There is a second major source of early hagiographical writing about Ravidās, Kabīr, and a number of other *nirguṇa* saints: the *paricayīs* ("accounts") of Anantdās, which purport to have been written near the end of the sixteenth century and therefore to have been approximately contemporary with the core text of the *Bhaktamāl*—Nābhādās's own verse. Anantdās's *paricayīs* are considerably less well known than the *Bhaktamāl* and have never been published, so we will focus on the *Bhaktamāl* here, but valuable work on Anantdās has been done by Trilokī Nārāyaṇ Dīkṣit, *Paricayī Sāhitya* (Lucknow: Lucknow University, 1957) and Lalitā Prasād Dūbe, *Hindī Bhakta-Vārtā Sāhitya* (Dehra Dun: Sāhitya Sadan, 1968). A forthcoming book by David N. Lorenzen and Jagdish Kumar will provide an edition and translation of Anantdās's *paricayī* on Kabīr, and I am grateful to David Lorenzen for the chance to read portions of an unpublished paper entitled "Kabīr Legends," in which he analyzes some of this material.
17. See, e.g., Pṛthvī Siṃh Āzād, *Ravidās Darśan* (Chandigarh: Śrī Guru Ravidās Saṃsthān, 1973), p. 72. If one adopts a later dating for Rāmānand, of course, the problem is not so acute. This position has most recently been argued by David Lorenzen in "Kabīr Legends." Other scholars, however, disagree: among recent writings, see Paraśurām Caturvedī, *Uttarī Bhārat kī Sant-Paramparā* (Allahabad: Leader Press, 1972), pp. 224–32, and Charlotte Vaudeville, *Kabīr* (Oxford: Clarendon Press, 1974) vol. 1, pp. 30–31. Rāmānand, about whom very little—especially very little that is consistent—is known, seems all too handy a device for

establishing a link between one of the four "classical" Vaiṣṇava monastic traditions (*sampradāys*) of south India and a much later and theologically divergent branch of north Indian *bhakti*. (See Richard Burghart, "The Founding of the Ramanandi Sect," *Ethnohistory* 25:2 [1978], pp. 121–39.) Comparisons might well be made with dubious efforts to associate Caitanya with Madhva, or Vallabha with Viṣṇusvāmī. (On the former, see Friedhelm Hardy, "Mādhavêndra Purī: A Link Between Bengal Vaiṣṇavism and South Indian *Bhakti*," *Journal of the Royal Asiatic Society* 1974:1, pp. 25–26.) The early date proposed for Nimbārka, the fourth member of the quartet, by members of his *sampradāy* is similarly doubtful.

18. Priyādās's account is found in Nābhādās, *Bhaktamāl,* pp. 477–78. In recent times, perhaps because of renewed awareness of the *Bhaktamāl,* there have been different attempts to clarify the relation between the two queens of Cittor. One oral tradition, alive at the temple of Mīrābāī in Brindavan, specifies that Jhālī was Mīrā's mother-in-law and states, following Priyādās, that it was she, not Mīrā, who took initiation from Ravidās. The conclusion drawn in Brindavan is that Mīrā herself was not Ravidās's pupil and that the popular legend to that effect is a case of mistaken identity. (Pradyumna Pratāp Siṃh, interview, Brindavan, August 30, 1985.) On the other side are those who are committed to retaining the tradition that Mīrā accepted Ravidās as her guru, for example, the author of the *Ravidās Rāmāyaṇa*. He retains both stories, but recounts that of Mīrā first and at greater length, relegating Jhālī's encounter with the master to the end of the book and giving the queen's name not as Jhālī but as Yogavatī. (Bakhsīdās, *Ravidās Rāmāyaṇa,* pp. 111, 117–19, cf. Miśra, *Raidās Rāmāyaṇa,* pp. 114–16.)
19. An influential example is V. Raghavan, *The Great Integrators: The Saint-Singers of India* (New Delhi: Publications Division, Government of India, 1966), pp. 52–54. This book is based on a series of lectures broadcast over All India Radio on December 11–14, 1964.
20. Priyādās in Nābhādās, *Bhaktamāl,* pp. 477–78. His account is extremely condensed at points; it is reported here as interpreted by Sītārāmśaraṇ Bhagavānprasād Rūpkalā, in Nābhādās, *Bhaktamāl,* pp. 477–78.
21. Priyādās in Nābhādās, *Bhaktamāl,* p. 478. It is possible that the model for this story was provided by an incident included in relatively recent tellings of the *Rāmāyaṇa,* in which Hanumān's unparalleled devotion to Rām, Sītā, and Lakṣmaṇ is proved by his tearing open his chest to reveal their images ensconced within. See K. C. and Subhashini Aryan, *Hanuman in Art and Mythology* (Delhi: Rekha Prakashan, n.d.), p. 78, pls. 31, 111, 112.
22. Dhannū Rām et al., interview, Śrī Govardhanpur, August 13, 1983. Versions of this story appear in Bakhsīdas, *Ravidās Rāmāyaṇa,* pp. 51–52, and Miśra, *Raidās Rāmāyaṇa,* pp. 57–60, and the temple to Ravidās now being built in memory of Jagjīvan Rām at Rājghāṭ in Benares (see further text discussion) is said to mark the spot where this miracle occurred.
23. Gherā, *Saṃkṣipt Itihās,* p. 1. Gherā reports (p. 3) that it was not Ravidās who sought instruction from Rāmānand, in fact, but precisely the other way around. In other Ravidāsī communities it is not disputed that Rāmānand was Ravidās's teacher, but it may be pointed out that Ravidās substantially changed the nature

of what he was taught. This view has been expressed by Mahadeo Prashad Kureel, interview, Lucknow, November 28, 1986.

24. See Priyādās's commentary in Nābhādās, *Bhaktamāl,* pp. 471–72.
25. AG 31.
26. AG 29, translated here; cf. AG 28.
27. In "signing" his poems, he refers to himself in AG 3, 4 (both translated here), 5, 9, and 19 as "Ravidās the leatherworker" (*ravidās camār, ravidās camārā*) and as "Ravidās the slave" (*ravidās dās, ravidās . . . dāsā*). Or he may speak of his low birth directly, as in AG 2, 30, 38, and 39.
28. AG 29.
29. AG 9, 30, 33.
30. AG 3.
31. AG 4.
32. AG 4, 26.
33. AG 27.
34. AG 19, 12.
35. AG 5.
36. AG 10, 15, 18.
37. B. R. Gherā, *All India Ādi Dharm Mission* (New Delhi: All India Ādi Dharm Mission, n.d.), p. 5.
38. Gherā, *Mission,* p. 6.
39. Juergensmeyer, *Social Vision,* pp. 33–155.
40. B. R. Gherā, personal communication, December 9, 1983. Cf. Juergensmeyer, *Social Vision,* p. 254.
41. Some traditions also attribute *dohās* —couplets—to Ravidās, but only one of these is found in the *Ādi Granth.*
42. Poem no. 2 in the *Guru Ravidās Granth* (handwritten in Devanagari on the basis of a published original in Gurmukhi) as transcribed for Virendra Singh. I am grateful to Virendra Singh for permission to make use of this copy.
43. B. R. Gherā, personal communication, December 9, 1983. Another anthology of Ravidās poems in current use is that of Candrikāprasād Jijñāsu, *Sant Pravar Raidās Sāhab.* It contains 102 *pads* (poems) and 18 *sākhīs* (couplets).
44. Dhannū Rām, interview, Śrī Govardhanpur, August 15, 1983.
45. Jagjīvan Rām, "Appeal: Nirmāṇādhīn Guru Ravidās Mandir, Kāśī," [Varanasi], [1985].
46. Rām Lakhan, interview, Varanasi, August 19, 1985.
47. On Sarvan Dās and his *derā* at Ballan, see Juergensmeyer, *Social Vision,* pp. 84–85, 260–61, 264, and the sixth unnumbered plate.
48. Other figures included in that genealogy are Lonī Devī, the goddess of "the original inhabitants" (*ādivāsīs*) of India, whose power is in effect from the beginning of time; Sudarśaṇ, belonging to the second world age (*dvāpar yug*); Śaṃbuk, belonging to the third world age (*tret yug*); and Dhanā and Cetā in our own era, the *kali yug.*
49. F. Max Müller, *Lectures on the Origin and Growth of Religion* (London: Longmans, Green, 1882), p. 277.

Chapter 1: Poems of Ravidās.

Texts

A full, systematic study of manuscripts containing poems of Ravidās is yet to be attempted, though an awareness of textual variants is displayed in various studies; for example, Yogendra Siṃh's *Sant Raidās* (Delhi: Akṣar Prakāśan, 1971), pp. 141–204. A major resource is to be found in the scriptural anthologies (*Pañcvāṇī, Sarvāṅgī*) of the Dādū Panth, a sect headquartered in Rajasthan that considered Ravidās one of the four great *bhaktas* whose words were to be revered alongside those of their preeminent guru, Dādū. For an index of the relevant manuscripts, see W. M. Callewaert and L. de Brabandere, "*Nirguṇ* Literature on Microfilm in Leuven, Belgium," *IAVRI Bulletin* 9 (1980), pp. 28–48. Other early anthologies preserve a poem or two of Ravidās; a series of four from the Fatehpur manuscript of A.D. 1582 (discussed in chapter 4) is translated here. Our main source here—and the one with the earliest date after the Fatehpur manuscript—is the scriptural anthology created for the Sikh community. This is the *Ādi Granth,* probably compiled in A.D. 1604. (For further information, see chapter 3, the "Texts" section in the notes accompanying Nānak's poems.) Citations to the *Ādi Granth* (AG) are numbered sequentially as in P. G. Siṃh, *Sant Ravidās,* pp. 191–204.

Poems

AG 20

In Ravidās's usage, the term Rām refers not to Rāmacandra, the hero of the *Rāmāyaṇa* and the seventh avatar of Vishnu, but to God in general. In part because it rhymes with the Hindi word for "name" (*nām*), Rām is a name of God especially worthy of human contemplation. The phrase *rām nām* is also used in AG 19, 27, below.

The large, hooked needle (*ār*) and pear-shaped cutting device (*rā̃bī*) mentioned by the poet are the two essential tools of a shoemaker's trade.

AG 33

Govind and Hari are both names of God derived from Vaiṣṇava terminology. The former normally refers specifically to Krishna and the latter refers to any manifestation of Vishnu, including his avatars Krishna and Rām. Here, however, neither name is used in a sectarian sense; these are general designations for God.

Nāmdev, Kabīr, Trilocan, Sadhnā, and Sain (also called Sen or Senā) are "saints" (*sants*) contemporary with or slightly preceding Ravidās. When he addresses his hearers as "saints" in a similar way, he is implicitly bidding them to join their company.

AG 38

The *Bhāgavata Purāṇa,* composed in the ninth or tenth century A.D., was the standard Vaiṣṇava scripture in Ravidās's day and remains so in ours. In eastern India, many manuscripts, including those of the *Bhāgavata Purāṇa,* are written on palm leaves.

Ravidās is "born among those who carry carrion" because the occupational responsibilities of *camārs* begin at the moment an animal dies and extend through the manufacture of any products derived from their hides.

AG 29

The word "exalts" translates the verb *tār-,* both here and in AG 33 (*tarai*). Literally it means "to cause to cross over," and describes God's action of enabling creatures to vault over the troubled, inhibiting sea of existence in which we all find ourselves (cf. AG 4 and Fatehpur, pp. 190–91, below).

In the phrase "Priests or merchants, laborers or warriors" Ravidās lists the four classical divisions (*varṇa*) of Indian society. But even beneath the lowest of these, the laborers, are others: "halfbreeds" (*caṇḍār*), "outcastes" (*malech*), and "those who tend the cremation fires" (*ḍom*). These are all Untouchables.

AG 13

Sandalwood has the power to cool whatever it comes into contact with. For that reason, Hindus say, poisonous snakes are attracted to it: they seek relief from the heat that builds up because of the poison stored inside them. The mention of this phenomenon introduces the similar motif of "nectar and poison." In Hindu mythology it is said that the world in its present form was generated from a common desire on the part of both gods and demons to obtain the nectar of immortality (*amṛt*). They cooperated with one another in churning the primeval milk-ocean to obtain it, but found that their efforts produced not only the elixir they sought but a deadly poison (*bikhu,* i.e., *viṣ*) as well.

AG 23

The various ritual gestures listed in this poem are associated with the lamp ceremony (*āratī*) by means of which images in Hindu temples and homes are illuminated so that their devotees can see them. The priest or householder lifts a cruse of oil or a series of candles with a circular motion that reveals the enthroned deity. Hari is a name of Vishnu that can be applied to either Rām or Krishna; Murāri is a title reserved for Krishna.

There is room for different interpretations in translating the phrase *cāre khāṇī.* The option chosen here is "the direction points," of which there are four, as the original specifies. To Hindus these four have a religious significance, and cities identified with each have become major places of pilgrimage. Other possibilities for giving sense to the number four are the four Vedas and the four species of living beings: plants, birds, animals, and humans (interviews: Krishna Caitanya Bhatt, Brindavan, November 18, 1986; Sant Jñān Prakāś, Benares, November 27, 1986). The apparent association of flower garlands with the number eighteen, as the original seems to require, is as yet unexplained.

AG 19

"The dimensions of a grave" are calculated as "three and a half hands," the phrase used in the original. A hand (*hāth*) is the distance from the fingertips to the elbow.

AG 27

The "scaffold made of grass" (*ghās kī ṭāṭī*) evidently expands upon the image of a house, with which the poet begins. In addition, however, it suggests the way in which an effigy (*ṭaṭiyā*) is constructed.

AG 4

The animal of which Ravidās speaks in the first verse is his *niraguṇ bailu*, his *nirguṇa* bullock. In one sense this creature is the appropriate vehicle of his theological trade since it is "without attributes," but in another sense, precisely because it lacks good attributes (*guṇ*), it is "worthless." So the poet-peddler turns to a higher power, Rām, as he travels along the road of life, which he implicitly homologizes to the sea of existence. When he asks Rām to chart his course along that road, he uses an expression (*āl patālu*) that emphasizes the possibility of his having to deal with hell. Death, the ruler of that underworld kingdom, appears in the following verse.

The saffron or, more generally, yellow (*kasuṃbh*) dye mentioned near the end of the poem provides a brilliant hue but is not colorfast. It is derived from flower petals, while the dye associated with Rām (*majīṭh*) is extracted from a root and is extremely long lasting. Its color is deeper, too.

Fatehpur, pp. 190–92

A variant form—somewhat fuller—can be found in various printed editions; for example, Yogendra Siṃh, *Sant Raidās,* pp. 175–76.

These four poems, addressed to the same sort of peddler (*banjārā*) Ravidās styles himself in AG 4, aim to describe the four watches of night. Each is a unit of time about three hours long, and each is made to correspond to a fourth of a human life: infancy, youth, maturity, and old age. There is a sense of urgency here, for the *banjārā* stays but a day in one place, packs his things before morning, and is gone. Thus, too, a human life.

The "child-god" form of Hari is Dāmodar, whose name means "the one with a rope around his belly." He is the hyperactive baby Krishna, whom his foster mother tries to restrain in this manner (see Sūrdās NPS 984 in chap. 4), and his presence in the poems concerning infancy and youth is apt. The name Hari is a more general designation for Krishna or Rām, so it can appropriately be used not only in the first two poems but in the last. In the second poem, attention is drawn to the value of the name Hari itself. It is made part of a pun, for the word *nāu* can mean either "name" or "boat." It recurs, and is translated one way in one line and the other in the next. Nautical imagery is employed in the first poem, too, where the peddler finds himself launched on the sea of existence.

Hindus often think of the god Yama, Death, as a keeper of the books. He records good deeds and bad, and distributes rewards and punishments accordingly. Here Hari himself is also cast in that role, and the interplay between that simile and the one likening a human being to a peddler gives the fourth poem its final thrust: the peddler is to be tried as a smuggler.

AG 3

The phrase "Queen City, a place with no pain" translates the Hindi *begam purā.*

Purā means plainly "city," but *begam* has two possibilities. The easiest way to construe it is as the Urdu word meaning "a lady of nobility"—whence the translation "queen"—since Indian cities with a Muslim past often have names such as this. The second alternative, however, is to hear it as a compound of *be,* "without," and *gam,* "pain." The translation attempts to preserve the ambiguity.

This poem is notable for the extent of its Urdu vocabulary, but that should occasion no surprise. If Ravidās has a poem that borders on being genuinely political, it is this, and the political institutions of his time were Muslim.

The friend or friends mentioned in the last line may be any companion in Queen City or it may be that special companion, God.

Chapter 2: Kabīr

1. Hazārīprasād Dvivedī, *Kabīr* (New Delhi: Rājkamal Prakāśan, 1976), pp. 17–36, esp. pp. 23–25, and Charlotte Vaudeville, *Kabīr,* vol. 1, pp. 82–89.
2. Kabīr's lack of business acumen is suggested at more than one point by Priyādās, *Bhaktamāl,* pp. 483–84. In Kabīr's own poetry, see KG *pad* 12, translated here; cf. vol. 2 of Pāras Nāth Tivārī, *Kabīr Granthāvalī* [hereinafter KG] (Allahabad: Allahabad University, 1961), *pad* 111.9–10. A translation of *pads* in the KG will be found in the second volume of Charlotte Vaudeville's *Kabīr* when it appears. On Priyādās, see chap. 1, n. 16. For a full listing of hagiographical material having to do with Kabīr, see David N. Lorenzen, "Kabīr Legends," forthcoming. Lorenzen deals in particularly great detail with the Kabīr story as told by Anantdās, a figure who may have been roughly contemporary with Nābhādās. Anantdās's and Priyādās's accounts agree very closely.
3. In regard to Priyādās's attitude to generosity, particularly as reflected in his life of Narasī Mehtā, see J. S. Hawley, "Morality Beyond Morality in the Lives of Three Hindu Saints," in Hawley, ed., *Saints and Virtues* (Berkeley: University of California Press, 1987), pp. 53–73.
4. Priyādās in Nābhādās, *Bhaktamāl,* p. 487.
5. Anon., *Kabir* (Bombay: Amar Chitra Katha, n.d.).
6. Priyādās in Nābhādās, *Bhaktamāl,* pp. 487–90.
7. Priyādās in Nābhādās, *Bhaktamāl,* pp. 490–91.
8. See, e.g., Gangāśaraṇ Śāstrī, *Kabīr Jīvancaritra* (Varanasi: Kabīrvāṇī Prakāśan Kendra, 1976), pp. 255–58.
9. Muhammad Hedayetullah, *Kabir: The Apostle of Hindu-Muslim Unity* (Delhi: Motilal Banarsidass, 1977). The subtitle of the English version of the Kabīr volume in the Amar Chitra Katha series is similar: "The Mystic Who Tried to Bring the Hindus and the Muslims Together."
10. KG *pads* 191 and 178, translated here.
11. KG *pad* 61, translated here.
12. On the prostitute, see Priyādās, *Bhaktamāl,* p. 485.
13. KG *pad* 46 is translated here. Cf. also KG 200.

14. KG *pad* 177.9–10; a full translation appears in R. S. McGregor, *Hindi Literature from its Beginnings to the Nineteenth Century* (Wiesbaden: Otto Harrassowitz, 1984), p. 51. KG *pad* 178.7; full translation in this chapter.
15. On this genre, see Linda Hess, *The Bījak of Kabīr* (San Francisco: North Point Press, 1983), pp. 135–61.
16. Compare, e.g., KG *pad* 150, translated in this chapter. In regard to "spontaneity" Kabīr is heir to the Nāth and Sahajiyā traditions. See Vaudeville, *Kabīr,* vol. 1, pp. 85–89; Shashibhusan Das Gupta, *Obscure Religious Cults* (Calcutta: K. L. Mukhopadhyay, 1969), pp. 3–255; Edward C. Dimock, Jr., *The Place of the Hidden Moon* (Chicago: University of Chicago Press, 1966); and George Weston Briggs, *Gorakhnāth and the Kānpaṭha Yogīs* (Delhi: Motilal Banarsidass, 1973 [orig. pub. 1938]).
17. KG *sākhīs* 17.1 and 16.1.
18. On Kālī see, e.g., KG *sākhī* 24.2, translated below, and KG *pad* 161.4, 168.1–2. On avatars, see *Bījak ramainī* 75 and KG *pad* 103 (= *Bījak śabd* 45). The latter is translated in Hess, *Bījak,* p. 57.
19. KG *pad* 50, translated in J. S. Hawley, *Sūr Dās: Poet, Singer, Saint* (Seattle: University of Washington Press and Delhi: Oxford University Press, 1984), pp. 139–40.
20. Priyādās in Nābhādās, *Bhaktamāl,* pp. 480–81. The story is also found in Anantdās's *paricayī.*
21. On this usage of the word "Rām," see Vaudeville, *Kabīr,* vol. 1, pp. 105–6; F. R. Allchin, "The Place of Tulsī Dās in North Indian Devotional Tradition," *Journal of the Royal Asiatic Society* 1966:3–4, pp. 132–34.
22. Vaudeville, *Kabīr,* vol. 1, pp. 81–89.
23. On Gorakhnāth's dates, see John I. Millis, "Malik Muhammad Jāyasī: Allegory and Religious Symbolism in His *Padmāvat,*" diss., University of Chicago, 1984, p. 84.
24. A description of a Nāth Yogī from the pen of Jāyasī is presented in Millis, *Jāyasī,* p. 158.
25. On householder Nāths in the present day, see Daniel Gold and Ann Grodzins Gold, "The Fate of the Householder Nāth," *History of Religions* 24:2 (1984), pp. 113–32; see also Ann Grodzins Gold, "Life Aims and Fruitful Journeys: The Ways of Rajasthani Pilgrims," diss., University of Chicago, 1984, pp. 140–71.
26. The Kabīr Panth is particularly strong in advocating this tradition. For them it becomes a geographical expression of Ravidās's proximity—in a subordinate role—to Kabīr.
27. It is usually attributed to the *nirguṇa* poet Sen, who was probably a younger contemporary of Kabīr's and could therefore have observed the dialogue, but there is no internal evidence of Sen's authorship. The oldest manuscript yet discovered comes from the Rajasthan Oriental Research Institute, Jaipur, and bears the date V.S. 1743 (A.D. 1686). The text is printed in B. P. Śarmā, *Sant Guru Ravidās-Vāṇī,* pp. 144–46; textual information is on pp. 6, 11. Anantdās knew of this dialogue: the relevant passage is printed in Śarmā, *Ravidās-Vāṇī,* p. 143.

28. *Ravidās-Kabīr Goṣṭhī* v. 8. Śarmā, *Ravidās-Vāṇī,* p. 144.
29. *Ravidās-Kabīr Goṣṭhī* v. 22. Śarmā, *Ravidās-Vāṇī,* p. 145.
30. *Ravidās-Kabīr Goṣṭhī* vv. 25–26. Śarmā, *Ravidās-Vāṇī,* p. 145.
31. *Ravidās-Kabīr Goṣṭhī* vv. 27–39. Śarmā, *Ravidās-Vāṇī,* p. 146.
32. Bakhsīdās, *Ravidās Rāmāyaṇa,* pp. 52–62.
33. E.g., Śukdev Siṃh, *Kabīr ke Smaraṇ Tīrtha* (Varanasi: Kabīrvāṇī Prakāśan Kendra, 1981), pp. 26–27, where the author notes that Kabīr was the recipient of Gorakhnāth's (*nirguṇa*) trident and Rāmānand's (*saguṇa*) necklace. Perhaps this relatively bland mood in modern interpretations of Kabīr is partly responsible for stimulating a latitudinarian attitude toward Kabīr in Jagjīvan Rām's Ravidās organization. A volume it recently issued to commemorate Ravidās's birthday includes a version of the traditional *Ravidās-Kabīr Goṣṭhī,* and Ravidās's deference to Kabīr, which is so evident in the Jaipur manuscript, is only slightly masked by occasional alterations of format and phraseology. See Śukdev Siṃh, ed., *Ravidās* (Varanasi: Ravidās Smārak Society, 1986), pp. 37–40.
34. Officials of this sect insist that such statues are memorials (*smārak*) rather than living beings that would correspond exactly to images of gods in Hindu temples, but the visual analogy and the way in which they are treated discourages lay adherents from giving too much weight to this delicate distinction. (David N. Lorenzen, personal communication, October 7, 1986.)
35. *Saṃskṛt hai kūp jal / bhāṣā bahatā nīr.* A translation is given in Vaudeville, *Kabīr,* vol. 1, p. 50.
36. The most recent writings in English on the Kabīr Panth, to which this monastary belongs, are by David N. Lorenzen: "The Kabīr Panth: Heretics to Hindus," in Lorenzen, ed., *Religious Change and Cultural Domination* (Mexico City: El Colegio de México, 1981), pp. 151–71; "The Kabīr Panth and Social Protest," in Karine Schomer and W. H. McLeod, eds., *The Sants: Studies in a Devotional Tradition in India* (Delhi: Motilal Banarsidass, 1987, pp. 281–303); and "Traditions of Non-caste Hinduism: The Kabīr Panth," *Contributions to Indian Sociology* 21:2 (1987), pp. 263–83. In the last-mentioned article Lorenzen notes that if images of Kabīr are permitted in the Dharmadās sect, even pictures are forbidden in the Panth's Burhānpur sect, and observes that the *Bījak* itself, a collection of Kabīr's poetry, serves as an object of worship in the mainstream Kabīr Panth tradition, a practice that reminds one of the veneration of the *Ādi Granth* among Sikhs, on which see chap. 3 of this book. On the cultivation of Sanskrit in the Kabīr Panth, see Lorenzen, "The Kabīr Panth," pp. 162–64.
37. See, e.g., sec. 3 of "The Social Psychology of the World Religions," in H. H. Gerth and C. Wright Mills, trans. and eds., *From Max Weber: Essays in Sociology* (New York: Oxford University Press, 1946), pp. 297ff.
38. Anon.: *Kabīr Sāhab kā Anurāg Sāgar* (Allahabad: Belvedere Printing Works, 1975), translated as *The Ocean of Love* by Raj Kumar Bagga, Partap Singh, and Kent Bicknell (Sanbornton, N.H.: Sant Bani Ashram, 1982). See also Mark Juergensmeyer, "The Radhasoami Revival of the Sant Tradition," in Schomer and McLeod, eds., *The Sants,* pp. 352–54.

Chapter 2: Poems and Epigrams of Kabīr

Texts

Poetry attributed to Kabīr is preserved in three principal recensions: the eastern, as attested in the *Bījak* of the Kabīr Panth; the western, as found primarily in the *Pañc-Vāṇī* and *Sarvāṅgī* of the Dādū Panth; and the *Ādi Granth* of the Sikh Panth. Among the poems (*pads*) chosen for translation here, five appear in two recensions and the remainder in all three. All the epigrams (*sākhīs*) translated appear in all three recensions, with a single exception: AG *sākhī* 82, which is confined to the *Ādi Granth*. Obviously, our effort has been to translate poems whose representation in more than one recension serves as a good indication of their age, if not as an absolute guarantee of their authenticity.

The most extensive critical work on Kabīr is that of Pāras Nāth Tivārī, *Kabīr Granthāvalī* [KG], and it is his edition that we adopt. Poems are cited according to his system of enumeration. Tivārī's critically edited texts have been reprinted (without apparatus) in Charlotte Vaudeville, *Kabīr-Vāṇī* (Pondicherry: Institut français d'Indologie, 1982), pp. 54–97, 224–80, and it is Vaudeville's text and enumeration that are used in the case of AG *sākhī* 82. All the epigrams presented here have also been translated by Vaudeville in her *Kabīr,* vol. 1, and she provides editorial notations and a discussion of editorial problems that may be of help to the English reader. In recent work, Linda Hess and Śukdev Siṃh have challenged the prestige of the western recension, which Tivārī and Vaudeville have favored primarily on the basis of the age of the manuscripts involved. Siṃh's proposal for a critical text of the *Bījak* can be found in his *Kabīr-Bījak* (Allahabad: Nīlam Prakāśan, 1972), and Hess's beautiful translations of selections from the *Bījak* are worth the attention of every reader (Hess, *The Bījak of Kabīr*).

Poems

KG *pad* 174

The practices of wandering naked, shaving the head, and learning to retain the semen all pertain to yoga in some form. The word translated "eunuchs" (*khusarai*) might also be interpreted as referring to castrated bulls and the like. If that was what the poet intended, he was reserving his hypothetical heaven exclusively for animals.

KG *pad* 191

Vedas and Purāṇas are fundamental Hindu religious texts. Hindus believe that in the vast cycle of births and deaths, to be born a human being is a rare and precious chance because it provides access to salvation—release from the cycle. Nārad, Vyās, and Śukdev are sages to whom various portions of the Hindu scriptural tradition are ascribed. Kabīr depicts his presumed interlocutor as falling back on them for authority. "Great Saint" is a translation of the term *munivar,* which might also be rendered "great sage."

KG *pad* 178
The book to which reference is made is, of course, *the* book: the Qur'ān.

KG *pad* 12
It is possible that Kabīr's mother's lament is not for Kabīr's children but her own child: Kabīr himself. Both singular and plural meanings are possible. The "three worlds"—an ancient formula summing up the universe—are the earth, the heavens, and the atmosphere that separates them.

KG *pad* 46
The privilege of living in Benares is sometimes explained as the result of acts of merit or self-abnegation performed in past lives. One of the city's several names is Kāśī, "the luminous one," and Śiva is held to be its special guardian: see Diana L. Eck, *Banaras: City of Light* (New York: Alfred A. Knopf, 1982), pp. 94–145. If one dies in Benares, Śiva himself can be assumed to pronounce the *tāraka* mantra, facilitating one's passage beyond the trials of this life and all lives like it. (Eck, *Banaras,* pp. 331–34.)

KG *pad* 182
Three horizontal lines of ash applied to the forehead are the most familiar insignia of a worshiper of Śiva. They are sometimes said to represent the prongs of his weapon, the trident, or the three "attributes" (*guṇ*) from which he weaves the world. For further information see Alan W. Entwistle, *Vaiṣṇava Tilakas: Sectarian Marks Worn by Worshippers of Viṣṇu, IAVRI Bulletin* 11 and 12 (1981–82), pp. 6–10.

KG *pad* 62
"Death's club" is both mythological and literal. Yama, the god of death, is said to carry such an implement (*ḍaṇḍ,* a general word denoting a stick or staff), and it is used in the rite of cremation to crack the dead person's skull and provide a way of escape for the soul trapped within.

KG *pad* 61
Several important variants in the final verse suggest an alternate translation:

> Kabīr says: A pot tends to wobble if half-full,
> but fill it to the brim and it's firm.

KG *pad* 150
"Easy spontaneity" is *sahaj,* on which see the introduction.

KG *pad* 139
On the notion of God as a thief (*ṭhag*), cf. Sūrdās NPS 901, 2490, and 3821, translated in chap. 4.

KG *pad* 119

"God" translates Govind, a title usually reserved for Krishna but used more loosely by Kabīr. The leaves without which worship could not be are presumably those of the *bel* tree, sacred to Śiva, and the *tulsī,* sacred to Vishnu.

Epigrams

AG *sākhī* 82

"Lord" translates the term Gopāl, which, like Govind, is normally confined to Krishna but is used with far less precision by Kabīr, as befits his *nirguṇa* theology.

KG *sākhī* 1.5

"The true Master" is the *satguru,* on which see the introduction.

KG *sākhī* 4.1

The words *ḍhāk* and *palās* refer to the same tree: one word names the plant before its flowering, the other, afterward. The tree is extremely common, but of minimal worth. At most, its leaves are made into the leaf plates that are ubiquitous in north India: these are used briefly and then discarded. The sandal tree, by contrast, is both valuable and rare.

KG *sākhī* 15.5

On the importance of human birth, see the note to KG *pad* 191 above.

KG *sākhī* 16.3

Life is fragile and tentative, like a deer. The enjoyments that nourish it expose it at the same time to numerous dangers: hunters are poised to kill it in areas where it would like to feed.

KG *sākhī* 16.2

Traditionally this forest fire has been interpreted as *saṃsāra,* "the sufferings of worldly existence;" and the blacksmith as *kāl,* death. The blacksmith is mentioned, of course, because he fires his furnace with charcoal. See Mātāprasād Gupta, *Kabīr-Granthāvalī* (Allahabad: Sāhitya Bhavan, 1985 [orig. publ. 1969]), p. 121; Vaudeville, *Kabīr,* vol. 1, p. 246. The sense of the poem also points, however, to the cycle of multiple existences: suffering in this world earns one further suffering the next time around.

KG *sākhī* 15.7

A significant variant in the western recension is *sab tan* ("the whole body") for *jag* ("world").

KG *sākhī* 17.1

"Boundless knowledge" (*brahma giān*) is literally "the knowledge of Brahman."

KG *sākhī* 2.1

On *viraha* ("separation"), see the introduction to chapter 4 and poems of Sūrdās (NPS 2490, 3122, 3821, 3886) and Mīrābāī (Caturvedī 82, 84, 117, 153, 166) translated in chaps. 4 and 5.

KG *sākhī* 18.1

"God is the jewel" translates the phrase *hari hīrā,* an important one in Kabīr that refers to the innermost truth.

KG *sākhī* 24.2

The "tree of thorns" is the *ber* (here, *beri*) tree. "Goddess-worshipers" are Śāktas, a term that points to the extraordinary power (*śakti*) associated with certain goddesses. Kabīr is probably thinking of Kālī and Durgā, since particularly in eastern India their cult is marked by blood sacrifice and tantrism.

KG *sākhī* 21.11

The hut mentioned here may signify the body, which, according to ancient Indian reckoning, has five internal organs of sense (*jñānendriya*) to supplement the five external ones (*karmendriya*). At the same time, the hut may represent the world with its ten directions—eight horizontal ones (east, southeast, south, etc.) and two vertical (up and down).

KG *sākhī* 20.4

The phrase "and they're gone" refers to the term *bahīr* and presents a contrast to the stability that Kabīr claims for his own path. Another interpretation would emphasize that *bahīr* means "outside" in the sense of "exoteric," which suggests by contrast that Kabīr's approach is an esoteric one. The phrase *aughaṭ ghāṭī* ("impossible pass") seems to confirm this interpretation.

KG *sākhī* 16.1

For a treatment of the same metaphor in a *saguṇa* context, see Sūrdās NPS 3982.

Chapter 3: Nānak

1. A series of essays on Sikh dispersion, together with a bibliography on the subject, can be found in Mark Juergensmeyer and N. Gerald Barrier, eds., *Sikh Studies: Comparative Perspectives on a Changing Tradition* (Berkeley: Berkeley Religious Studies Series, 1979), pp. 127–208. Among more recent publications one should cite A. W. Helweg, *Sikhs in England* (Delhi: Oxford University Press, 1979); Paramatma Saran and Edwin Eames, eds., *The New Ethnics: Asian Indians in the United States* (New York: Praeger, 1980); W. H. McLeod, *Punjabis in New Zealand* (Amritsar: Guru Nanak Dev University Press, 1986); Joan M. Jensen, *Passage from India: Asian Indian Immigrants in North America* (New Haven: Yale University Press, 1988); and S. Chandrasekhar, ed., *From India to America* (La Jolla, Calif.: Population Review Publications, 1982). The most convenient guide

to the Sikh tradition as a whole is provided in W. Owen Cole and Piara Singh Sambhi, *The Sikhs: Their Religious Beliefs and Practices* (London: Routledge & Kegan Paul, 1978).

2. The foregoing paragraph owes a great deal to the historical overview of central elements in the establishment of Sikh identity that is provided in W. H. McLeod, *The Evolution of the Sikh Community: Five Essays* (Delhi: Oxford University Press, 1975), pp. 1–19. Indeed, as subsequent notes will make clear, a deep debt is owed to McLeod's innovative and thorough scholarship throughout this chapter.
3. This refrain occurs in *Japjī* 4–8, all of which are translated here.
4. The brightness of Nānak's face is also reported in the *janam sākhīs* ("birth-witnesses," i.e., hagiographical accounts) concerning him. See W. H. McLeod, *Gurū Nānak and the Sikh Religion* (Oxford: Clarendon Press, 1968), p. 40, on *sākhī* 22 in the Puratan series. McLeod provides elegant studies of the *janam sākhīs* in chap. 2 of *Evolution,* chaps. 2–4 of *Gurū Nānak,* and in the entirety of his *Early Sikh Tradition: A Study of the Janam-sākhīs* (Oxford: Clarendon Press, 1980) and *The B40 Janam-sākhī* (Amritsar: Guru Nanak Dev University, 1980).
5. See *Japjī* 34–37, translated in this chapter.
6. See McLeod, *Gurū Nānak,* pp. 5, 146.
7. See McLeod, *Gurū Nānak,* p. 47 (*sākhī* 47) and p. 50 (*sākhī* 54). There is a bloodthirstiness—even a flirtation with cannibalism—in these tales that reminds one vividly of Gobind Singh's invitation to human sacrifice. In both Nānak's and Gobind Singh's cases, of course, the sacrifice is ultimately averted.
8. McLeod, *Gurū Nānak,* pp. 36, 52–53.
9. McLeod, *Gurū Nānak,* pp. 39, 49, 51.
10. McLeod, *Gurū Nānak,* p. 49, *sākhī* 52.
11. McLeod, *Gurū Nānak,* p. 40, *sākhī* 18, and p. 49, *sākhī* 50.
12. McLeod, *Gurū Nānak,* p. 49, *sākhī* 50.
13. McLeod, *Gurū Nānak,* p. 42, *sākhī* 28.
14. McLeod, *Gurū Nānak,* pp. 37–38, *sākhī* 10.
15. McLeod, *Gurū Nānak,* pp. 38–39, *sākhī* 13.
16. McLeod, *Gurū Nānak,* p. 39, *sākhī* 16.
17. McLeod, *Gurū Nānak,* pp. 123–24.
18. McLeod, *Gurū Nānak,* p. 35.
19. McLeod, *Gurū Nānak,* pp. 119–22.
20. McLeod, *Gurū Nānak,* p. 11.
21. McLeod, *Gurū Nānak,* pp. 191–92.
22. McLeod, *Gurū Nānak,* pp. 37–38, *sākhī* 10.
23. See *Japjī* 2, translated in this chapter.
24. See *Japjī* 34, translated here, which is described in *Japjī* 35 (also translated here) as having to do with "religion." Cf. McLeod, *Gurū Nānak,* p. 194. Cosmological poetry in a somewhat similar vein has also been attributed to Kabīr; in fact, it looms large in the *ramainīs* that have been placed at the very beginning of the version of the *Bījak* used today in the Kabīr Panth headquartered at Benares. This poetry contrasts so markedly with the remainder of the corpus, however, that doubts have been expressed about its authenticity. See esp. *ramainīs* 1–5 in Hujūr

Uditnām Sāheb and Prakāśamaṇinām Sāheb, eds., *Kabīr Sāhab kā Bījak Granth* (Varanasi: Kabīr Panth, 1982), pp. 1–29; cf. Ahmad Shah, *The Bijak of Kabir* (New Delhi: Asian Publications Services, 1979 [orig. publ. 1911]), pp. 52–54, and Hess, *Bījak,* pp. 79–80.

25. McLeod, *Gurū Nānak,* p. 199. For a study of the effect of this conviction on the shaping of Nānak's own language, see Michael C. Shapiro, "The Rhetorical Structure of the *Japjī,*" paper presented at the Second Berkeley Conference on Sikh Studies, Berkeley, February 1987. *Japjī* 28, translated here, concerns the Word.
26. This translation of *haumai* is discussed by McLeod in *Gurū Nānak,* p. 183. The term occurs in the last verse of *Japjī* 2, translated here.
27. *Japjī* 19, 24.
28. See *sirī rāgu* 9.3, translated here and in McLeod, *Gurū Nānak,* p. 197; also *āsā chhant* 2 (3), translated in McLeod, *Gurū Nānak,* p. 220.
29. See J. S. Hawley, "Asceticism Denounced and Embraced: Rhetoric and Reality in North Indian *Bhakti,*" in Austin Creel and Vasudha Narayanan, eds., *Monastism in the Christian and Hindu Traditions: A Comparative Study* (forthcoming).
30. John Campbell Oman, *The Mystics, Ascetics, and Saints of India* (London: T. Fisher Unwin, 1903), pp. 195–96; cf. G. S. Ghurye, *Indian Sadhus* (Bombay: Popular Prakashan, 1964), pp. 142–44.
31. Interview, Udāsī Āśram, Hardwar, August 24, 1983. Cf. also Hawley, "Asceticism."

Chapter 3: Poems of Nānak

Texts

Textual problems relating to the poems of Nānak, as recorded in the *Ādi Granth,* are by no means as severe as those affecting the utterances of Kabīr. There are three principal versions of the *Ādi Granth,* but they are much more closely related than the three recensions of Kabīr, and there is little reason to doubt that one of them (the Kartārpur manuscript) is the bearer of the date (A.D. 1604) on which the *Ādi Granth* is traditionally said to have been compiled. For an overview of texts of the *Ādi Granth,* see McLeod, *Evolution,* pp. 60–63, 73–79; also relevant are Pritam Singh, "Bhāī Banno's Copy of the Sikh Scripture," in Monika Thiel-Horstmann, ed., *Bhakti in Current Research, 1979–1982* (Berlin: Dietrich Reimer Verlag, 1983), pp. 325–48, and C. H. Loehlin, "Textual Criticism of the Kartarpur Granth," in Juergensmeyer and Barrier, eds., *Sikh Studies,* pp. 113–18. The text upon which the present translations are based is *Ādi Śrī Guru Granth Sāhib,* 4 vols. (Lucknow: Bhuvan Vāṇī Trust, 1978–82).

Poems

Ek Omkār

The first section of the "root mantra" is indeed mantralike in structure. It is composed of syntactically unrelated terms, all of which are traditionally understood as characterizations of Ultimate Reality, or God. This is certainly true with regard to most, but it may be that the first and last of the series originally referred to something different. The syllable *om,* representing to Hindus the sum of all sound, language, and meaning, usually serves the function of an auspicious prefatory utterance, and it may originally have played that role here too. The numeral 1 may also have been prefatory at some point in the early history of the text: a beginning enumeration on the page. The concluding phrase "the guru's grace" is similarly ambiguous. Although it may be interpreted as a characterization of the divine—God as mediated by the guru's teachings—it may also be understood as a framing device for the mantra it concludes: "[all this by] the guru's grace."

The second part of the root mantra contains the signature of Nānak and functions as a sort of doxology. Because of its repetition of the word "truth" (*sacu*), it moves in the direction of poetry, but it is still far from being metrical, rhymed verse such as one finds in the remainder of the *Ādi Granth.*

Japjī 2

On *hukam,* the "order" that gives structure to this composition, see the introduction. At one point that order is described as being written (*likhi*). If Nānak has in mind a document of some sort, he would seem to be building on a concept of scripture that arose in religions of the Near East, including Islam. If he has in mind the sort of inscription that is thought to be indelibly but invisibly inscribed on each human forehead, then he is apparently drawing on the Hindu tradition that assigns such a role to the creator god Brahmā. Or perhaps he is somewhere between the two, thinking of a destiny inscribed on creation as a whole.

The expression *haumai* (on which see the introduction) occurs in the last verse and is translated simply "I".

Japjī 8

Siddhas are realized Hindu adepts; Pīrs are their Islamic counterparts. It is notable that here, as elsewhere, Nānak appears to include the gods at the same level of veneration as such sages and yogīs. Like many Hindu and Buddhist teachers before him, he thereby demotes the gods from a level of ultimacy.

The "white foundation" of the earth is literally only "the white one" (*dhaval*), but the term would have been understood to mean the white bull upon whose horns the earth is sometimes said to rest. As in the case of the gods, Nānak is eager to devalue any such mythical being. Here he does so by asserting that it, along with the levels of the universe that lie above it, is supported by something of a different nature altogether—listening. In another poem of the *Japjī* (16.4–5), rather than devaluing this subterranean bull, he revalues it. He explains that the true meaning of that bull is *dharma:* righteousness upholds the world.

Japjī 9

Śiva, Brahmā, and Indra are among the chief Hindu gods and are mentioned by Nānak for that reason. Of the three, the warrior Indra is the one with the strongest Vedic associations; in Vedic times he was often considered captain of the pantheon.

The Śāstras, Smṛti, and Vedas are Hindu texts possessing various degrees of authority; theoretically, the Śāstras are at the lower end, the Vedas at the higher.

Japjī 10

"All the holy places" are the *tīrthas* ("fords," "crossing places") of Hindu tradition, which are sometimes said to number sixty-eight, as in the original of this poem. They include India's major places of pilgrimage, and Nānak is not the only *bhakta* to question their efficacy. In fact, he does so in only a muted way: he conceives their power as derivative and capable of being had by other means.

Japjī 11

"Those revered as masters" is a gloss to explain why *sheikhs* and *pīrs* (heads of Sūfī orders) belong in the same list with *bādshāhs* (emperors). All three terms are Muslim.

Japjī 12

"Immaculately clear" translates the word *nirañjan* (here, *nirañjanu*), a common designation for the Ultimate in *nirguṇa* vocabulary, meaning "faultless," "spotless."

Japjī 15

It is notable that in the first two verses of this composition two major goals in Hindu life—deliverance (*mokṣa* > *mokhu*) from the duties of this world and the fulfilling of those same duties (*dharma*)—are set side by side. The vocabulary of transformation is adopted in the following verse to translate two forms of the root *tṛ*, "to cross over," on which see Diana L. Eck, "India's *Tīrthas:* 'Crossings' in Sacred Geography," *History of Religions* 20:4 (1981), pp. 323–44.

Japjī 18

Other meditations on things that are "beyond number" (*asaṃkh*) are found in *Japjī* 17 and 19. "Barbarians" translates the standard Hindu term for outsiders (*mleccha* > *malech*), and it is telling to see that Nānak characterizes them by what they eat, as a Hindu might well do. When Nānak contemplates sacrificing himself, he is, of course, addressing God.

Sirī rāgu 9.3

Images of rafts and fords (*tīrtha;* cf. *Japjī* 10) as tools to cross the "ocean of existence" (*bhav sāgar*) are ancient in Hindu and Buddhist lore. Here Nānak expands the range of metaphor and applies it to the guru. For a comparable image in a *saguṇa* idiom, see Sūrdās NPS 181, translated in chap. 4.

Vār mājh, Pauṛī 25

"Life's nine great jewels" (*nav nidhi*) are the nine treasures classically associated with Kubera, the god of wealth, and sometimes personified as attendents upon either him or Lakṣmī, the goddess of fortune and wellbeing. They are a stylized group including the conch, the crocodile (*makara*), and various forms of lotus.

Japjī 34

This is the first of four—some would say five—poems that form a sequence describing the realms (*khaṇḍ*) encountered in the course of spiritual ascent. The first, labeled *dharma* (cf. *Japjī* 35.1) is this world itself, which offers human beings the opportunity to gain insight into what lies beyond and, implicitly, to escape the great round of rebirth that has brought them into their present, human form. Because it has this intermediary quality, Nānak characterizes this realm as a *dharmaśālā* (here, *dharamasāl*), which we translate as "a place to rest from travel and practice religion." *Dharmaśālās* are low-cost religious hotels built to shelter travelers who visit Indian places of pilgrimage. Nānak seems to accept this meaning, though in Sikh usage the word comes quickly to denote a house of worship. The imagery takes a juridical turn halfway through the poem as actions (*karma*) are emphasized. In that context Nānak compares God to a judge or monarch: he is "the Vigilant One" (*nadarī,* "one who sees") surrounded by his council (*pañc,* literally "five") of "proven ones" (*paravāṇu*).

Japjī 35

The second realm is the realm of wisdom (*jñāna* > *giān*), as labeled in *Japjī* 36.1. We have already encountered most of the gods and worthies who have made their way there. Dhruv, the pole-star, is the exception. He attained that lofty position as a boon from Vishnu, who applauded the strict regimen of self-abnegation he adopted as a human being—indeed, as a young boy. Dhruv was the recipient of a formidable sermon on religious propriety from Nārad, the envoy of the gods, and in some sources Nārad is also said to have transmitted to him the mantra that granted him initiation as a Vaiṣṇava (cf. *Bhāgavata Purāṇa* 4.8.27–61). In Hindu cosmology Mount Meru is the axial mountain of the universe.

Japjī 36

The third realm is called "the realm of effort" (*saram*), but the reason for this is far from clear. Consequently some interpreters have derived the term *saram* not from Sanskrit *śrama* ("effort") but from Persian *śaram* ("shame," "humility") or Sanskrit *śarma* ("joy"). For bibliography, see McLeod, *Gurū Nānak,* p. 222.

Japjī 37

This poem presents us with the two final realms, those of action (*karma* > *karam*) and truth (*satya* > *sac*), or so traditional interpretation affirms. The link between them seems to be particularly close, for already in the realm of action "truth is in their minds," and the two realms are sketched out in a single poem. One notable difference between the two is the presence of multiple divine figures in the realm of action, as contrasted with a single, central entity in the realm of truth. The former are especially associated with the mythology of Rām, whose value Nānak implicitly praises by giving him such an elevated rank. At the same time, however, he diffuses the reality of Rām and multiplies his wife Sītā into many Sītās, suggesting that the Rām and Sītā commonly worshiped are not their true, esoteric form. In the realm of truth, such appearances are transcended. Though the Ultimate Being "looks" (*nadari, vekhai*) upon all else, there is the sense that he himself cannot be seen. In a term that is foundational in *nirguṇa* theology, Nānak calls him "formless" (*nirankār* > *nirankāru*). One can still be a "lover of God" (*bhakta* > *bhagat*) in the realm of action, but there is no mention of such a thing in the realm of truth.

Japjī 38
Sikh commentators often interpret this poem as belonging to the series describing the five realms, as if five realms ought by rights to command five poems. In this poem Nānak is seen to be looking back over the path of ascent he has described and encouraging his flock to attempt the difficult journey. See, for example, Gurbachan Singh Talib, *Japuji: The Immortal Prayer-chant* (New Delhi: Munshiram Manoharlal, 1977), pp. 20–21.

Chapter 4: Sūrdās

1. The couplet is as follows:

   Sūr is the sun, Tulsī the moon, and Keśav Dās the stars.
   Modern poets only flicker around like fireflies.

2. A number of examples are clustered together among the second group of *pads* and the second group of *sākhīs* recorded in the *Pañcvāṇī*. See Tivārī, *Kabīr-Granthāvalī,* vol. 2, pp. 5–12, 140–48, reprinted without apparatus in Vaudeville, *Kabīr-Vāṇī,* pp. 56–58, 225–29, and translated in Vaudeville, *Kabīr,* vol. 1, pp. 160–71. Linda Hess discusses the paucity of such poems in the *Bījak* and *Ādi Granth* in "Studies in Kabīr: Texts, Traditions, Styles and Skills," diss., University of California, Berkeley, 1980, pp. 49–50.
3. I shall cite from the edition of the *Vārtā* prepared by Dvārkādās Parīkh (Mathura: Śrī Bajarang Pustakālay, 1970). Information about the Vallabhite sect in European languages may be found in Richard Barz, *The Bhakti Sect of Vallabhācārya* (Faridabad: Thomson Press, 1976); Helmuth von Glasenapp, "Die Lehre Vallabhâcāryas," *Zeitschrift für Indologie und Iranistik* 9 (1933–34), pp. 322–30); Mrudula M. Marfatia, *The Philosophy of Vallabhācārya* (Delhi: Munshiram Manoharlal, 1967); J. G. Shah, *Shri Vallabhacharya: His Philosophy and Religion* (Nadiad: Pushtimargiya Pustakalay, 1969); Richard J. Cohen, "Sectarian Vaishnavism: The Vallabha *Saṃpradāya,*" in Peter Gaeffke and David A. Utz, eds., *Identity and Division in Cults and Sects in South Asia* (Dept. of South Asia Regional Studies, 1984), pp. 65–72; and N. A. Thoothi, *The Vaishṇavas of Gujarat* (Calcutta: Longmans, Green, 1935).
4. A more detailed analysis of matters discussed in this paragraph appears in Hawley, *Sūr Dās,* pp. 18, 38–41.
5. *Vārtā,* pp. 418–19.
6. *Vārtā,* pp. 400–404.
7. From the manuscript research undertaken by Kenneth E. Bryant and J. S. Hawley. See Hawley, *Sūr Dās,* p. 29, n.62.
8. For a fuller consideration of the evidence and for translations of the poetry in question, see Hawley, *Sūr Dās,* pp. 29–32.

9. The effort to give an accurate description of Nānak's language is ongoing. Various possibilities have been reviewed by Michael C. Shapiro, "Linguistic Aspects of the *Ādigranth*," paper presented to the American Oriental Society, New Haven, March, 1986. Shapiro concludes that it is an anachronism to categorize Nānak's speech as either Hindi, Punjabi, or Braj: these languages attained recognizably distinct forms only somewhat after Nānak's time. A similarly measured approach is adopted by Christopher Shackle in the preface to *An Introduction to the Sacred Language of the Sikhs* (London: School of Oriental and African Studies, University of London, 1983). As for Kabīr, poems that could be said to fall within the range of Braj Bhāṣā are principally found among the *pads* of the Rajasthani recension, that is, the one especially associated with the *Pañcvāṇī* of the Dādū Panth. See Tivārī, *Kabīr-Granthāvalī,* vol. 2, pp. 1–219; Vaudeville, *Kabīr-Vāṇī,* pp. 224–80.
10. Esp. Charlotte Vaudeville, *Pastorales par Soûr-Dâs* (Paris: Gallimard, 1971), pp. 35–37, 42; cf. R. S. McGregor, *NandDas: The Round Dance of Krishna and Uddhav's Message* (London: Luzac, 1973), pp. 23–24.
11. Gopāl Nārāyaṇ Bahurā, ed., *Pad Sūrdāsjī kā / The Padas of Surdas* (Jaipur: Maharaja Sawai Man Singh II Museum, 1982), with an essay by Kenneth E. Bryant.
12. A listing of these manuscripts is presented in Hawley, *Sūr Dās,* p. xviii. Also relevant are two manuscripts of a later date discovered in Dādū Panthī archives; their readings seem to be more conservative than their date would indicate, as has been observed by Kenneth E. Bryant in "The Poems of Sūrdās" (Grant application to the National Endowment for the Humanities, 1984), p. 15.
13. Prabhudayāl Mītal, "Sūr Kṛt Padõ kī Sabse Prācīn Prati," *Nāgarīpracāriṇī Patrikā* 67:3 (1962), p. 267. *Vātsalya* poems translated here are NPS 901 and 984. A great many other examples—some from earlier strata of the *Sūr Sāgar,* some not—can be found in Kenneth E. Bryant, *Poems to the Child-God: Structures and Strategies in the Poetry of Sūrdās* (Berkeley: University of California Press, 1978). Bryant's book also contains an extended, subtle analysis of the poetic invention at work in these poems.
14. *Mādhurya* poems translated here are NPS 1774, 1806, 2415, and 2741.
15. For a consideration of Sūr's *viraha* poems, see Hawley, *Sūr Dās,* pp. 93–118. *Viraha* poems translated here are NPS 2490, 3122, 3821, 3886, and 3908. NPS 3399 is an exceptional poem depicting not the *gopīs*' longing, but Krishna's.
16. For details, see Hawley, *Sūr Dās,* pp. 127–28. *Vinaya* poems translated here are NPS 56, 138, 181, 292, 368, and Jodhpur 1359/14. Some would also classify NPS 371 in this group, since it does not pertain to specific events in the life of Krishna or Rām.
17. See, e.g., NPS 2490, translated here. On theft as a motif in Sūr's poems, see Hawley, *Krishna, the Butter Thief* (Princeton: Princeton University Press, 1983), pp. 99–177.
18. Dramatic representations of this can be very powerful. See "The Coming of Akrūr," introduced and translated in Hawley (in association with Shrivatsa Goswami), *At Play with Krishna: Pilgrimage Dramas from Brindavan* (Princeton: Princeton University Press, 1981), pp. 225–74.
19. Again one has access to a dramatic rendition of this moment in the Krishna story.

See "The Uddhav Līlā of Svāmī Kuñvar Pāl" in Norvin Hein, *The Miracle Plays of Mathurā* (New Haven: Yale University Press, 1972), pp. 179–221. Poetry of Nand Dās on the same theme is translated in McGregor, *NandDas,* pp. 85–105.

20. On history of this genre, see McGregor, *NandDas,* pp. 47–54.
21. *Bhramargīt* poems translated here are NPS 4184 and 4208. Further examples may be found in Hawley, *Sūr Dās,* pp. 104–13, and Bryant, *Child-God,* pp. 202–4.
22. A more extended version of this argument may be found in Hawley, *Sūr Dās,* pp. 121–60.
23. See Hawley, *At Play,* pp. 242–43, 260–61, and Hein, *Miracle Plays,* pp. 182–83, 188–89, 196–97, 216–17.
24. Two such "ballets" were presented in connection with the celebration of the five-hundredth anniversary of the year in which Sūr is traditionally thought to have been born, 1478. The scripts for both performances were written by Vasant Yāmadagni. The first, called "Sūrdās," was presented at the Kamani Auditorium under the auspices of the Śrīrām Bhāratīya Kalākendra. The second performance, called "Bhakta Sūrdās," took place in the Pyarelāl Auditorium and was sponsored by the Nāṭya-Ballet Center, under the direction of Kamalā Lāl. I am grateful to Vasant Yāmadagni for a personal communication (December 12, 1986) explaining these events.

Chapter 4: Poems of Sūrdās

Texts

The poems translated here are based on critical texts produced by Kenneth E. Bryant with assistance from Vidyut Aklujkar, Mandukranta Bose, Thomas B. Ridgeway, and John Hawley. The search for manuscripts on which these texts are based was initiated by Hawley in 1974; Bryant joined forces in 1977. All poems presented here—except for the Jodhpur entry at the end, in the note to which relevant information is provided—are found in the first anthology of compositions attributed to Sūr, the Fatehpur manuscript of A.D. 1582. The critical readings, however, are based on a comparison of versions of the same poem found in the fifteen oldest extant manuscripts of the *Sūr Sāgar.* The method employed will be fully laid out in Bryant's introduction to the forthcoming critical edition, to appear in the Harvard Oriental Series, but in general it can be said to involve a comparison between eastern (primarily Braj) and western (Rajasthani) manuscripts of the *Sūr Sāgar.* Though the Fatehpur manuscript stands closer to the latter group than the former, it is placed in a sufficiently median position to serve as an important arbitrator in instances of dispute, and its age gives it a prestige that makes it noteworthy in any case. On the general disposition of old manuscripts of the *Sūr Sāgar* one can consult Hawley, *Sūr Dās,* pp. 35–52; on the position of the Fatehpur manuscript within that group, see Bryant, "The Manuscript Tradition of the Sursagar: The Fatehpur Manuscript," in Bahurā, ed., *Pad Sūrdāsjī kā,* pp. vii–xx.

Poems

NPS 792

Gopāl is a title of Krishna meaning "cowherd." Here he is addressed as a little boy by his foster mother, Yaśodā, who, like every Indian mother, wants to have a nice plump baby. She attempts to convince Krishna that milk from a black cow, a rarer species among Indian cattle than the white, will have the effect of lengthening his hair, which is also black. "Kans [Kaṃsa] and Keśī and the crane" are three of the enemies Krishna will have to deal with in the course of his childhood and adolescence. Yaśodā urges Krishna—rather prematurely!—to prepare for these battles. Kaṃsa is the usurper king of Mathura; Keśī is a demonic horse who, like the demonic crane also mentioned, attacks Krishna as he plays his boyish games.

NPS 901

In this composition one *gopī* urges another to look at the child called Gopāl and Śyām, a title meaning "dusk-toned." Hence the poem is, in good *saguṇa* fashion, a *darśan* poem. The metaphors chosen to illuminate the vision it offers are familiar ones. Krishna's face, luminous and pleasingly round, is likened to the full moon, while his tender, dark hands are compared to lotuses. When the *gopī* makes reference to a "feud" between the moon and the lotus, she is thinking of the fact that most lotuses bloom by day and retreat into themselves at night (cf. NPS 2415, just below). For further information on Krishna's fondness for butter, which is ultimately a symbol for love, see Hawley, *Butter Thief,* passim.

NPS 2415

This is *darśan* in a different mode. Now the *gopīs* contemplate an adolescent Krishna, a cowherd playing his flute. Hari, meaning "remover," is a title of Vishnu that is inherited by both Krishna and Rām. It is usually explained as referring to the one who removes his devotees' troubles, but it also connotes Krishna's ability to steal away the hearts of those who love him, as here. In Hindu mythology the moon is thought of as having a chariot pulled across the sky by deer, but deer are frequently mentioned in another connection in Indian literature: their wide eyes are a standard of beauty. Here, then, the deer are Krishna's eyes, which seem momentarily to elude the control of their charioteer, the moon—his face. They do so when they hear his flute, for deer are especially sensitive to sound.

NPS 2741

The dominant note in poems of Krishna's adolescence is the sweetness (*mādhurya*) that attracts lovers to one another, and here, in Sūr's description of Rādhā's reaction to Krishna, we have mention of the root concept *madhu:* honey. The poem is a fine example of a genre (*prem vaicitrya*) in which the intensity of love is celebrated by showing that the lover longs for the beloved not only under conditions in which he is absent but also when he is near. This separation-in-union manifests itself as a debate between belief and doubt, reality and hallucination.

NPS 1744

This poem celebrates new love, as Krishna ("Joy of the Yadus") is moved to the same act of sympathy for Rādhā that all nature feels. The *cakor* is a mythological bird said to live entirely on moonbeams, here likened to Rādhā's tears.

NPS 3908

Among the animals whose behavior is cited as exemplifying the costliness of love is the deer. Its weakness for sweet sound (cf. NPS 2415) causes it to stop short—and therefore become an easy target—when hunters play a raga. Deer are said to be particularly susceptible to *rāg sārang,* the "deer" raga.

The cuckoo (*papīhā*) displays fearlessness of another sort. Separated from its mate at night, it is irrepressible in its call *pīu, pīu,* which is understood by the "lonely woman" who listens as a variant of *priya, priya:* "my love! my love!" This love wounds twice, then. It strikes the bird and it strikes the woman.

NPS 1806

Here Rādhā herself speaks—or perhaps some other, nameless *gopī*—as she observes the pyrotechnics of the monsoon season, the time especially associated with love in Indian lore. Two titles of Krishna appear in the poem: Kānh, an affectionate vernacular derivative of the name Krishna, and Śyām, which means "dark" or "dusk-toned" (cf. NPS 901) and refers to the color of his skin. Kāma ("desire") is the god of love; like Cupid, he carries a bow from which he shoots flower-arrows.

NPS 2490

The hero of this poem is again Krishna the thief, but now in a more developed version than that depicted in butter-thief poems such as NPS 901. Krishna is not the only culprit: as is typical, the *gopī* who speaks accuses her eyes of having aided his cause as "inside men."

NPS 3886

In this *viraha* poem, the heroine explains to a friend her delusions of Krishna's being present. She refers to him as Nandanandan, a title meaning the "joy" or "delight" of his foster father Nanda. The sheldrake (*cakaī*) appears frequently in *viraha* poems because it spends its nights separated from its mate, with whom it reunites when morning comes.

NPS 3821

In the battle for love, it is sometimes the woman's part to lure her beloved by resisting his advances—perhaps with some justification: Krishna's profligacy is proverbial. Here she succeeds in winning from him the gesture of submission in which he touches his hand to her feet, but she presses her advantage too far: she spurns him still. He turns away, and although he returns to consummate his passion, the next thing she knows—on awakening—he is gone. Perhaps she should not have played so hard to get.

NPS 3122

Here we see another response than remorse to the painful realities of *viraha*. A *gopī* expresses her anger when Krishna (Manmohan, "beguiler of the mind") reappears after a night away.

NPS 3399

This poem is quite unusual, in that it focuses on Krishna's longing for one of the *gopīs* from whom he is separated—Rādhā—rather than on the *gopīs'* yearning for him. It is spoken to Rādhā by a friend who acts as a go-between. Her purpose is to draw Rādhā out of the sulking anger into which she frequently falls upon learning of Krishna's attachments to other women, and it is possible that the picture she gives of Krishna is one that she has invented merely to arouse Rādhā's sympathy. Elsewhere there is very little in Krishna's behavior to suggest the yogi.

NPS 4184

This is a *bhramargīt* poem—a "song to the bee"—in which the metaphor of yoga is used in a way much more familiar to the *Sūr Sāgar* than what we have seen in NPS 3399. Here the rigors of the *gopīs'* separation from Krishna are shown to have turned them into ascetics. It is therefore no wonder, as the penultimate line says, that they understand what Ūdho is talking about. "Those who are clad with the sky" are *digambars,* an order of Jain ascetics whose rule it is never to wear any clothing. The "simple concentration" (*sahaj samādhi*) of the *gopīs'* eyes is also a reference to yogic practice. In meditation, yogis typically train their eyes not to move, an action the *gopīs* have no need to cultivate artificially, since they constantly stare down the road to see if Krishna will return. But *sahaj samādhi* is also a standard form of burial that is used for yogis: rather than being cremated, they are interred in a meditative position. The *gopīs* manage to achieve this death while still alive.

NPS 4208

Defiance is another of the responses that the *gopīs* offer Ūdho in the *bhramargīt* poems. The hunchback to whom they refer—their new rival, they allege—is a woman Krishna met on the way into the city of Mathura and cured of her deformity. As for their response to his diagnosis of what they need to overcome their own deformity, they question his professional competence when he prescribes yoga.

NPS 371

We have seen a poem of Ravidās (AG 23) in which saying the name of God is identified as the valid analogue to the practice of illuminating an image by waving lamps before it (*āratī*). Ravidās proposes the substitution of a *nirguṇa* for a *saguṇa* approach to worship. Here is the *saguṇa* answer: the whole creation is perceived as *āratī* offered by God to God, so all its attributes (*guṇ*)—not just the divine name—are intrinsically sacred.

The tortoise refers to the avatar assumed by Vishnu/Krishna to support the churning stick that was used to generate all created things, according to one major cosmogony. Here it is likened to the throne on which a divine image is seated in a temple. The rope used to turn the churning stick was a great snake (here called Śeṣ, "remainder," itself a portion of Vishnu). The creation is called Island Earth not only because in Hindu cosmology the earth is conceived as an island (*dvīpa* > *dīp*) but because the word for a shallow vessel containing a flame can take the same form (*dīpa* > *dīp*). Earth-Island Jambudvīp is surrounded by seven seas, and the mountain to which reference is made is axial Mt. Mandara, which was upended to serve as the cosmogonic churning stick.

NPS 138

Here is an example of the genre in which Sūr vaunts himself as the quintessential sinner and challenges his Lord to live up to his reputation as savior of the fallen. The four persons who are listed as among the saved in the penultimate verse may be taken either as representing roles in life that imply ethically questionable acts or as something more specific. If the latter, the vulture would be Jaṭāyu, who fought to prevent Rām's enemy, Rāvaṇ, from carrying away his wife Sītā but was mortally wounded in the combat. Rām performed his obsequies and ushered him into heaven. The prostitute would probably be Pingalā, about whom various stories are told. According to one, Pingalā was granted salvation simply on the basis of having taught her parrot to repeat the name of Rām. According to another, a prostitute named Pingalā attempted to lure away Rām himself and was therefore cursed by Sītā. Rām forgave her, granting her a birth in the presence of Krishna in her next life.

NPS 181

Again the poet criticizes Krishna, whom he addresses with the title Mādhav, for not saving him. More than that, he alleges that none of the worthless ones he is so famous for rescuing has in fact been saved. The poet often uses the image of a racing river or flood to signify what life is like in this world; classically it is called "the ocean of existence" (*bhav sāgar*).

NPS 56

Here the appeal is to Krishna as a cowherd, and the cow is the cow of this life. She is sensuality, appetite, or what Hindus often call *māyā*—magic, delusion. The Veda and the Purāṇas (of which there are classically eighteen) are texts revered by Hindus, and the poem is full of other enumerations: the six basic tastes, the fourteen worlds (seven above the earth, seven below), and the "three qualities" (*triguṇ*)—sloth, passion, and truth—that weave this world into what it is. These are often characterized by means of colors associated with them—dark (here *nīl,* blue), red, and white—and the poet associates them in turn with portions of the cow who has conquered the world. The word *triguṇ* is a pun. On the one hand it denotes these three qualities, which are manifest in the cow as hooves, belly, and horns, and a little bit later as the body parts most closely aligned with these three: nails, heart, and head. On the other hand the word *triguṇ* means "threefold," suggesting the enormous size to which the cow has grown—a size that makes it easy for her to take on the threefold world. Divine sages such as Nārad and ascetics such as Śuk and Sanak are powerless against her; so is Sūr. A popular etymology of the title Mādhav, however, suggests who should be powerful enough to herd this cow. "Mādhav" is often said to be constructed from the words *māyā* and *dhav,* and therefore to mean "master of illusion."

The implication is that Sūr is not the only one unable to control this cow. Apparently Mādhav, the great cowherd, cannot either.

NPS 292

In this poem *māyā* ("illusion") makes an explicit appearance. Often personified as female, she is the Trickster who makes of her human victims little diplomats and acrobats, performers on a stage they delight in designing for themselves.

NPS 368

It is possible that the poet remonstrates with his audience here, but even more likely that he is addressing his own mind, as in other, similar poems. Indeed, the mind is openly identified in the next to last verse: it has seen something, but too late. The reference to blindness here is about as specific as anything one finds in early strata of the *Sūr Sāgar*.

Jodhpur 1359/14

This recently discovered poem (see Hawley, *Sūr Dās,* pp. 31–32, 180–81), is presumably somewhat more recent than the others quoted here; the anthology in which it was found bears a date equivalent to A.D. 1736. Some may interpret it as the first clear reference to the poet's blindness, but it is obvious that the blindness has a meaning more spiritual than physical. The pairing of blindness and willful ignorance in the title line almost forces one to that conclusion, and the rest of the poem bears it out. The sinister enemy *kāl* has a name that means not only "Time," as translated (v. 4), but "Death" (for which a different term, *jam,* i.e., Yama, is chosen in v. 6); the one ushers in the other.

Chapter 5: Mīrābāī

1. M. S. Subbalaxmi, *Meera Bhajans,* serial number EALP 1297 (Dum Dum: Gramophone Company of India, 1965).
2. A listing is provided in Kusum Gokarn, "Popularity of Devotional Films (Hindi)," National Film Archive of India Research Project 689/5/84. This study is available at the National Film Archive of India, in Pune.
3. *Meera,* produced by T. Sadashivam, Chandraprabha Cine, Madras, 1947. The original dialogue is in Tamil but has been dubbed in various Indian languages; the music is Hindi in all versions.
4. Of especial interest among Vaswani's own voluminous publications are *The Call of Mira Education* (Poona: Mira, n.d.) and *Saint Mira* (Poona: St. Mira's English Medium School, n.d.). A brief description of the institutions he established can be found in *Sadhu Vasvani Mission and its Activities* (Poona: Sadhu Vaswani Mission, n.d.). I am grateful to Mrs. R. A. Vaswani and Mr. Atma Vaswani for interviews concerning the founder's philosophy (Pune, August 26, 1985).
5. The text is printed in T. L. Vaswani, *The Call of Mira Education,* p. 62.
6. Mrs. R. A. Vaswani, interview, Pune, August 26, 1985. The choice of June 4th as Mīrā's birthday is entirely arbitrary, so far as I have been able to determine.
7. One Indian scholar, a Punjabi and a Sikh, confessed that for him Mīrā serves as

"almost a divine consort and goddess. . . ." Darshan Singh, private communication, March 1, 1984.

8. The contrast between Mīrā and Sūr is developed in J. S. Hawley, "Images of Gender in the Poetry of Krishna," in Caroline Walker Bynum, Stevan Harrell, and Paula Richman, eds., *Gender and Religion: On the Complexity of Symbols* (Boston: Beacon Press, 1986), pp. 231–56.

9. One answer would seem to be given by an edition of poems ascribed to Mīrā that was originally published by Lalitāprasād Sukul under the title *Mīrā Smṛti Granth* (Calcutta: Bangīa Hindī Pariṣad, 1949). Its contents have been reprinted and amplified with a critical apparatus in Bhagavāndās Tivārī's *Mīrā kī Prāmāṇik Padāvalī* (Allahabad: Sāhitya Bhavan, 1974). Both these books purport to record the contents of two manuscripts of Mīrā's poetry which would, if genuine, constitute an old manuscript tradition for Mīrā, since the earlier, from Ḍākor (in Gujarat), is said to bear the date V.S. 1642 (A.D. 1585) and the later, from Benares, is said to be dated to V.S. 1727 (A.D. 1670). I regret that I have not yet been able to examine the manuscripts themselves, since the information published about them causes me to doubt their authenticity. The early dating of the Ḍakor manuscript, in particular, would make it remarkable, considering that the great manuscript libraries of north India (e.g., the Nāgarīpracāriṇī Sabhā in Benares, the royal Pothīkhānā in Jaipur, and the Vrindaban Research Institute) contain no early manuscripts exclusively devoted to Mīrā; she does not even appear in anthologies until the late eighteenth century. Further doubt is cast by the fact that these two manuscripts were obtained from a single source and that, despite the disparate provenances claimed for them, they contain a common store of poems with apparently identical readings. Kalyāṇsiṃh Śekhāvat (in his *Mīrābāī kā Jīvanvṛtt evam Kāvya* [Jodhpur: Hindī Sāhitya Mandir, n.d.], p. 15) was bothered by the occurrence of *ḍ* in some of the poems. I am struck more by the frequent substitution of *ś* for *s*, a fact that would seem to suggest Sukul's place of publication—Calcutta—rather than the cities with which the manuscripts themselves are said to be associated, unless hypercorrection is involved. At the very least such circumstances force us to question the authenticity of these two manuscripts until the originals can be examined.

As for the five poems attributed to Mīrā before 1700, one is much older than the rest. This poem of separation and longing appears in the Kartarpur manuscript of the *Gurū Granth Sāhib* (A.D. 1604), as has been shown by Gurinder Singh Mann, *The Making of Sikh Scripture* (New York: Oxford University Press, forthcoming). Mann's analysis of this heretofore only partially accessible manuscript supersedes the scholarship offered in McLeod, *Evolution*, pp. 72–75, and Pritam Singh, "Bhāī Banno's Copy of the Sikh Scripture," in Thiel-Horstmann, ed., *Bhakti in Current Research*, pp. 325–27, 331–32.

Three of the remaining seventeenth-century poems are found on folios 43, 44, and 51 of manuscript 30346 (*sphuṭapadaḥ*) in the Rajasthani and Hindi collection of the Rajasthan Oriental Research Institute, Jodhpur. This manuscript is assigned the dates V.S. 1713–14 (A.D. 1656–57) by the Institute, but the colophon that would confirm them seems absent. The Mīrā poems have been translated by Nancy Martin, "Dyed in the Color of Her Lord: Multiple Representations in the Mīrābāī Tradition," Ph.D. diss., Graduate Theological Union, 1995, pp. 138–39. Finally, Winand Callewaert (personal communication, November 1994) has recently discovered a fifth poem attributed to Mīrābāī in a Jaipuri anthology dating to A.D. 1673. For Nābhādās's statement on Mīrā, see *Bhaktamal*, pp. 712–13.

10. Nābhādās, *Bhaktamāl*, pp. 712–13.
11. The best known deity in present-day Rajasthan is of this type: the image of Krishna as Srī Nāth Jī, at Nāthdvārā. There is also, however, a substantial series of pillars representing the Mountain Lifter that stretches through the region. See Vijayśaṃkar Śrīvāstav, "Rajasthānī Mūrtikalā mẽ Kṛṣṇalīlā Abhiprāy," *Bhāratīya Saṃskṛti kī Rūparekhā* (Bikaner: Sadul Rajasthani Research Institute, 1969), pp. 63–76.
12. Priyādās in Nābhādās, *Bhaktamāl*, p. 717. In modern Hindi the term *sādhū* (or *sādhu*) has come to refer specifically to a religious mendicant. Here, however, it is translated as "saint," because the term's meaning was not restricted to ascetics in medieval Hindi. The gloss provided by the text itself—concerning obedience to Śyām's will—also suggests this interpretation.
13. Priyādās in Nābhādās, *Bhaktamāl*, p. 718.
14. Priyādās in Nābhādās, *Bhaktamāl*, p. 719.
15. Some recent commentators have urged that the meeting must have been with Jīv's uncle Rūp Gosvāmī since, according to traditional reckoning, Mīrā's life would have been more closely contemporary with Rūp's than Jīv's. Furthermore there is a verse attributed to Mīrā in which she praises Brindavan and mentions "the sight of Govind":

    ālī mhāṇe lāgā vṛndāvaṇ nīkā̃
    ghar-ghar tulasī ṭhākur pūjā, darasaṇ govindajī kā̃.

    (Paraśurām Caturvedī, ed., *Mīrā̃bāī kī Padāvalī* [Allahabad: Hindī Sāhitya Sammelan, 1973], no. 160.) If this "Govind" is interpreted as the temple of Govindadev, there is a hint of Rūp, since he was priest there. This, however, is a thin thread, and Jīv's vow of lifelong celibacy makes the story fit better with him than with Rūp, who was married. And whichever *gosvāmī* one prefers as Mīrā's antagonist, the outline of the tale remains unchanged.
16. Priyādās in Nābhādās, *Bhaktamāl*, p. 722.
17. James Tod, who lived in Rajasthan as a servant of the British government from 1805 to 1822, evidently reflected the opinion prevalent in his day when he reported that Rāṇā Kumbha was Mīrā's husband. (James Tod, *Annals and Antiquities of Rajasthan* [London: Milford, 1920] vol. 1, pp. 337–38; orig. ed., 1829.) A century later, however, the Rajput historian Har Bilas Sarda had asserted the Bhojrāj view in his *Maharana Sāngā* (Ajmer: Scottish Mission Industries, 1918), pp. 95–96, as was noted in William Crooke's updated edition of Tod's *Annals*, p. 337. The matter is reconsidered in Hermann Goetz, *Mira Bai: Her Life and Times* (Bombay: Bharatiya Vidya Bhavan, 1966), pp. 4–5; S. M. Pandey, "Mīrābāī and Her Contributions to the Bhakti Movement," *History of Religions* 5:1 (1965), pp. 55–56; and Kalyāṇsiṃh Śekhāvat, *Mīrā̃bāī kā Jīvanvṛtt evam Kāvya* (Jodhpur: Hindī Sāhitya Mandir, n.d.), pp. 45–46.
18. Kamala Chandrakant, *Mirabai* [Amar Chitra Katha, no. 36] (Bombay: India Book House, n.d.), p. 4; cf. also p. 11.
19. Chandrakant, *Mirabai*, p. 4.

20. The Mīrā temple in the fort at Cittor was originally dedicated to Vishnu, as was the Mīrā temple at Ahār on the outskirts of Udaipur.
21. In a pamphlet issued at the temple, it is said to grant the wishes of devotees who come to see it. Pradyumna Pratāp Siṃh, "Bhakta-Śiromaṇi Śrīmīrābāī Mandir, Vṛndāvan kā Jīrṇoddhār," p. 5.
22. Caturvedī, *Mīrābāī,* nos. 140.1–8, 199.1, 200.1–2; Kalyāṇsiṃh Śekhāvat, ed., *Mīrā -Bṛhatpadāvalī* (Jodhpur: Rajasthan Oriental Research Institute, 1975) vol. 2., no. 131.8.
23. Śekhāvat, *Bṛhatpadāvalī,* nos. 16.1, 21.2, 98.2, 146.1, 155.2.
24. Caturvedī, *Mīrābāī,* no. 196.5–6; cf. Śekhāvat, *Bṛhatpadāvalī,* no. 99.
25. Caturvedī, *Mīrābāī,* no. 18.4–5; Śekhāvat, *Bṛhatpadāvalī,* no. 155.10.
26. Caturvedī, *Mīrābāī,* nos. 158, 159; Śekhāvat, *Bṛhatpadāvalī,* no. 4.
27. Caturvedī, *Mīrābāī,* nos. 145.1, 169.6, 42.2, 51.3–6. The last two poems are translated here.
28. Caturvedī, *Mīrābāī,* nos. 81–85, 146, 147, 149; cf. 92, 115–17; Śekhāvat, *Bṛhatpadāvalī* no. 75. One song of the monsoon season (Caturvedī 82) is translated here; cf. also Caturvedī 117, below.
29. Caturvedī, *Mīrābāī,* no. 171.5. On the theology involved, see Donna M. Wulff, *Drama as a Mode of Religious Realization: The* Vidagdhamādhava *of Rūpa Gosvāmī* (Chico, Calif.: Scholars Press, 1984), pp. 29–34, and David L. Haberman, *Acting as a Way of Salvation: A Study of Raganuga Bhakti Sadhana* (New York: Oxford University Press, forthcoming), chaps. 5 and 6.
30. Caturvedī, *Mīrābāī,* no. 186.8–9. The poem is translated here.
31. Matters considered in this paragraph are discussed at somewhat greater length in J. S. Hawley, "Author and Authority in the Bhakti Poetry of North India," *The Journal of Asian Studies* 47, no. 2 (1988), pp. 269–90. Examples of the standard Mountain Lifter refrain appear in Caturvedī 37, 42, 153 and Śekhāvat 76, all translated in this chapter.
32. See Sūrdās NPS 3399, translated in chap. 4.
33. Caturvedī, *Mīrābāī,* nos. 26.7–13, 27.1–5, 32.4–5, 39.5, 51.3–6, 141.3, 141.8, 150.3–4, 154.9, 201.3–4; cf. 43.4. Nos. 27 and 51 are translated here.
34. Caturvedī, *Mīrābāī,* no. 80.2, 117, 188; Śekhāvat, *Bṛhatpadāvalī,* no. 74.2–4, 85.5, 149.1–3.
35. Caturvedī, *Mīrābāī,* no. 117, 153; cf. 25.2, 49.1–3, 68.3; Śekhāvat, *Bṛhatpadāvalī,* no. 85.5–7, 149.1–3. Caturvedī 117 and 153 are translated here. A rare exception to the Hindu insistance that yogis be celibate has existed in the Nāth Yogī tradition since at least the eighteenth century. See D. and A. G. Gold, "The Fate of the Householder Nāth," p. 116, passim. Also worth noting are the *makānvāle* ("house-dwelling") monks of the Dādū Panth, who sometimes—unofficially—have wives and children. (Monika Thiel-Horstmann, "Modes of Renunciation in the Dādūpanth," paper delivered at the conference "Ascetics and Asceticism in India: A Comparative Study," held at the University of Florida, February 1988; W. G. Orr, *A Sixteenth-Century Indian Mystic: Dadu and His Followers* (London: Lutherworth, 1947), p. 218.
36. Recent research by Lindsey Harlan suggests that among Rajput women in Rajasthan Mīrā's bravery is understood as having to do with her caste as well. The Rajputs are warriors by tradition, and their women are praised for showing a heroism defiant enough to match their men's, as in famous cases of suttee. There

is nothing in Rajput lore to justify a woman's departing from her husband or becoming a yogi to do so, but Mīrā's action displays a quality of determination that is perceived by Rajput women as not unrelated to their caste ideals. (Lindsey Harlan, personal communication, December 23, 1985; cf. Harlan, "Satīmātā Veneration in Rajasthan," paper presented to the Conference on Religion in South India, Craigville, Mass., June, 1986.)

37. Caturvedī, *Mīrābāī*, nos. 37.3, 39.5, 97.3, 99.4, 130.2; cf. Śekhāvat, *Bṛhatpadāvalī*, no. 71.1. Mīrā is not the only saint whose poems speak of madness: cf., e.g., Kabīr in KG *pad* 190.3.

Chapter 5: Poems of Mīrābāī

Texts

Mīrābāī's poetry, unlike that of the other five poets translated in this book, cannot be traced back to a secure manuscript tradition. A search for poems bearing her name in Rajasthani manuscripts was recently undertaken by Kalyāṇsimh Śekhāvat (*Mīrā-Bṛhatpadāvalī*, cited above, vol. 2; cf. Śekhāvat, *Mīrābāī*, pp. 75–134), but Śekhāvat was unable to unearth dated manuscripts written earlier than the latter half of the eighteenth century. One of the oldest he found (A.D. 1779) is translated here. To my knowledge no similarly rigorous study of manuscripts outside Rajasthan has yet been attempted. One does have the critical edition of Bhagavāndās Tivārī, which is focused on two purportedly old manuscripts, but there seems good reason to doubt that these manuscripts are as genuine as claimed (see n. 9). In the absence of secure sources, we have based all but one of our translations on the edition most widely used at present: Paraśurām Caturvedī's *Mīrābāī kī Padāvalī*, cited earlier. It contains no apparatus, but one can find variant readings for poems 27, 37, 82, 166, and 193 in Tivārī (*Mīrā kī Prāmāṇik Padāvalī*, nos. 36, 48, 49, 94, and 71). An English translation of the full Caturvedī edition can be found in A. J. Alston, *The Devotional Poems of Mīrābāī* (Delhi: Motilal Banarsidass, 1980).

Poems

Caturvedī, no. 37

The word *sāvariyo* is a variant on *śyām*, a title of Krishna that means "the dark one." The repetition of the phrase in which this word occurs creates an opportunity to translate it in both its senses, as "the color of dusk" and "the color of my Lord." Mīrā adopts a metaphor that is frequent in Krishna poetry when she implies that she is so indelibly dyed with his color that she can never return to what she was before.

In translating this particularly musical poem, we have repeated the refrain not only in the opening verse, where it is indicated in the printed edition, but after every subsequent verse as well. We hope thereby to give an impression of how many poems of Mīrā—and of other poets—sound when actually performed.

On "the saints," see note 12 above. The "Maddening One" is probably to be understood as Krishna identified by the title Madan—someone who exhilarates or intoxicates. It is possible, however, that the poet means Kāma, who also bears the title Madan. In that case Mīrā is adjudged mad with passion.

Śekhāvat, no. 76

"The game of Spring" is *holī*, a festival that occurs in February or March in which the normal rules of social behavior are tossed aside in several days of abandon. Because it unleashes natural urges, *holī* is a festival of love; and as a celebration of love, it is closely associated with Krishna and his milkmaids.

The sort of message articulated in this poem is normally addressed to the heroine by one of her confidantes, as a stimulus to a meeting between the heroine and her lover. (Cf. Sūrdās NPS 3399, in chap. 4.) Here perhaps Mīrā assumes that role in relation to Rādhā, but Rādhā is not specifically mentioned, so it is possible that Mīrā is merely sharing with a friend the enthusiasm she enjoys as a "latter-day *gopī*." When she says that Krishna is her friend's "best blessing" (*param suhāg*), she means not only that, but that he makes a fine husband; for in traditional usage the phrase "blessed woman" (*suhāginī;* cf. *suhāgavatī,* p. 147) designates a woman who has a husband. When she mentions the crow, she is drawing on a convention of Indian love poetry that takes the call of the crow as a harbinger of the arrival of an absent lover. The basil garden where the cowherds gather is Brindavan (*vrandāban vāg*).

Caturvedī, no. 82

Lurking behind the vivid colors associated with the rainy season are colors associated with Krishna as well. When the poet sees the dark (*syām*) clouds she also sees the other Śyām, and when she sees the earth turn green (*harī*) she can scarcely help thinking of the other Hari. Etymologically the title Hari has nothing to do with greenness—it refers to one who delivers, who takes away ills—but that scarcely matters to a woman in love.

Caturvedī, no. 166

Muralī is the name of the bamboo flute that Krishna plays to attract his women to his side. It is often personified as feminine, and is said to possess irresistable powers, as here. The three darknesses pertain to the muddy waters of the River Jumna, the cloak (*kamariyā*) in which Krishna sometimes wraps himself, and the color of his skin.

Caturvedī, no. 84

The male *papīhā* bird, a member of the cuckoo family, calls with an especially piercing sound in the rainy season. In Indian lore its cry is heard as *pīu, pīu,* which sounds like *priya, priya,* "my love, my love." It is this, then, that Mīrā herself cries, as she confesses near the end of the poem. (Cf. Sūrdās NPS 3908.)

"The one who sees inside" (*antarjāmī*) is a frequent designation for Krishna or Rām. When this term first became significant—in the ancient Upaniṣads—it meant "inner controller," but by the sixteenth century it referred to the divine power to know what was in a devotee's heart.

Caturvedī, no. 186

The Bhīls, a tribal group of southwest Rajasthan, are traditionally looked down upon as being beyond the caste structure of Hindu society. Therefore when the Bhīl woman named Śabarī offered the exiled king Rām fruits that she had been careful to taste before he did, to make sure they were sweet, she presented him with a double challenge to ritual purity. Not only was he asked to accept food from the hands of an outcaste, but from her very mouth. The poem celebrates Rām's response.

The fruit she offers is that of the prickly *ber* tree—something between a plum and a large berry, and often a bit sour. It is understandable, therefore, that the woman desires to test the taste before presenting an offering to Rām.

Caturvedī, no. 27

In a traditional Hindu wedding a decorative arch, often woven of mango leaves, is erected in front of the doorway to welcome guests—notably, the bridegroom and his party. The ceremony itself takes place beneath a pavilion constructed in the courtyard of the bride's house. There, as one of the central events, the bridegroom places the bride's hand in his own, palm up, so that various auspicious substances can be poured into them both. Then he leads his bride around the Vedic *homa* fire, solemnizing the marriage.

Caturvedī, no. 51

The "altar of pearl tears" (*motī cauk*) refers to the area on the bride's courtyard floor that is demarked as sacred by auspicious designs laid out with flour. This area, just in front of the *homa* fire, serves as the focus of the wedding ceremony. From it various offerings and sacrifices are made into the fire, according to ancient prescriptions.

Caturvedī, no. 153

Red is the traditional color of the wedding sari, and it is contrasted here with yellow, the ascetic's color. To decorate the part in the hair with a string of jewels is a traditional aspect of the bride's appearance, and in the course of the wedding ceremony her part receives further attention when the groom marks it with red powder to signify her wedded status. By contrast, again, a yogi's hair is normally left totally unattended. Thus the poem achieves a thorough intermixture of yoga and marriage, at Krishna's pleasure.

Caturvedī, no. 117

Here, as in Śekhāvat no. 76, Mīrā speaks to an unnamed female friend. In contrast to what we have in Caturvedī no. 186, the term Rām is not in this context a reference to Rāmacandra, the hero of the *Rāmāyaṇa*, but to Rām in the general sense—a designation for God. Mention is made of Śiva, the archetypal yogi, for he is the natural patron deity of ascetics. Snakes form part of Śiva's rough, forbidding dress—they are his necklaces and garlands—and the serpent named here seems to share in these associations. He is Śeṣ, who serves as the vehicle and shield of Vishnu.

Caturvedī, no. 193

We have seen Ravidās's "regal realm" (AG 3); here is Mīrā's "realm beyond going," her impossible, indestructible, unapproachable land (*agam des,* i.e., *agamya deś*). Unlike Ravidās, she evinces no concern about its social structure, except to portray it as the place where all devotees (*sādhā, sant*) gather and dance a dance of common concentration as Krishna's women. The "high-flying birds" are *haṃsas,* geese that fly at unusually high altitudes and are said to make their home in the highest reaches of the Himalayas—in particular at Mānsarovar, the "spiritual lake" that lies at the base of Mount Kailās, where Śiva sits in eternal meditation. The "sixteen signs / Of beauty" are those that befit a married woman: mascara, a forehead mark, a pearl set in the nostril, and so forth.

Chapter 6: Tulsīdās

1. Several accounts of the Rāmnagar *rām līlā* have recently become available. They are: Richard Schechner, "Ramlila of Ramnagar: An Introduction," in his *Performative Circumstances from the Avant Garde to Ramlila* (Calcutta: Seagull Books, 1983), pp. 238–88; Linda Hess, "Rām Līlā: The Audience Experience," in Monika Thiel-Horstmann, ed., *Bhakti in Current Research, 1979–1982* (Berlin: Dietrich Reimer Verlag, 1983), pp. 171–94; Schechner and Hess, "The Ramlila of Ramnagar," *The Drama Review* 21:3 (1977), pp. 51–82; Philip Lutgendorf, "The Life of a Text: Tulsidas' *Rāmcaritmānas* in Performance" (diss., University of Chicago, 1987), chap. 5; and Anuradha Kapur, "Actors, pilgrims, kings, and gods: The Ramlila at Ramnagar," in Veena Das, ed., *The Word and the World: Fantasy, Symbol and Record* (New Delhi: Sage Publications, 1986), pp. 57–74. I am indebted to Linda Hess for personal communications on the subject in March, 1986. For historical depth on the *rām līlā* genre, see Norvin Hein, *The Miracle Plays of Mathurā* pp. 70–125, especially p. 72n.
2. Philip Lutgendorf, "The Quest for the Legendary Tulsīdās," paper presented to the American Academy of Religion, Los Angeles, November, 1985, pp. 12–13.
3. *Kavitāvalī* 7.176, 7.182, 7.183; the last of these is translated in this volume. Much of the *Kavitāvalī* has been translated in F. R. Allchin, *Tulsī Dās: Kavitāvalī* (London: Allen and Unwin, 1964.
4. *Kavitāvalī* 7.177. Cf. *Vinaya Patrikā* 8, also translated here.
5. *Kavitāvalī* 7.183.
6. *Kavitāvalī* 7.57, 7.72, 7.73; *Vinaya Patrikā* 275. *Kavitāvalī* 7.72 and 7.73 are translated here. The entire *Vinaya Patrikā* has been rendered into English by Allchin as *Tulsī Dās: The Petition to Rām* (London: Allen and Unwin, 1966).
7. *Kavitāvalī* 7.72.
8. *Rāmcaritmānas* 1, *soraṭhā* 5. This name is generally interpreted as referring to Naraharidās, the man said to have been Tulsī's guru in a work called the *Gautam Candrikā*. The problem is that the *Gautam Candrikā,* despite the early date of composition it claims for itself, was only discovered in 1955, which casts doubt, as does much else, upon its authenticity. See Lutgendorf, "Quest," pp. 7–8; Viśvanāth Prasād Miśra, "Gautam-Candrikā mẽ Tulsīdās kā Vṛttānt," *Nāgarīpracāriṇī Patrikā* 60:1 (1954), pp. 1–22. Several English translations of the *Rāmcaritmānas* exist. The most recent is that of W. D. P. Hill, *The Holy Lake of the Acts of Rāma* (Bombay: Oxford University Press, 1952).
9. *Rāmcaritmānas* 1.4.1–1.8.10.
10. *Rāmcaritmānas* 1.9.1.
11. Cf. esp. *Rāmcaritmānas* 1.9.4: *bhāṣā bhaniti.* This may also be in the background of *Vinaya Patrikā* 142.15–16, where Tulsī draws a contrast between the tensions he

experienced with Brahmins and his creativity "among the saints" (*santan mā̃jh*). There is nothing in Tulsī's own writings to force one to the conclusion that Tulsī himself was a Brahmin, but tradition assumes it universally and there seems no reason to doubt the fact.

12. Nābhādās, *Bhaktamāl,* p. 756. On the contemporaneity of Tulsīdās and Nābhādās, see Gilbert Pollet, "Early Evidence on Tulsīdās and his Epic," *Orientalia Lovaniensia Periodica* 5 (1974), pp. 157–59. Reservations must be voiced, however, about Pollet's acceptance of the *Mūl Gosāī̃ Carit* and the *Gautam Candrikā* as providing evidence on the period that precedes the testimony of Priyādās ("Early Evidence," pp. 160–62); cf. Lutgendorf, "Quest," pp. 4–9, and Kiśorīlāl Gupta, *Gosāī̃-Carit* (Varanasi: Vāṇī-Vitān Prakāśan, 1964), pp. 4–5. To the contrary, in relation to the *Mūl Gosāī̃ Carit*, see Chandra Kumari Handoo, *Tulasīdāsa: Poet, Saint and Philosopher of the Sixteenth Century* (Bombay: Orient Longmans, 1964), pp. 4–6, 35, *et passim.* Handoo's study is based primarily on materials given in the *Mūl Gosāī̃ Carit.*
13. Only Jayadeva, the author of the *Gītagovinda,* precedes him. See Justin E. Abbott and Narhar R. Godbole, *Stories of Indian Saints: Translation of Mahipati's Marathi Bhaktavijava* (Delhi: Motilal Banarsidass, 1982 [orig. publ. 1933]), vol. 1, p. 32.
14. *Bhaktamāl,* pp. 756, 764. There is room for some difference of opinion as to whether Priyādās means a murderer of a Brahmin, a Brahmin who has committed a murder, or both when he says *hatyā kari vipra ek* (*Bhaktamāl,* p. 764). Context leads me to favor the last possibility.
15. *Bhaktamāl,* p. 764. Again, the meaning of Priyādās' words—in this case, *sudh gāyau pyāre kāu*—is not self-evident.
16. Priyādās in Nābhādās, *Bhaktamāl,* pp. 764–66. On *prasād,* cf. *Kavitāvalī* 7.74, translated here.
17. Priyādās in Nābhādās, *Bhaktamāl,* p. 767.
18. Priyādās in Nābhādās, *Bhaktamāl,* pp. 767–68.
19. One can see this vividly represented in the comic-book version of Tulsī's life: Suresh Chandra Sharma: *Tulsidas* [Amar Chitra Katha, no. 62] (Bombay: India Book House, n.d.), pp. 15–17.
20. Priyādās in Nābhādās, *Bhaktamāl,* p. 759.
21. *Rāmāyaṇ kathā* (Priyādās in Nābhādās, *Bhaktamāl,* p. 762).
22. Priyādās in Nābhādās, *Bhaktamāl,* p. 763.
23. There are problems with assuming this to have been Akbar, as has traditionally been done. (See Pollet, "Early Evidence," p. 160; cf. *Bhaktamāl,* p. 768.) Jahāngīr is more likely, if indeed the story has a basis in fact.
24. On Priyādās' sectarian affiliations, see R. D. Gupta, "Priyā Dās, Author of the *Bhaktirasabodhinī,*" *Bulletin of the School of Oriental and African Studies* 32:1 (1969), p. 61; also Philip Lutgendorf, "Kṛṣṇa Caitanya and his Companions as presented in the *Bhaktamāla* of Nābhā Jī and the *Bhaktirasabodhinī* of Priyā Dāsa," master's essay, University of Chicago, 1981. As a location for Tulsīdās's great vision of Rām, the temple of Madan Mohan is not undisputed. A small temple in Jñān Gudaḍī, Brindavan, calls itself the Tulsī Rām Darśan Sthal ("Place Where Tulsī Saw Rām") and claims that honor.

25. It is also possible to interpret this typically terse passage from Priyādās in a somewhat different way, and many have chosen to do so. One can understand Tulsī's response to mean that before his heckler pointed out the divinity of Rām, Tulsī had merely regarded Rām as the incomparably handsome son of Daśarath. To be told of his divinity, on top of that, merely deepens Tulsī's devotion. If there is a difficulty in this reading, it is that it forces one to understand Tulsī's initial request to see his "chosen one" (*iṣṭ*) as if it were something other than a request to see his chosen divinity (*iṣṭadevatā*), whereas the latter would be the normal way of construing the reference of the term *iṣṭ*. I am grateful to Philip Lutgendorf for calling this problem of interpretation to my attention (personal communication, January 14, 1987).
26. On this work, see Ronald Stuart McGregor, "Tulsīdās' Śrīkṛṣṇagītāvalī," *Journal of the American Oriental Society* 96:4 (1976), pp. 520–26. Tulsīdās's devotion to Krishna is popularly said to have been fostered in a period when he lived near the Vallabhite temple of Gopāljī, in Benares. Cf. Lutgendorf, "Life of a Text," p. 455, n. 73.
27. *Vinaya Patrikā* 279; cf. *Vinaya Patrikā* 277, translated here along with a number of other poems from the *Vinaya Patrikā*. A range of divinities also appears in *Kavitāvalī* 7.136–68.
28. See Charlotte Vaudeville, *Étude sur les sources et la composition du Rāmāyaṇa de Tulsī-Dās* (Paris: Librairie d'Amérique et d'Orient, 1955), pp. 170–73, 319–20. She builds on the earlier scholarship of Rām Nareś Tripāṭhī, *Tulsīdās aur unkī Kavitā*, vol. 1 (Allahabad: Hindī Mandir, 1937), pp. 220ff., and Mātāprasād Gupta, *Gosvāmī Tulsīdās* (Allahabad: Indian Press, 1946), pp. 264ff.
29. *Rāmcaritmānas* 1.115–1.121.
30. *Rāmcaritmānas* 7.53ff.
31. *Rāmcaritmānas* 7.2–3; cf. *Adhyātma Rāmāyaṇa* 6.4.1–2.
32. See *Kavitāvalī* 7.72–74, 7.76; *Vinaya Patrikā* 66, 69.
33. *Vinaya Patrikā* 111.
34. On the Rām Rājya Pariṣad, see Lutgendorf, "Life of a Text," pp. 634–38. For an example of the attitude maintained toward Tulsīdās on the part of its founder, Svāmī Karpātrī, see pp. 606–07 of the same work.
35. *Rāmcaritmānas* 3.34.1–2. The translation is the one made by Linda Hess in her study "For the Sake of Brahmans, Gods, and Cows: Tulsīdās between Bhakti and Orthodoxy," p. 12. This paper was presented to the American Academy of Religion, Dallas, December, 1983, and to the Society for Asian and Comparative Philosophy, Honolulu, August, 1984.
36. Hess, "Brahmans, Gods, and Cows," pp. 23–29.
37. *Rāmcaritmānas* 3.35.4–6, translated by Hess, "Brahmins, Gods, and Cows," p. 15.
38. Such themes are well represented in the *Kavitāvalī* and *Vinaya Patrikā:* e.g., VP 65–70 and Kav. 7.178 on the name; VP 84 and 203 on teachers and good company; and VP 87–92, 114, 208, 271, 275, and 276 on the poet's baseness. VP 66, 69, and 92 are translated here.
39. *Kavitāvalī* 7.165 and *Vinaya Patrikā* 8. The latter is translated here.
40. Striking examples of Tulsī's ecumenism are passages such as the one in which he seems to equate Śiva's greatest mantra with the name of Rām (*Kavitāvalī* 7.74,

translated here) and the poem whose every line is divided between the praise of Rām and the praise of Śiva (*Vinaya Patrikā* 52). One can, however, discover moments in which Tulsī seems to disavow the formulaic catholicity of Smārta Brahmins in favor of a more intense and focused devotional life (*Kavitāvalī* 7.78, *Vinaya Patrikā* 250).

41. Such expositions (*kathās*) constitute a major genre in which the *Mānas* is performed. See Lutgendorf, "Life of a Text," chapters 3–4, and Añjanīnandan Śaran, "*Mānas* ke Prācīn Ṭīkākār," *Kalyāṇ: Mānasānk* (Gorakhpur: Gītā Press, 1938), pp. 908–28.
42. All this is eloquently argued by Lutgendorf in "Quest," pp. 2–9.
43. Lutgendorf, "Quest," p. 16.
44. *Hindustān,* August 17, 1983.
45. *Mūl Gosāī̃ Carit,* attributed to Benī Mādhavdās, *dohās* 29–30 and the accompanying *caupāīs,* in Gupta, *Gosāī̃-Carit,* p. 285. For the Sūr poem, see Handoo, *Tulasīdāsa,* p. 34.
46. *Mūl Gosāī̃ Carit, dohās* 31–32 and following *caupāīs,* in Gupta, *Gosāī̃-Carit,* p. 285. In Tulsī's case, the letter is said to have taken the form of two poems. The *Mūl Gosāī̃ Carit* does not specify which these were, but it has come to be assumed that *Vinaya Patrikā* 174 was one of them, since it is written in the epistolary format and concerns incidents in which devotees of Rām and Krishna had to leave behind the persons dearest to them in order to be true to their Lord. (Handoo, *Tulasīdāsa,* pp. 35–36; Siṃh, "Bhakta-Śiromaṇi Śrīmīrābāī Mandir," p. 5.) It is significant that the legend of this correspondence is reported not just in circles where Tulsī is praised but at the temple to Mīrā in Brindavan, as the latter reference indicates. See also Caturvedī, *Mīrābāī,* pp. 212–14.
47. Louisa Wright et al., "Help for the Stream of Nectar," *Time,* international ed., April 22, 1985, p. 21; Geoffrey Ward, "Benares, India's Most Holy City, Faces an Unholy Problem," *Smithsonian,* September, 1985, pp. 83, 90–92; Santha Rama Rau, "Banaras: India's City of Light," *National Geographic* 169:2 (February, 1986), pp. 244–45. I am grateful to Linda Hess and Vijaya Nagarajan for their help in locating these materials.
48. *Mūl Gosāī̃ Carit, caupāīs* following *dohā* 49 and *ślok* 1, in Gupta, *Gosāī̃-Carit,* p. 291. Cf. Handoo, *Tulasīdāsa,* pp. 47–48.

Chapter 6: Poems of Tulsīdās

Texts

Manuscript evidence relating to the poetry of Tulsīdās has been subjected to relatively close scrutiny. Tulsī's acclaim in his own time and the fact that in all probability he not only sang but wrote make it likely that text criticism can bring us fairly close to the words of the poet himself. In the case of the *Vinaya Patrikā* one is aided by a closely related manuscript entitled *Rām Gītāvalī* that bears a date (A.D. 1609) locating it within the lifetime of the poet himself; manuscripts of the *Kavitāvalī* go back to A.D. 1660. Such matters are taken into account in the Nāgarīpracāriṇī Sabhā editions of the *Kavitāvalī* and *Vinaya Patrikā,* which form the basis for the translations presented here. They are found in volume 2 of Rāmcandra Śukla et al., eds., *Tulsī-Granthāvalī* (Varanasi: Nāgarīpracāriṇī Sabhā, 1974). Also relevant is Mātāprasād Gupta, *Tulsīdās* (Allahabad: Allahabad University, 1935), pp. 225–29, 232–33.

Poems

Kavitāvalī 7.72

The grammar of this poem is such that one can read its first two sections either in the first person or in the third. What pulls one ultimately toward the former option is the signature verse, which makes it clear that Tulsī is speaking about himself in all he says here. His reference at that point to a "great sage" (*mahāmunī*) has traditionally been understood to mean Vālmīki, but since no name is given we have adopted the more conservative, indefinite translation. It is possible that in the last stanza he is speaking not only of but to himself: he is the fool who receives this undeserved adulation and still does not cling to the feet of Rām as he ought.

Kavitāvalī 7.73

Traditional Hindus say that fate, often personified as the god Brahmā, inscribes its dictates on a person's forehead at birth. Traditional prognosticators are normally called in to decipher such secrets in advance. Everything about Tulsī's birth seems to confirm that his is to be a sad destiny, but his devotion to the name of Rām overturns fate.

Kavitāvalī 7.74

Śiva, as we have seen, is the presiding deity of Benares, and he exercises his power in the most critical way at the moment of death. Death in Benares is said to present the chance of immediate liberation from the cycles of worldly existence, and it is Śiva who makes such liberation possible by acting as guru in the moment of death. He whispers the *tāraka mantra,* the "formula for crossing beyond," in the ear of the person who dies. According to Tulsīdās and others, that mantra is "Rām, Rām." Cf. *Vinaya Patrikā* 184.4 and Eck, *Banaras, City of Light* pp. 332–34.

No explicit mention is made of Tulsīdās himself in this poem, but there is a tradition that the last verse refers to him. According to this interpretation, the leather (*cām*) he mentions—a substance Hindus consider so lowly that they regard those who work with it (*camārs*) as untouchable—would be a humble allusion to his own condition before the name of Rām dramatically altered his worth. This is the reading presented by Allchin, *Kavitāvalī,* p. 160. Since the original is not specific, however, we have chosen the more conservative interpretation: anything stamped with the name of Rām—even a piece of leather—becomes valuable currency.

Kavitāvalī 7.76

The secret of this poem is hidden in what the old Muslim shouts: *harām harām. Harām* is a word of Arabic derivation meaning "unclean" or "forbidden," but it is commonly used as an ejaculation of disgust and despair, somewhat like the English "Oh God!" The two meanings are combined in translation because the syllables *harām harām* also contain the name of Rām, which, in its general sense, means God. In fact, the expression *he rām, he rām,* which is only slightly different from what the Muslim says, is a much-used Hindu exclamation of despair. Though he does not mean to, then, he utters the name of Rām, and that takes him straight to heaven—quite the opposite fate from the one he fears will befall him on account of having touched the animal Muslims most despise. The pig is so hateful that "son of a pig" has become a familiar way of swearing in the languages of north India, but the name of Rām is so powerful that if one says it at the moment of death, however inadvertently, it brings salvation.

The last word of the poem, *agamāi* (Sanskrit *agamya*), also holds a little secret. Frequently it means "not to be gone beyond," hence "unsurpassable," but it can also mean "not to be gone to," hence a place "where it's impossible to go." When pious people assert that the name of Rām is *agamya,* they have the former meaning in mind, but in this instance it suits the poet's purpose to misunderstand what they are saying when they do.

Vinaya Patrikā 66

The "sick age" to which reference is made is the *kali yug,* which creates conditions so bad that it is no longer possible for disciplines successful in earlier ages to have any effect. In the original, the poet lists three examples: yoga (*jog*), the restraining of one's senses (*sanjam*), and trance (*samādhi*). In one sense this decline of spiritual possibility is obviously a bad thing, but in another it is not. All that can be expected of a right-minded person in the *kali yug* is a technique that is within the reach of all—the repetition of God's name—and that, indeed, works.

Vinaya Patrikā 69

It is notable that when Tulsī extols the name of Rām here, he means it not only as a general designation for God but the name of someone more particular: King Rām, the hero of the *Rāmāyaṇa.* "Rescuer of the Fallen" (*patit-pāvan*) is the most common title referring to the salvific power of Krishna or Rām as a savior; cf., e.g., Caturvedī 86, translated above.

Vinaya Patrikā 8

Of the great gods in the Hindu pantheon, Śiva is the strangest, the least polished. Though unpredictable, he can be the most direct in his responses to worldly events—whether it be an urge to generosity or revenge. The terms with which Tulsī addresses Śiva in this poem draw attention to these traits. He calls him Bāmadev (i.e., Vāmadev), a title that properly means "the fair god" but also has the sense of "god of the left," owing to two distinct meanings of *vāma.* These two meanings are far apart, for in Indian society what is left-handed is dark and suspicious, and the second seems apt here. At the same time, however, Tulsī also calls Śiva a god "of great simplicity" (*baḍe bhore*), alluding to his title *bholānāth,* "Lord of the simple." The name refers to Śiva's ingenuousness, as reflected in his willingness to accept such simple offerings as the *bel* leaf, to which reference is made in verse 3. It also suggests the absence of a certain sense of proportion, as shown in the incommensurability of the offering and its reward.

There is room for disagreement about who the poet means when he speaks of Śiva's servants. They may be "earthly trials" in a general sense, for Śiva is often thought of as causing unhappy events, such as diseases that accomplish his malevolent purposes. Or Tulsī may have something more specific in mind: the traditionalist Śaivite Brahmins of Benares. There may also be a sectarian dimension to his final remark, for Tulsī's own name refers to the sweet, medicinal basil tree sacred to Vishnu and his avatars, while the *āk* (Skt. *arka*) leaves dear to Śiva are poisonous and come from a tree that bristles with thorns.

Vinaya Patrikā 19

The "river of the gods" is the Ganges, to whom this poem is dedicated. The "threefold fire" it extinguishes is the pain of life, classically understood as experienced in reference to heaven, earth, and the body (*daivik, bhautik, daihik*). The "fluid of undying life" refers to the elixir of immortality that is possessed by the gods but eagerly sought by demons and humans. Hindu mythology pictures it as stored in the moon, and the poet expands the image by suggesting a connection with moonlight.

Vinaya Patrikā 30

Several traits that make Hanumān an attractive object of devotion are stressed here: his reliability (vv. 1–2), his strength (v. 3), and the fact that because of his animal side—he is not just the general of Rām's armies but in some sense a pet—one thinks of him as patronized by other, "greater" deities (v. 5). His devotees hope that this accessible devotee-god will be able to pass on to them the favor in which he is held by relevant members of the rest of the pantheon (v. 6).

Vinaya Patrikā 48

The flame that serves as the subject of this poem is the focal point of the *āratī* offering. The *āratī* ceremony was evidently first performed at evening, as the word's Sanskrit etymology indicates; the persistent nocturnal imagery of this poem reflects that past. Today, however, the importance of the *āratī* as an adjunct to the worship of images has come to be so great that it plays a role in services of worship conducted at all times of the day and night. It casts a special spell as a plate of little lamps—sometimes a candelabra in modern practice—is lifted with slow, sweeping motions to illuminate the deities in the mysterious niches where they often reside. Cf. Ravidās AG 23 and Sūrdās NPS 371.

The great goddess Kālī (or alternatively Durgā) is often pictured subduing an unruly buffalo demon who threatened the hegemony of the gods, hence her title "buffalo-killer" (Mahiṣamardinī). Here Tulsī places himself on the enemy's turf.

Vinaya Patrikā 79

The contrast between the contentious intimacy of many of Sūr's *vinaya* poems (e.g., NPS 138 above) and the confident, almost restful intimacy of this one is worthy of notice. Here, in a very well-known poem, we have complementarity, not combat.

Vinaya Patrikā 92

As the last verse of this poem makes clear, Tulsī here addresses himself to the Lord—his Lord—who "rescues the destitute" (*patit-pāvan,* cf. *Vinaya Patrikā* 69:

"Rescuer of the Fallen"), and he seems genuinely to apologize for his condition. Although he, like Sūr, advertises himself as one who excels in dullness (v. 1), his tone seems full of regret, not contestation.

Initially he addresses his Lord as Mādhav (v. 1), a name that usually refers to Vishnu or Krishna but may by extension signify Rām. The "Goddess of Learning" upon whom he calls near the end of the poem is Sarasvatī. She bears a special relation to Brahmins because of their scholarly calling, so it is as a failed Brahmin that Tulsī turns to Rām—in the last verse—for his ultimate refuge.

Garuḍ, "the bird that Hari rides," is Vishnu's avian vehicle and the legendary enemy of snakes. The snake here is existence itself (*bhav byāl,* a version of the more frequent expression *kāl vyāl,* "the snake of time"). The frog symbolizes timorousness, and fish, to whom allusion is made under the heading of "water creatures" (*jalacar bṛnd*), are the exemplars of what in India is called "fish logic" (*matsya nyāya*), that is, "dog eat dog."

Kavitāvalī 7.120

This poem makes its point cogently enough in English, but the original is even stronger because the word translated "tomorrow" (*kālhi*) is almost exactly the same as a word that means either "time" or "death" (*kāl*). The broad dimensions of time are explored in the third section of the poem, though the word *kāl* is not used there. It is reserved for the very last phrase in the fourth section, where it occurs as part of a quotation that takes in all three meanings: "Tomorrow, the time to die." This comprehensive understanding of *kāl,* in which time is seen as implying both tomorrow and death, is just what eludes the person about whom Tulsī speaks in this composition.

Mount Meru (v. 2) is the mythological mountain located at the center of the earth: its largest, most impressive, and heaviest formation. Raghuvar means "best of the Raghu clan" and is a title of Rām.

Vinaya Patrikā 200

The meaning of the reference to copper is not entirely plain: armor would normally be cast from iron. Copper, however, is favored as a metal that does not contaminate food cooked in it or water stored in it. Perhaps this is the conceit the poet intends to expose: the illusion that a splendidly arrayed body, like a copper-plated vessel, is capable of shielding its contents from decay.

The "ruler of the realm of death" is the god Yama. On Śiva as a devotee of Rām, see the introduction.

Vinaya Patrikā 277

This poem is the third to last in the *Vinaya Patrikā,* and the one in which Tulsī looks back and calls the entire series a "letter of petition" (*vinaya patrikā*). His reference to "my master" (*svāmī*) is apparently a reference to Rām himself, and is so interpreted here. The others included in the "all" whom he addresses are apparently those seated in the divine court (see below). The "false fruit / in the heart of a banana tree" is its bright red flower, much larger than any of the bananas themselves and more prominently placed, near the tip of the stalk.

In the concluding verses, as the poet prepares to hand his petition to Rām, he draws nearer to his Lord than at any other point in the *Vinaya Patrikā*. Accordingly, he addresses him intimately as "Father" (*bāpu*) and asks him to intercede before the rest of the assembled court (*pāñco,* "the five," a term with judicial overtones) by making right (*sahī*) anything that might have been imperfectly stated owing to the inevitable imperfections of Tulsī's human nature. The five persons comprising the court are traditionally taken to be Rām's three brothers together with Hanumān and Sītā. In *Vinaya Patrikā* 279, the last poem in the series, Tulsī's petition is accepted.

Kavitāvalī 7.183

This is the last poem in the *Kavitāvalī* and, like its counterpart in the *Vinaya Patrikā,* it ends with an affirmation of Tulsī by Rām. In the *Vinaya Patrikā* this comes upon receipt of a complex and elaborately phrased petition. Here the juxtaposition of a statement of Tulsī's need (and that of all Benares, as *Kavitāvalī* 7.182 explains) and the divine response is much more simple and direct.

The "black-magic curse" attributed to unknown gods here is a tantric spell directed against a person one wants to kill. The tantric adept focuses on a mantra bearing the name of the victim, takes it to the cremation ground, and there implants it in a small earthen pot. The pot is thought to fly through the air like an arrow until it lands on the condemned person; death ensues. The making of such a curse is an elaborate, secretive procedure, while the gesture of dismissal that answers it is open and consummately simple.

Select Bibliography

Publications and Other Written Documents

Abbott, Justin E., and Narhar R. Godbole. *Stories of Indian Saints: Translation of Mahipati's Marathi Bhaktavijaya.* Delhi: Motilal Banarsidass, 1982 (orig. publ. 1933).

Adhyātmarāmāyaṇam. Calcutta Sanskrit Series, no. 9 (two parts). Calcutta: Metropolitan Printing and Publishing House, 1935.

Ādi Śrī Guru Granth Sahib. 4 vols. Lucknow: Bhuvan Vāṇī Trust, 1978–82.

Allchin, F. R. *Tulsī Dās: Kavitāvalī.* London: Allen and Unwin, 1964.

———. "The Place of Tulsī Dās in North Indian Devotional Tradition." *Journal of the Royal Asiatic Society* 1966:3–4, pp. 132–34.

———. *Tulsī Dās: The Petition to Rām.* London: Allen and Unwin, 1966.

Alston, A. J. *The Devotional Poems of Mīrābāī.* Delhi: Motilal Banarsidass, 1980.

Aryan, K. C., and Subhashini. *Hanuman in Art and Mythology.* Delhi: Rekha Prakashan, n.d.

Āzād, Pṛthvī Siṃh. *Ravidās Darśan.* Chandigarh: Śrī Guru Ravidās Saṃsthān, 1979.

Babb, Lawrence A. *Redemptive Encounters: Three Modern Styles in the Hindu Tradition.* Berkeley: University of California Press, 1986.

Bahurā, Gopāl Nārāyaṇ, ed. *Pad Sūrdāsjī kā/The Padas of Surdas.* With an introductory essay by Kenneth E. Bryant. Jaipur: Maharaja Sawai Man Singh II Museum, 1982.

Bakhsīdās. *Ravidās Rāmāyaṇa.* Edited by Rājā Rām Miśra. Mathura: Śyām Kāśī Press, 1970.

Barz, Richard. *The Bhakti Sect of Vallabhācārya.* Faridabad: Thomson Press, 1976.

Briggs, George Weston. *Gorakhnāth and the Kānpaṭha Yogīs.* Delhi: Motilal Banarsidass, 1973 (orig. publ. 1938).

Bryant, Kenneth E. *Poems to the Child-God: Structures and Strategies in the Poetry of Sūrdās.* Berkeley: University of California Press, 1978.

———. "The Manuscript Tradition of the Sursagar: The Fatehpur Manuscript." In G. N. Bahurā, ed., *Pad Sūrdāsjī kā/The Padas of Surdas,* pp. vii–xx. Jaipur: Maharaja Sawai Man Singh II Museum, 1982.

———, and John Stratton Hawley. "The Poems of Sūrdās." Grant application to the National Endowment for the Humanities, 1984.

Burghart, Richard. "The Founding of the Ramanandi Sect." *Ethnohistory* 25:2 (1978), pp. 121–39.

Callewaert, W. M. *The Sarvāṅgī of the Dādūpanthī Rajab.* Leuven: Departement Orientalistiek, Katholieke Universiteit, 1978.

———, and L. de Brabandere. "*Nirguṇ* Literature on Microfilm in Leuven, Belgium." *IAVRI Bulletin* 9 (1980), pp. 28–48.

Caturvedī, Paraśurām. *Uttarī Bhārat kī Sant-Paramparā.* Allahabad: Leader Press, 1972.

———, ed. *Mīrābāī kī Padāvalī.* Allahabad: Hindī Sāhitya Sammelan, 1973.

Chandrakant, Kamala. *Mirabai.* Amar Chitra Katha, no. 36. Bombay: India Book House. n.d.

Chandrasekhar, S., ed. *From India to America.* La Jolla, Calif.: Population Review Publications, 1982.

Cohen, Richard J. "Sectarian Vaishnavism: The Vallabha *Saṃpradāya.*" In Peter Gaeffke and David A. Utz, eds., *Identity and Division in Cults and Sects in South Asia,* pp. 65–72. Philadelphia: Department of South Asia Regional Studies, 1984.

Cole, W. Owen, and Piara Singh Sambhi. *The Sikhs: Their Religious Beliefs and Practices.* London: Routledge & Kegan Paul, 1978.

Das Gupta, Shashibhusan. *Obscure Religious Cults.* Calcutta: K. L. Mukhopadhyay, 1969.

Dīkṣit, Trilokī Nārāyaṇ. *Paricayī Sāhitya.* Lucknow: Lucknow University, 1957.

Dimock, Edward C., Jr. *The Place of the Hidden Moon.* Chicago: University of Chicago Press, 1966.

Dūbe, Lalitā Prasād. *Hindī Bhakta-Vārtā Sāhitya.* Dehra Dun: Sāhitya Sadan, 1968.

Dvārkādās Parīkh, ed. *Caurāsī Vaiṣṇavan kī Vārtā.* Mathura: Śrī Bajarang Pustakālay, 1970.

Dvivedī, Hazārīprasād. *Kabīr.* New Delhi: Rājkamal Prakāśan, 1976.

Eck, Diana L. "India's *Tīrthas:* 'Crossings' in Sacred Geography." *History of Religions* 20:4 (1981), pp. 323–44.

———. *Banaras, City of Light.* New York: Alfred A. Knopf, 1982.

Entwistle, Alan W. *Vaiṣṇava Tilakas: Sectarian Marks Worn by Worshippers of Viṣṇu. IAVRI Bulletin* 11–12 (1981–82).

Gherā, B. R. *All India Ādi Dharm Mission.* New Delhi: All India Adi Dharm Mission, n.d.

———. *Śrī Guru Ravidās jī kā Saṃkṣipt Itihās.* [New Delhi]: All India Adi Dharm Mission, n.d.

Ghurye, G. S. *Indian Sadhus.* Bombay: Popular Prakashan, 1964.

Glasenapp, Helmuth von. "Die Lehre Vallabhâcāryas." *Zeitscrift für Indologie und Iranistik* 9 (1933–34), pp. 193–248.

Goetz, Hermann. *Mira Bai: Her Life and Times.* Bombay: Bharatiya Vidya Bhavan, 1966.

Gokarn, Kusum. "Popularity of Devotional Films (Hindi)." National Film Archive of India Research Project 689/5/84. Unpublished paper deposited in the National Film Archive of India, Pune.

Gold, Ann Grodzins, "Life Aims and Fruitful Journeys: The Ways of Rajasthani Pilgrims." Diss., University of Chicago, 1984.

Gold, Daniel. *The Lord as Guru: Hindi* Sants *in the Northern Indian Tradition.* New York: Oxford University Press, 1987.

———, and Ann Grodzins Gold. "The Fate of the Householder Nāth," *History of Religions* 24:2 (1984), pp. 113–32.

Gupta, Kiśorīlāl. *Gosāī-Carit.* Varanasi: Vāṇī-Vitān Prakāśan, 1964.

Gupta, Mātāprasād. *Tulsīdās.* Allahabad: Allahabad University, 1935.

———. *Gosvāmī Tulsīdās.* Allahabad: Indian Press, 1946.

———. *Kabīr-Granthāvalī.* Allahabad: Sāhitya Bhavan, 1985 (orig. publ. 1969).

Gupta, R. D. "Priyā Dās, Author of the *Bhaktirasabodhinī.*" *Bulletin of the School of Oriental and African Studies* 32:1 (1969), pp. 57–70.

Haberman, David L. *Acting as a Way of Salvation: A Study of Raganuga Bhakti Sadhana.* New York: Oxford University Press, 1988.

Handoo, Chandra Kumari. *Tulasīdāsa: Poet, Saint and Philosopher of the Sixteenth Century.* Bombay: Orient Longmans, 1964.

Hardy, Friedhelm. "Mādhavêndra Purī: A Link Between Bengal Vaiṣṇavism and South Indian *Bhakti.*" *Journal of the Royal Asiatic Society* (1974), pp. 23–41.

———. "The Tamil Veda of a *Śūdra* Saint (The Śrīvaiṣṇava Interpretation of Nammāḻvār). In G. Krishna, ed., *Contributions to South Asian Studies,* vol. 1, pp. 29–87. Delhi: Oxford University Press, 1978.

Harlan, Lindsey. "Satīmātā Veneration in Rajasthan." Paper presented to the Conference on Religion in South India, Craigville, Mass., June, 1986.

Hawley, John Stratton. *At Play with Krishna: Pilgrimage Dramas from Brindavan.* In association with Shrivatsa Goswami. Princeton: Princeton University Press, 1981.

———. *Krishna, the Butter Thief.* Princeton: Princeton University Press, 1983.

———. *Sūr Dās: Poet, Singer, Saint.* Seattle: University of Washington Press, and Delhi: Oxford University Press, 1984.

———. "Images of Gender in the Poetry of Krishna." In Caroline Walker Bynum, Stevan Harrell, and Paula Richman, eds., *Gender and Religion: On the Complexity of Symbols,* pp. 231–56. Boston: Beacon Press, 1986.

———. "Morality Beyond Morality in the Lives of Three Hindu Saints." In J. S. Hawley, ed., *Saints and Virtues,* pp. 53–73. Berkeley: University of California Press, 1987.

———. "Author and Authority in the Bhakti Poetry of North India." *The Journal of Asian Studies* 47:2 (1988), pp. 269–90.

———. "Asceticism Denounced and Embraced: Rhetoric and Reality in North Indian *Bhakti.*" In Austin Creel and Vasudha Narayanan, eds., *Monasticism in the Christian and Hindu Traditions: A Comparative Study.* Forthcoming.

Hedayetullah, Muhammad. *Kabir: The Apostle of Hindu-Muslim Unity.* Delhi: Motilal Banarsidass, 1977.

Hein, Norvin. *The Miracle Plays of Mathurā.* New Haven: Yale University Press, 1972.

Helweg, A. W. *Sikhs in England.* Delhi: Oxford University Press, 1979.

Hess, Linda. "Studies in Kabīr: Texts, Traditions, Styles and Skills." Diss., University of California, Berkeley, 1980.

———. *The Bījak of Kabīr.* In association with Shukdev Singh. San Francisco: North Point Press, 1983.

———. "Rām Līlā: The Audience Experience." In Monika Thiel-Horstmann, ed., *Bhakti in Current Research, 1979–1982.* Berlin: Dietrich Reimer Verlag, 1983.

———. "For the Sake of Brahmans, Gods, and Cows: Tulsīdās between Bhakti and Orthodoxy." Paper presented to the American Academy of Religion, Dallas, December, 1983, and to the Society for Asian and Comparative Philosophy, Honolulu, August, 1984.

Hill, W. D. P. *The Holy Lake of the Acts of Rāma.* Bombay: Oxford University Press, 1952.

Hujūr Uditnām Sāheb and Prakāśamaṇinām Sāheb, eds. *Kabīr Sāhab kā Bījak Granth.* Varanasi: Kabīr Panth, 1982.

Jagjīvan Rām. "Appeal: Nirmāṇādhīn Guru Ravidās Mandir Kāśī." Varanasi: Guru Ravidās Mandir, [1985].

Jensen, Joan M. *Passage from India: Asian Indian Immigrants in North America.* New Haven: Yale University Press, 1988.

Jijñāsu, Candrikāprasād. *Sant Pravar Raidās Sāhab.* Rev. ed. Lucknow: Bahujan Kalyāṇ Prakāśan, 1969 (orig. publ. 1959).

Juergensmeyer, Mark. *Religion as Social Vision: The Movement Against Untouchability in 20th-Century Punjab.* Berkeley: University of California Press, 1982.

———. "The Radhasoami Revival of the Sant Tradition." In Karine Schomer and W. H. McLeod, eds., *The Sants: Studies in a Devotional Tradition of India,* pp. 329–55. Berkeley: Berkeley Religious Studies Series, and Delhi: Motilal Banarsidass, 1987.

———. *Radhasoami Reality: The Logic of a Modern Faith.* Forthcoming.

———, and N. Gerald Barrier, eds. *Sikh Studies: Comparative Perspectives on a Changing Tradition.* Berkeley: Berkeley Religious Studies Series, 1979.

Kabīr. *Kabīr-Bījak.* Edited by Śukdev Siṃh. Allahabad: Nīlam Prakāśan, 1972.

Kabīr Sāhab kā Anurāg Sāgar. Allahabad: Belvedere Printing Works, 1975. Translated as *The Ocean of Love* by Raj Kumar Bagga, Partap Singh, and Kent Bicknell. Sanbornton, N.H.: Sant Bani Ashram, 1982.

Kapur, Anuradha. "Actors, pilgrims, kings, and gods: The Ramlila at Ramnagar." In Veena Das, ed., *The Word and the World: Fantasy, Symbol and Record.* New Delhi: Sage Publications, 1986.

Khare, R. S. *The Untouchable as Himself: Ideology, Identity, and Pragmatism Among the Lucknow Chamars.* Cambridge: Cambridge University Press, 1984.

Loehlin, C. H. "Textual Criticism of the Kartarpur Granth." In Mark Juergensmeyer and N. Gerald Barrier, eds., *Sikh Studies: Comparative Perspectives on a Changing Tradition,* pp. 113–18. Berkeley: Berkeley Religious Studies Series, 1979.

Lorenzen, David N. "The Kabīr Panth: Heretics to Hindus." In D. N. Lorenzen, ed., *Religious Change and Cultural Domination,* pp. 151–71. Mexico City: El Colegio de México, 1981.

———. "The Kabīr Panth and Social Protest." In Karine Schomer and W. H. McLeod, eds., *The Sants: Studies in a Devotional Tradition in India,* Berkeley: Berkeley Religious Studies Series, and Delhi: Motilal Banarsidass, 1987. pp. 281–303.

———. "The Social Ideologies of Hagiography: Śaṅkara, Tukārām and Kabīr." In Milton Israel and N. K. Wagle, eds., *Religion and Society in Maharashtra,* pp. 92–114. Toronto: University of Toronto Centre for South Asian Studies, 1987.

———. "Traditions of non-caste Hinduism: The Kabīr Panth. *Contributions to Indian Sociology* 21:2 (1987), pp. 263–83

Lutgendorf, Philip. "Kṛṣṇa Caitanya and His Companions as presented in the *Bhaktamāla* of Nābhā Jī and the *Bhaktirasabodhinī* of Priyā Dāsa." Master's thesis, University of Chicago, 1981.

———. "The Quest for the Legendary Tulsīdās." Paper presented to the American Academy of Religion, Los Angeles, November 1985.

———. "The Life of a Text: Tulsīdās' *Rāmcaritmānas* in Performance." Diss., University of Chicago, 1987.

Marfatia, Mrudula M. *The Philosophy of Vallabhācārya*. Delhi: Munshiram Manoharlal, 1967.

McGregor, R. S. *NandDas: The Round Dance of Krishna and Uddhav's Message*. London: Luzac, 1973.

———. "Tulsīdās' Śrīkṛṣṇagītāvalī." *Journal of the American Oriental Society* 96:4 (1976), pp. 520–26.

———. *Hindi Literature from Its Beginnings to the Nineteenth Century*. Wiesbaden: Otto Harrassowitz, 1984.

McLeod, W. H. *Gurū Nanak and the Sikh Religion*. Oxford: Clarendon Press, 1968.

———. *The Evolution of the Sikh Community: Five Essays*. Delhi: Oxford University Press, 1975.

———. *The B40 Janam-sakhi*. Amritsar: Guru Nanak Dev University, 1980.

———. *Early Sikh Tradition: A Study of the Janam-sākhīs*. Oxford: Clarendon Press, 1980.

———. *Punjabis in New Zealand*. Amritsar: Guru Nanak Dev University Press, 1986.

Millis, John I. "Malik Muhammad Jāyasī: Allegory and Religious Symbolism in His *Padmāvat*." Diss., University of Chicago, 1984.

Miśra, Girjāśaṃkar. *Raidās Rāmāyaṇa*. Mathura: Bhagavatī Prakāśan, 1981.

Miśra, Viśvanāth Prasād. "Gautam-Candrikā mẽ Tulsīdās kā Vṛttānt." *Nāgarīpracāriṇī Patrikā* 60:1 (1954), pp. 1–22.

Mītal, Prabhudayāl. "Sūr Kṛt Padõ kī Sabse Prācīn Prati." *Nāgarīpracāriṇī Patrikā* 67:3 (1962), pp. 262–67.

Müller, F. Max. *Lectures on the Origin and Growth of Religion*. London: Longmans, Green, 1882.

Nābhādās. *Śrī Bhaktamāl,* with the *Bhaktirasabodhinī* commentary of Priyādās. Lucknow: Tejkumār Press, 1969.

Oman, John Campbell. *The Mystics, Ascetics, and Saints of India*. London: T. Fisher Unwin, 1903.

Orr, W. G. *A Sixteenth-Century Indian Mystic: Dadu and His Followers*. London: Lutterworth, 1947.

Pandey, S. M. "Mīrābāī and Her Contributions to the Bhakti Movement." *History of Religions* 5:1 (1965), pp. 54–73.

Pollet, Gilbert. "Early Evidence on Tulsīdās and his Epic." *Orientalia Lovaniensia Periodica* 5 (1974), pp. 153–62.

Raghavan, V. *The Great Integrators: The Singer-Saints of India*. New Delhi: Publications Division, Government of India, 1966.

Rām, Jagjīvan. "Appeal: Nirmāṇādhīn Guru Ravidās Mandir, Kāśī." [Varanasi], [1985].

Rama Rau, Santha. "Banaras: India's City of Light." *National Geographic* 169:2 (February, 1986), pp. 244–45.

Sadhu Vasvani Mission and its Activities. Poona: Sadhu Vaswani Mission, n.d.

Saran, Paramatma, and Edwin Eames, eds. *The New Ethnics: Asian Indians in the United States.* New York: Praeger, 1980.

Sarda, Har Bilas. *Maharana Sāngā.* Ajmer: Scottish Mission Industries, 1918.

Śarmā, B. P. *Sant Guru Ravidās-Vāṇī.* Delhi: Sūrya Prakāśan, 1978.

Śarmā, Harinārāyaṇ. *Mīrā-Bṛhatpadāvalī.* Vol. 1. Jodhpur: Rajasthan Oriental Research Institute, 1968.

Śāstrī, Gangāśaraṇ. *Kabīr Jīvancaritra.* Varanasi: Kabīrvāṇī Prakāśan Kendra, 1976.

Schechner, Richard, and Linda Hess. "The Ramlila of Ramnagar." *The Drama Review* 21:3 (1977), pp. 51–82.

———. *Performative Circumstances from the Avant Garde to Ramlila.* Calcutta: Seagull Books, 1983.

Schomer, Karine, and W. H. McLeod, eds. *The Sants: Studies in a Devotional Tradition of India.* Berkeley: Berkeley Religious Studies Series, and Delhi: Motilal Banarsidass, 1987.

Śekhāvat, Kalyāṇsiṃh, ed. *Mīrābāī kā Jīvanvṛtt evam Kāvya.* Jodhpur: Hindī Sāhitya Mandir, n.d.

———. *Mīrā-Bṛhatpadāvalī.* Vol. 2. Jodhpur: Rajasthan Oriental Research Institute, 1975.

Shackle, Christopher. *An Introduction to the Sacred Language of the Sikhs.* London: School of Oriental and African Studies, University of London, 1983.

Shah, Ahmad. *The Bijak of Kabir.* New Delhi: Asian Publications Services, 1979 (orig. publ. 1911).

Shah, J. G. *Shri Vallabhacharya: His Philosophy and Religion.* Nadiad: Pushtimargiya Pustakalay, 1969.

Shapiro, Michael C. "Linguistic Aspects of the *Ādigranth.*" Paper presented to the American Oriental Society, New Haven, Conn., March 1986.

———. "The Rhetorical Structure of the *Japjī.*" Paper presented to the Second Berkeley Conference on Sikh Studies, Berkeley, February, 1987.

Sharma, Suresh Chandra. *Tulsidas.* Amar Chitra Katha, no. 62. Bombay: India Book House, n.d.

Siṃh, Padam Gurcaran. *Sant Ravidās: Vicārak aur Kavi.* Jullundur: Nav-Cintan Prakāśan, 1977.

Siṃh, Pradyumna Pratāp. "Bhakta-Śiromaṇi Śrīmīrābāī Mandir, Vṛndāvan kā Jīrṇoddhār." Vrindaban: n.p., n.d.

Siṃh, Śukdev, ed. *Kabīr ke Smaraṇ Tīrtha.* Varanasi: Kabīrvāṇī Prakāśan Kendra, 1981.

———. *Ravidās.* Varanasi: Ravidās Smārak Society, 1986.

Siṃh, Yogendra: *Sant Raidās.* Delhi: Akṣar Prakāśan, 1971.

Singh, Darshan. *A Study of Bhakta Ravidāsa.* Patiala: Punjabi University, 1981.

Singh, Pritam. "Bhāī Banno's Copy of the Sikh Scripture." In Monika Thiel-Horstmann, ed., *Bhakti in Current Research, 1979–1982.* Berlin: Dietrich Reimer Verlag, 1983.

Śrīmadbhāgavata-Mahāpurāṇa. 2 vols. Gorakhpur: Gītā Press, 1970.

Śrīvāstav, Vijayśaṃkar. "Rajasthānī Mūrtikalā mẽ Kṛṣṇalīlā Abhiprāy." In *Bhāratīya Saṃskṛti kī Rūparekhā,* pp. 63–76. Bikaner: Sadul Rajasthani Research Institute, 1969.

Śukla, Rāmcandra, et al., eds. *Tulsī-Granthāvalī.* Varanasi: Nāgarīpracāriṇī Sabhā, 1974.

Sukul, Lalitāprasād. *Mīrā̃ Smṛti Granth.* Calcutta: Bangīya Hindī Pariṣad, 1949.

Talib, Gurbachan Singh. *Japuji: The Immortal Prayer-chant.* New Delhi: Munshiram Manoharlal, 1977.

Thiel-Horstmann, Monika. "Modes of Renunciation in the Dādūpanth." Paper presented at the conference "Ascetics and Asceticism in India: A Comparative Study," held at the University of Florida, February 1988.

Thoothi, N. A. *The Vaishṇavas of Gujarat.* Calcutta: Longmans, Green, 1935.

Tivārī, Bhagavāndās. *Mīrā kī Prāmāṇik Padāvalī.* Allahabad: Sāhitya Bhavan, 1974.

Tivārī, Pāras Nāth. *Kabīr Granthāvalī.* Allahabad: Allahabad University, 1961.

Tod, James. *Annals and Antiquities of Rajasthan.* Vol. 1. Revised by William Crooke. London: Milford, 1920 (orig. ed. 1829).

Tripāṭhī, Rām Nareś. *Tulsīdās aur unkī Kavitā.* Vol. 1. Allahabad: Hindī Mandir, 1937.

Tulsīdās. *Rāmcaritmānas.* Edited by Viśvanāthprasād Miśra. Varanasi: Kāśīrāj Samskaran, [1962].

Upadhyaya, K. N. *Guru Ravidas: Life and Teachings.* Beas: Radha Soami Satsang Beas, 1982.

Vaswani, T. L. *The Call of Mira Education.* Poona: Mira, n.d.

———. *Saint Mira.* Poona: St. Mira's English Medium School, n.d.

Vaudeville, Charlotte. *Étude sur les sources et la composition du Rāmāyaṇa de Tulsī-Dās.* Paris: Librairie d'Amérique et d'Orient, 1955.

———. *Pastorales par Soûr-Dâs.* Paris: Gallimard, 1971.

———. *Kabir.* Vol. 1. Oxford: Clarendon Press, 1974.

———. *Kabīr-Vāṇī.* Pondicherry: Institut français d'Indologie, 1982.

Ward, Geoffrey. "Benares, India's Most Holy City, Faces an Unholy Problem." *Smithsonian,* September 1985, pp. 83, 90–92.

Weber, Max. "The Social Psychology of the World Religions." In H. H. Gerth and C. Wright Mills, trans. and eds., *From Max Weber: Essays in Sociology.* New York: Oxford University Press, 1946, pp. 267–301.

Weightman, S. C. R. "The Rāmcaritmānas as a Religious Event." In Gopal Krishna, ed., *Contributions to South Asian Studies 2.* Delhi: Oxford University Press, 1982, pp. 53–72.

Womack, Julie. "Ravidas and the Chamars of Banaras." Essay written for the Junior Year Abroad Program of the University of Wisconsin in Benares, 1983.

Wright, Louisa, et al. "Help for the Stream of Nectar." *Time,* International Edition, April 22, 1985, p. 21.

Wulff, Donna M. *Drama as a Mode of Religious Realization: The* Vidagdhamādhava *of Rūpa Gosvāmī.* Chico, Calif.: Scholars Press, 1984.

Miscellaneous Sources

Bhatt, Krishna Caitanya. Interview. Brindavan, November 18, 1986.
Dhannū Rām. Interview. Śrī Govardhanpur, August 15, 1983.
Dhannū Rām et al. Interview. Śrī Govardhanpur, August 13, 1983.
Gherā, Bantā Rām. Personal communication. December 9, 1983.
Harlan, Lindsey. Personal communication. December 23, 1985.
Hess, Linda. Personal communication. March 1986.
Jñān Prakāś, Sant. Interview. Benares, November 27, 1986.
Kāśī Dās. Interview. Varanasi, August 20, 1985.
Kureel, Mahadeo Prashad. Interview. Lucknow, November 28, 1986.
Lorenzen, David N. Personal communication. October 7, 1986.
Lutgendorf, Philip. Personal communication. January 14, 1987.
McLeod, W. H. Personal communication. February 1985.
Meera. Film produced by T. Sadashivam, Chandraprabha Cine, Madras, 1947.
Rām Lakhan. Interview. Varanasi, August 19, 1985.
Siṃh, Pradyumna Pratāp. Interview. Brindavan, August 30, 1985.
Singh, Darshan. Personal communication. March 1, 1984.
Subbalaxmi, M. S. *Meera Bhajans.* Gramophone Company of India EALP 1297. Dum Dum, 1965.
Vaswani, Mrs. R. A., and Atma Vaswani. Interviews. Pune, August 26, 1985.
Yāmadagni, Vasant. Personal communication. December 12, 1986.

Glossary

In the following list the name or term adopted for common use in the text is given first. Alternative versions, including other transliterations, are indicated in parentheses.

acal	Unmoving, stable
achūt (achut)	Intangible, incapable of being touched
Ādi Dharm (Ād Dharm, ādi dharma)	Original (*ādi*) religion or moral order (*dharma*); name of a movement of Untouchables who claim that their *dharma* forms the true basis of Indian religion and society
Ādi Dharmī	Follower of Ādi Dharm
Ādi Granth	"Primal Book": the poetic anthology that comprises the Sikh scriptures
akāl	Timeless; undying
Akbar	Mughul emperor who ruled from A.D. 1556 TO 1605
Āḻvār	One of a set of Vaiṣṇava poet-saints who flourished in south India ca. A.D. 600–900
Amritsar	City in the Punjab that is the major focus of Sikh pilgrimage; site of the Golden Temple
amṛt	"Immortal": the liquid of immortality
anādi	Beginningless, primordial
anahad śabd (anahadi śabad)	Primordial "unstruck sound" that is the basis for all other sounds
anahat (anahati)	Not struck, not to be struck, indestructible
anīl (anīlu)	Colorless, lacking attributes (lit., "without blue")
Āṇṭāl	Female Āḻvār poet-saint of Tamil south India
ant na (antu na)	Without end
Arjan (Arjun)	The fifth Sikh guru
asankh	Without number, innumerable

ātmārām	The Rām (i.e., God) within
avināsī (abināsī)	Undecaying
ayonī (ajūnī)	Unborn
Bādshāh (bādśāh)	A Muslim designation for an emperor or ruler
Balarām	Elder brother of Krishna
bedī khatrī	A merchant-caste community of the Punjab
Benares (Banāras)	A preeminent Hindu place of pilgrimage
Benarsi (Banārsī)	A resident of Benares
Bhagavad Gītā	Classic Hindu text embedded in the *Mahābhārata,* in which Krishna plays the role of teacher
Bhāgavata Purāṇa	Ninth- or tenth-century Purāṇa whose description of Krishna's life subsequently became the standard scripture for many Vaiṣṇavas
bhakta	Devotee, lover of God
Bhaktamāl	"Garland of *Bhaktas*": a hagiographical anthology composed in verse by Nābhādās in about A.D. 1600
bhakti	Devotion, passionate love for God
Bharat	Older half-brother of Rām
Bhīl	A tribe of southwestern Rajasthan and adjacent Madhya Pradesh
Bhuśuṇḍī	A crow who, in the *Rāmcaritmānas,* teaches and exemplifies devotion to Rām
bhramargīt	"Songs of [or to] the bee," found in the *Sūr Sāgar* and other Krishnaite works, so called because they are addressed to Ūdho, whom the *gopīs* liken to a black bee
Birla	A well-known family of Marwari industrialists.
Brahmā	The Hindu divinity most directly associated with processes of creation
Brahmin (brāhmaṇ)	The most highly ranked of India's castes, traditionally composed of specialists in ritual and learning
Braj (Vraja)	Region south of Delhi where Krishna is said to have grown up
Braj Bhāṣā	Language of the Braj region
Brindavan (Vrindā-ban, Vṛndā-vana)	Major focus of pilgrimage for Krishna worshipers and the spiritual center of modern-day Braj
Buddha	One who has awakened, is enlightened; Gautama the Buddha
būḍhā, būḍhe	Old, superior in age
Caitanya	Ecstatic saint from Bengal who inspired much of the "rediscovery" of Krishna's Braj in the early sixteenth century
camār	Low–ranked caste group whose name indicates their traditional occupation: working with leather (*cām*)
caraṇāmṛt	"Immortal liquid of the feet": a designation of liquid *prasād* that has

	literally or figuratively passed over the grace-giving feet of an image of a deity
Caurāsī Vaiṣṇavan kī Vārtā	"Conversations with [or Accounts of] Eighty-four Vaiṣṇavas;" a major seventeenth-century hagiographical text of the Vallabha Sampradāy
Citrakūṭ	Pilgrimage city located west of Benares, sacred to devotees of Rām
Cittor (Cittaur)	City in southwestern Rajasthan
Cokhāmeḷā	Untouchable poet-saint of west India
dasnāmī (daśanāmī)	An order of ascetics reputedly established by the eighth-century philosopher Śaṃkara, so called because it is comprised of ten (*das*) suborders
derā	Sacred enclosure, residence of a holy man
Dhruv	Young devotee of Vishnu who was elevated by the latter to become the pole-star
Dvārakā	Pilgrimage city in Gujarat, western India
ek omkār	"1 *Omkar*," the first two words in the *Ādi Granth* and the preeminent symbol of the Sikh faith
ektār	The one-stringed instrument traditionally said to have been played by Sūrdās
faqīr	"Poor man," a Muslim (i.e., Sūfī) mendicant
Farīd, Skeikh	Twelfth-century Sūfī poet-saint
Fatehpur	City in Rajasthan in which the oldest surviving anthology of north Indian *bhakti* poetry (A.D. 1582) was written
Garuḍ	Bird that serves as the vehicle of Vishnu
Gaṇeśa (Gaṇeś)	Elephant-headed god, son of Śiva and Pārvatī
ghāṭ	Bathing place at the side of a river
Giridhar	Lifter of the Mountain (i.e., Mount Govardhan), a title of Krishna
Gobind Singh (Govind Siṃh)	The tenth Sikh guru
Goindvāl	The first Sikh place of pilgrimage
Golden Temple	The central shrine of Sikhism, in Amritsar, called by Sikhs Harimandir or Darbār Sāhib
Gopāl	"Cowherd," a title of Krishna
gopī	One of the many cowherding women who lavished their affections on Krishna
Gorakhnāth	Tenth- to eleventh-century yogī revered by the Nāth Yogīs
Gosā̃ī	I.e., *gosvāmī* ("master of the senses"), a title of Tulsīdās
Gosā̃ī Carit	Late eighteenth-century(?) biography of Tulsīdās
goṣṭhī	Dialogue, discussion
gosvāmī	"Master of the senses," a title of Tulsīdās and of several of the Brahmin theologians of sixteenth-century Brindavan
granthī	Custodian of the *Ādi Granth* and of the *gurudvārā* in which it is kept

Gujarat	Westernmost state in India
guru	Teacher, revered master (lit., "weighty")
gurudvārā (gurdwara)	"Door of the guru" or "door to the guru": a Sikh place of worship
Hanumān	Monkey warrior who was a chief ally of Rām in his struggle to rescue Sītā, and who is revered as an unparalleled devotee of Rām
Hari	Title of Vishnu, Krishna, or Rām, frequently interpreted as meaning "the one who takes away" sin or evil
Harirāy	The major commentator on the *Caurāsī Vaiṣṇavan kī Vārtā;* traditional dates: A.D. 1590–1715
Harnām	Guru to Bantā Rām Gherā
haṭha yoga	"Forceful yoga," involving poses of considerable physical difficulty
haumai	Egotism, self-centeredness
hukam	Order, decree
Indra	Hindu deity often identified as captain of the gods; a major figure in the Vedic pantheon
Jagjīvan Rām	Major Untouchable political figure (d. 1986)
Jaṭ	The dominant caste of rural Punjab
Jhālī	Queen of Cittor, who appears in the *Bhaktamāl* as a patroness and devotee of Ravidās
Jīv Gosvāmī	Theologian of sixteenth-century Brindavan
julāhā	A caste of weavers; cf. *korī*
Jumna (Yamunā)	Sister river to the Ganges, which flows through Delhi and the Braj country
Kabīr	*Nirguṇa* poet-saint
kabīr caurā	Kabīr Square, a major intersection in Benares
kabīr maṭh	The major monastery of the Kabīr Panth in Benares
Kabīr Panth	The "path of Kabīr"; the group that identifies itself as adhering to Kabīr's teachings
Kāl (kāl)	"Death, time": the evil dimiurge according to certain Kabīr Panthī teachings
Kālī	The "black" or "deathly" one, a horrific goddess especially worshiped in eastern India
Kāma (Kām, Kāmdev)	Hindu god of amorous love, roughly corresponding to Cupid
Kānh	Vernacular form of the Sanskrit name Krishna, more familiar in tone than the latter
Kans (Kaṃsa)	Evil usurper of the throne of Mathurā, enemy of Krishna
kaṛāh prasād	Food set aside as sacred in Sikh worship, so called because it is perceived as God's grace (*prasād*) and is prepared in an iron bowl (*kaṛāhi*)
Kāshī (Kāśī)	"The luminous one," a Sanskrit designation for Benares
Kavīśvar	"Lord of poets" pilloried in the *Caurāsī Vaiṣṇavan kī Vārtā*
Kavitāvalī	"Garland of Poetry" composed by Tulsīdās
Keśī	Horse demon who threatened the Braj countryside and was vanquished by the boy Krishna

khālsā	The Sikh brotherhood said initially to have been formed by Gobind Singh
korī	Weaver caste; cf. *julāhā*
Krishna (Kṛṣṇa)	"Dark, black": Hindu god often understood as an avatar of Vishnu
Lahore (Lahaur)	Preeminent city of the Punjab, now in Pakistan
Lakhmī Dās	First son of Nānak
Lakṣmaṇ	Younger brother of Rām
līlā	Play, drama
Lodī	A Muslim dynasty that ruled northern India from Delhi in the fifteenth and early sixteenth centuries
Madan Gopāl	"Beguiling cowherd," a title of Krishna
Mādhav	A title of Krishna whose derivation is disputed; usually it is taken as a patronymic referring to Madhu, a putative ancestor of Krishna in the Yadu dynasty. The title can be applied, by extension, to Rām
mādhurya bhāva	The range of "honeyed" (*madhu*) emotions befitting lovers
Magahar	Town near Gorakhpur in Uttar Pradesh (northeastern India) where Kabīr is said to have spent his last days
Mahābhārata	The great epic of India
Maharashtra	Region of western India, in the vicinity of Bombay
Mahīpati	Eighteenth-century Marathi poet who composed the *Bhaktavijaya* ("Triumph of the Devotees"), a hagiographical anthology
Mānas	See *Rāmcaritmānas*
mandir	In modern Hindi usage, "temple"
mañjarī	Maidservant, an ancillary figure in the world of Braj whose position enables her to observe the amours of Krishna and the *gopīs,* especially Rādhā
Manmohan	"The one who disorients the mind," a title of Krishna
Marwārīs	A prominent group of merchants and industrialists who were originally from Marwār, the region surrounding Jodhpur in Rajasthan
Mathura (Mathurā)	Major city of the Braj region, located on the Jumna south of Delhi
Merta (Meḍtā)	City in Rajasthan that is believed to be the birthplace of Mīrābāī
Meru (Sumeru)	The axial mountain of the universe, according to Hindu mythology
Mīrā (Mīrā̃)	See Mīrābāī
Mīrābāī (Mīrā̃bāī)	*Saguṇa* poet-saint
Mughal (Moghal)	Muslim dynasty that controlled much of India from Delhi or Agra during the period from the mid-sixteenth century to the advent of British rule
Muralī	The name of Krishna's flute: it is personified as female
Mūl Gosāī̃ Carit	Text presenting the "essentials" (*mūl*) of the life of Tulsīdās

Murāri	"Enemy of [the demon] Mura," a title of Krishna
Nābhādās (Nābhā, Nābhājī)	Author of the *Bhaktamāl*
Nāmdev	Low-caste poet-saint of west India
Nānak	*Nirguṇa* poet-saint whom Sikhs regard as their first and foremost guru
Nanda	Headman of Braj, foster father of Krishna
Nārad	The emissary of the gods—a sagacious, musical, sometimes meddlesome figure
Nararūpahari	"Hari in human form," whom Tulsīdās salutes as his guru
Nāth Yogīs (Nāths)	A group of renunciants who trace their lineage to such "lords" (*nāth*) of spiritual attainment as Gorakhnāth
nirākār	Having no shape or form, unformed
Nirañjan (nirañjan)	Having no taint or blemish
nirguṇa (nirguṇ)	Without attributes; the view that God cannot be positively conceived and should not be worshiped through images or other visual forms
nirguṇī	Adherent of *nirguṇa* ideas
pad (pada)	Verse form involving lines of variable length whose final syllables either adopt a single rhyme or rhyme by couplets, and whose final or penultimate line normally includes the signature of the poet
Pārvatī	"Of the mountains": daughter of Himavān (i.e., the Himālayas) and wife of Śiva
patidev	Husband (*pati*) conceived as a god (*dev*) by his wife, as traditional Hindu canons say he ought to be
patit pāvan	One who finds or rescues the fallen, a title frequently applied to God in *bhakti* poetry
Pīr (pīr)	A sūfī saint; the leader of a Sūfī order
prabhu	Lord, master
Prajāpati	"Lord of creatures," a member of the Hindu pantheon especially associated with creation and sometimes therefore identified with Brahmā
prasād	"Grace": food offered to deities in Hindu *pūjā* rites and then returned to worshipers as a divine gift
Pravarṣaṇ	Mythical mountain that serves as the home of Bhuśuṇḍī
Priyādās	Commentator on the *Bhaktamāl* of Nābhādās
Pune (Poona)	City in Maharashtra
Punjab (Pañjāb)	Province of Pakistan and northwest India
pūjā	"Worship, praise": term characterizing the general vocabulary of worship in Hindu temples and homes
Purāṇa (Purāṇ)	A class of texts written primarily in Sanskrit that recount primordial events (*purāṇa* = "old") such as those having to do with the gods
Puri	Pilgrimage city in Orissa, eastern India
qāzī	Muslim judge or magistrate

Rādhā	Krishna's consort and favorite among the *gopīs*
rāgī	One who intones a rāga, that is, who recites verses from the *Ādi Granth* in a *gurudvārā*
Rajasthan	Province of northwest India
Rājpūt	Warrior, governor caste of Rajasthan
Rām (Rāma)	Short form of the name Rāmacandra, a god understood as an avatar of Vishnu; in its *nirguṇa* context, a general name for God
Rāmānand	Putative guru of Kabīr, Ravidās, and other *nirguṇa* saints
Rāmāyaṇa (Rāmāyaṇ)	Epic of Rām; by extension, any epic story
Rāmcarit-mānas	Verse epic in which Tulsīdās tells the story of Rām
Rām Lakhan	Chief administrator of the Jagjīvan Rām temple to Ravidās in Benares
rām līlā	Devotional enactment of episodes from the story of Rām
Rāmnagar	Settlement across the Ganges from Benares where India's most famous *rām līlā* is performed
rām rājya	The rule of Rām, symbolizing an ideal social order
Rām Rājya Pariṣad	Political party devoted to realizing *rām rājya*
rāṇā	Designation for a royal figure in the Mewar (southwestern) region of Rajasthan
rās līlā	Krishna's dance of abandon with the *gopīs,* performed in the forests of Braj, and the genre of musical drama in which it is reenacted
Rāvaṇ	Enemy of Rām in the *Rāmāyaṇa*
Ravidās (Raidās)	*Nirguṇa* poet-saint
Śabarī	Bhīl woman who displayed ingenuous love for Rām
śabd (śabad)	Word, especially the Word of God
sac (sacu, satya)	"Truth," the name of the highest realm of reality perceived by Nānak
Sadhnā	*Nirguṇa* poet-saint
sādhū (sādhu)	A Hindu ascetic (lit. "good person")
sādhu sang	A gathering of *sādhūs*—whether specifically ascetics or good people generally
saguṇa (saguṇ)	With attributes; the view that divine beings have positive—often human—attributes or qualities, through which they may properly be worshiped
saguṇī	Proponent of *saguṇa* ideas
sahaj	"Spontaneous, easy": a designation of the ultimate state of religious realization, especially according to *nirguṇa* traditions associated with the Nāth Yogīs
Sain (Sen)	*Nirguṇa* poet-saint
Śaivite (Śaiva)	Devotee of Śiva

śakti	"Power": a generic name applied to many Indian goddesses
śālagrām	A fossilized rock native to the Gaṇḍakī River in Nepal, which is held in special esteem by Vaiṣṇavas and can function in lieu of an image
sampradāy	Teaching tradition, religious community
saṃvād	Dialogue
Sanak	Exemplary ascetic in Hindu mythology
Sankaṭ Mocan	Temple in Benares whose name means release (*mocan*) from extremity (*sankaṭ*), this being accomplished through the assistance of Hanumān, to whom it is dedicated
sant	"Good, true": a term commonly used to describe poets and devotees of the *nirguṇa* persuasion
śāstra	Treatise espousing Hindu doctrines
satguru	"True Guru," a familiar *nirguṇa* designation for Absolute Reality (God) especially insofar as it reveals itself within the self
Siddha (siddha)	An "accomplished one": a realized Hindu adept who has attained special powers; a particular category of such adepts believed by Nāth Yogīs to have attained immortality through their yogic attainments
Sīhī	Reputed birthplace of Sūrdās
Sikh	"Learner, pupil": the community that identifies itself as pupils of Nānak and the gurus said to follow in his lineage
Sītā	Wife of Rām, paragon of conjugal faithfulness and seemly behavior
Śiva (Śiv)	One of Hinduism's high gods, possessing seemingly contradictory ascetic and erotic attributes
Smārta Brahmin	One of a "catholic" group of Brahmins who adhere to *smṛti* while adopting a theistic orientation that permits primary devotion to one of five divinities: Vishnu, Sūrya, Śiva, Gaṇeśa, and the Goddess
Smṛti (smṛti)	"What is remembered," a class of Hindu law and scripture
śrāvaṇ	Rainy month in the Hindu lunar calendar that corresponds most closely to July
Śrīcand	Second son of Nānak, said to have established the *udāsī* monastic order
Śrī Govardhanpur	Untouchable enclave south of Benares
Śūdra	The lowest of the four major caste groupings set out in the *Laws of Manu*
Śuk	See Śukdev
Śukdev	A sage of a bygone age, narrator of a number of epic and puranic passages
Sumeru	See Meru
Sūr	See Sūrdās
Sūrdās	*Saguṇa* poet-saint
Sūr Sāgar	"Sūr's Ocean," the collection of poetry attributed to Sūrdās
Sūrya	The sun; the sun-god
svāmī	Master
Śyām (Syām)	"The dark one," a title of Krishna

syām dhām	The home or dwelling of Śyām
Tirumaṅkai	Saint (*āḻvār*) of Tamil south India
Tiruppān	Untouchable saint (*āḻvār*) of Tamil south India
Trilocan	*Nirguṇa* poet-saint
tulsī	Plant of the basil family, sacred to Vishnu and his avatars
Tulsī	See Tulsīdās
Tulsī Carit	See *Gosāī̃ Carit*
Tulsīdās	*Saguṇa* poet-saint
Udāsī	"Withdrawers": an ascetic order that traces its origins to Śrīcand, the second son of Nānak
Ūdho (Uddhava)	Companion of Krishna during the period in which he was ruler of Mathurā; messenger of *nirguṇa* religion from Krishna to the *gopīs*
ulaṭbāṃsī	"Upside-down speech": the riddle-like verses of Kabīr
Vaiṣṇava	Worshiper of Vishnu
Vallabha (Vallabhā-cārya)	Major sixteenth-century theologian traditionally understood to have been the preceptor of Sūrdās
Vālmīki	Sage who is credited with composing the *Rāmāyaṇa* in Sanskrit
Vārtā	See *Caurāsī Vaiṣṇavan kī Vārtā*
vātsalya bhāva	The emotion of parental tenderness, as of a cow for her calf (*vatsa*)
Veda	"Knowledge": the name given collectively to the most ancient Hindu scriptures
vinaya	"Petition, humble submission": a genre of verse in which the poet addresses complaint, petition, or praise to God
Vinaya Patrikā	"Letter of Petition," an anthology of poems addressed by Tulsīdās to Rām and his court
Vishnu (Viṣṇu)	Great god of the Hindu pantheon, of whom Krishna and Rām are said to be avatars
Viśvanāth	"Lord of the universe": a title of Śiva and the name of the preeminent temple to him in Benares
Viṭṭhalnāth	Second son of Vallabha and a major figure in shaping the Vallabha Sampradāy
Vyās	Legendary sage who is said to have narrated the epic *Mahābhārata* and arranged the Purāṇas
Yadu (Yādav)	The dynasty of which Krishna is said to have been a member
Yaśodā	Wife of Nanda, foster mother of Krishna

Index